Understanding and Treating Sex Addiction

Sex addiction is on the increase – in the media as well as in the therapy room. But while more and more people seek help for their compulsive sexual behaviours, there is still confusion and debate about whether the condition even exists.

Understanding and Treating Sex Addiction explains why an increasing number of people are inadvertently finding their lives devastated by their sexual behaviours. It explores the latest scientific understandings and research into why pornography, cyber sex, visiting sex workers, fetishes and multiple affairs can come to control some people's lives to the point that they can't stop. It explains how sex addiction is not a moral issue, as some assume, but a health issue that we as a society need to start taking seriously. Throughout the book are the revealing statistics from the UK's latest survey on sex addiction. Three hundred and fifty people who struggle with this condition have bravely and candidly shared their experience for the benefit of their fellow sufferers and those who choose to help them.

This book contains support and advice for both the clinician and for those who suffer from sex addiction. As well as practical guidance and techniques for stopping compulsive behaviours and preventing relapse, there is also a thorough exploration of the deeper underlying causes and how these must be addressed.

Paula Hall is a UKCP registered psychotherapist who specialises in sex addiction and is CSAT trained. She provides individual and couple therapy and is the founder of The Hall Recovery Course. She is also a founder trustee of ATSAC – a professional association dedicated to providing education and information about sex addiction as well as promoting services around the UK.

Understanding and Treating Sex Addiction

A comprehensive guide for people who struggle with sex addiction and those who want to help them

Paula Hall

Routledge
Taylor & Francis Group

LONDON AND NEW YORK

First published 2013
by Routledge
27 Church Road, Hove, East Sussex BN3 2FA

Simultaneously published in the USA and Canada
by Routledge
711 Third Avenue, New York, NY 10017

Routledge is an imprint of the Taylor & Francis Group, an informa business

British Library Cataloguing in Publication Data
A catalogue record for this book is available from the British Library

Library of Congress Cataloging in Publication Data
Hall, Paula.
Understanding and treating sex addiction : a comprehensive guide for
people who struggle with sex addiction and those who want to help them /
Paula Hall.
    p. cm.
  ISBN 978-0-415-69190-1 (hardback) – ISBN 978-0-415-69191-8 (pbk.)
  1. Sex addiction. 2. Sex addiction – Treatment. I. Title.
  RC560.S43H35 2012
  616.85'833–dc23   2012019468

ISBN: 978-0-415-69190-1 (hbk)
ISBN: 978-0-415-69191-8 (pbk)
ISBN: 978-0-203-08090-0 (ebk)

Typeset in Times New Roman
by HWA Text and Data Management, London

Printed and bound in Great Britain by the MPG Books Group

Contents

List of illustrations   vii
Acknowledgements   ix

Introduction   1

PART I
Understanding sex addiction   3

1 Defining sex addiction   5

2 Assessment and diagnosis   18

3 How sex addiction starts   33

4 How addiction is maintained and reinforced   50

5 The partner's perspective   61

PART II
Breaking the chains of addiction   77

6 Treatment objectives and options   79

7 Making a commitment to recovery   91

8 Understanding the cycle of addiction   103

9 Identifying unresolved issues and unmet needs   118

PART III
Establishing relapse prevention strategies for life   129

10 Avoiding and managing triggers   131

11 Creating healthy couple relationships   144

12 Satisfying sexuality   155

13 Developing a healthy lifestyle   164

14 Recognising and overcoming blocks to recovery   178

Conclusion   191

Further reading and resources   192
References   196
Index   200

Illustrations

Figures

2.1	The stages of change	19
2.2	The OAT classification model	25
2.3	Measuring severity	30
3.1	The BERSC Model	35
4.1	The four-step cycle	51
4.2	Oscillating control/release cycle	52
4.3	The six-phase cycle of addiction	53
4.4	The window of tolerance	57
7.1	Identifying core beliefs	93
7.2	The circle exercise	98
8.1	The six-phase cycle of addiction	104
9.1	Ali's life line	119
11.1	The drama triangle	149
11.2	The PAC model	150
13.1	Life wheel	170

Tables

1.1	Harmful consequences	15
4.1	Common cognitive distortions	56
13.1	Emotional intelligence inventory	176
14.1	Cross addictions	186

Boxes

7.1	Reclaiming personal values	96
7.2	The circle exercise	98
7.3	Creating a vision	99

8.1	Evaluating unmet needs	105
8.2	Identifying triggers	107
8.3	Recognising cognitive distortions	109
8.4	Identifying SUDs	112
8.5	Identifying the positives of acting out	113
8.6	Identifying regrets	115
8.7	Identifying behaviours in the reconstitution phase	116
9.1	The life line exercise	120
10.1	The letter to self	141
11.1	The Accountability Contract	148
11.2	Ten rules of effective communication	153
13.1	Life balance inventory	171
13.2	Emotional intelligence inventory	175
14.1	Rock bottoms	180
14.2	Harmful consequences	181

Acknowledgements

My sincere thanks go to all the people who have helped me write this book. First I would like to thank my friend and mentor Thaddeus Birchard who inspired me to start working in this field, and Patrick Carnes and Robert Weiss who have helped me on the journey. I would also like to thank my fellow trustees in the Association for the Treatment of Sex Addiction and Compulsivity (ATSAC) who, like me, are committed to furthering the understanding of sex addiction in the UK and improving services. I would also like to thank the people who generously gave their time and emotional energy to complete the survey that is illustrated throughout this book. Finally, and most importantly, I want to thank my clients who have taught me more about sex addiction than anything else ever could. And especially the guys, the blokes, the men and the chaps (you know who you are!) who have been members of my recovery course. I couldn't have done any of this without you.

Acknowledgements

Introduction

Sex addiction is nothing new. The term may be a modern one, but the painful condition of feeling controlled by one's sexual desires and compelled to act on them has been described as far back in time as the third century by St Augustine. Human sexuality is a powerful drive and one that we've both celebrated and denigrated throughout history. It is one of the most healing forces known to man, and one of the most devastating. Sex can build self-esteem and create the closest couple bonds, but it can also break people and relationships in two. Sex is complex and mysterious – surely that's why we love it so much.

People who struggle with sex addiction have been taken over by their sexual appetites. Rather than being their master, they have become their slave. Rather than enjoying a sex life that fits their values and their goals, they're imprisoned by behaviours that damage their self worth and integrity. Relationships are often destroyed beyond repair and families divided. Yet amidst the wreckage that is left by sex addiction there are still the cynics who say it does not exist. Those who describe it as a lack of self-control, or a moral judgement made on those who enjoy sexual variety. It is my hope that this book will begin to quell those voices as well as give hope to those who struggle with this very real condition.

Although sex addiction has undoubtedly been around for centuries, it is only over the past few years that we have started to fully understand it. Advances in brain research and neuropsychology have helped us understand the nature of both chemical and behavioural addictions and appreciate the links with childhood experience and trauma. At the same time the unprecedented explosion of the internet and ever-growing availability of pornography is giving us a new breed of user who stumbled upon the drug by chance, without ever knowing they could become hooked. Throughout these pages you will learn how to identify, and more importantly overcome, sex addictions that are opportunity-induced, trauma-induced or attachment-induced – or indeed, a mixture of all three. You'll find assessment tools and practical resources for psycho education and relapse prevention as well as guidance on addressing the deeper underlying issues. There is also help for partners and couples, and suggestions for developing a fulfilling sexuality and a balanced lifestyle.

In preparation for this book I conducted a survey of people who describe themselves as struggling with sex addiction; 350 people replied, some of whom had gone through therapy, some were members of 12 step groups and others responded to an open invitation to complete the survey on the Relate website. This is the first UK survey of this kind and the results, which are scattered throughout this book, provide valuable insights into both the cause and effect of sex addiction. Many of the respondents have also generously shared their stories in their own words to further illuminate their experience.

First and foremost, this book has been written for the men and women whose lives have been hurt by sex addiction. Since the majority of my clinical experience has been with heterosexual men you will see they represent much of what's said. Although there are additional challenges for women who have sex addiction and for individuals and couples from other sexual orientations, what is written here still applies. There are also countless challenges for partners that I have not had space to address in this book – hopefully they will be tackled in the sequel.

This book has also been written for clinicians who want to help those with sex addiction. Unfortunately, the therapy field in the UK has been loitering in the shallows of unconscious incompetence for far too long and I hope this book will be the first of many UK resources to redress that. It should be noted by any professional working in this field that sex-offending behaviour is commonplace and hence additional skills and knowledge will be required. The treatment of sex addiction is a field that is currently in the middle of a massive growth spurt, and while I both welcome and applaud this, please be aware that the consequence may be that some of this book may soon become outdated.

And finally, please do not read this book as a warning against sexual experimentation or even sexual excess. There are many people who enjoy pornography and promiscuity without negative consequence or becoming addicted – in the same way as many people enjoy alcohol, and occasionally drink too much without becoming alcoholics. I hope you will see this as a sex-positive book. Overcoming sex addiction is not about fitting a societally imposed set of sex norms but about becoming free to become the person you want to be.

Part I

Understanding sex addiction

In Part I of this book we will look at the definition of sex addiction and consider both what it is and what it is not. Comprehensive assessment criteria are offered in Chapter 2 to identify someone who is struggling with an addiction and whether it is opportunity-, attachment- or trauma-induced. In Chapter 3 we look at how sex addiction gets set up from a biological, emotional, relational, social and cultural perspective. There is also an exploration of common childhood and adolescent themes. We then move on to consider how sex addiction is maintained and reinforced through a six-phase behavioural cycle that is common to all. We conclude Part I with the partners' perspectives and see the devastation sexual addiction can cause loved ones – and consider how a partner's reaction can affect successful addiction treatment.

1   Defining sex addiction

Sex addiction is possibly one of the most controversial problems to have entered the public arena in the past 50 years and one that has generated a huge amount of media attention. While a growing number of public figures and celebrities battle their condition in the face of public scorn and criticism, others claim it's nothing more than a made-up condition invented to excuse high-flying men who can't control their sex drives. And others sceptically say it's a problem created by sex-hating prudes who moralise sexual diversity and freedom.

Unlike other questionable conditions, the argument over the existence of sex addiction often becomes a moral one, rather than an issue of health. This is undoubtedly because the focus of public and clinical attention is on the word 'sex' rather than on the word 'addiction', which is the nub of where the problem truly lies. Hence numerous studies highlight the prevalence of cross-addiction (Carnes et al., 2005) and, in the UK, 36 per cent of sex addicts had experienced other addictions or compulsive behaviours (Hall, 2012). If one considers other addictions that have been thrown into the social ether, such as TV, gambling, shopping and even chocolate, they may be vilified but sufferers receive the help they need nonetheless. But when 'sex' is added to the title it becomes a matter of contention, and the first challenge facing many sufferers and the therapists who want to help them is to decide if they really are 'addicted' to sex or if they simply need to get a grip. Unfortunately, this moral debate over what the condition means and whether it truly exists results in many thousands of sufferers struggling to find help and many clinicians wasting hours of therapeutic time on definition and diagnosis rather than helping the client overcome the problem and move on with their life.

One argument that is proffered against sex addiction's existence is that it seems to have appeared on the social scene so recently, but sex has obviously been available since the dawn of time. 'If sex was "addictive" how come it's only happened so recently?' ask some. The answer to this is simple: the internet. The world wide web has made sex available and accessible to all, and accessible within relative anonymity, hence bypassing the usual social inhibitors. If crack cocaine was privately and freely available on every street corner, I'm sure the growth in coke addiction would soon hit the headlines. At no other time in history has it been so easy to become sexually addicted.

As millions of sufferers would testify, sex addiction definitely does exist, but like many conditions it is complex and not easily defined. There are some 'classic' cases that easily fit diagnostic criteria but others that do not. It's best to view sex addiction as a term that encompasses a range of problems and difficulties associated with a range of sexual behaviours. Those problems may be mild or severe, they may have existed for many years with no apparent cause or they may have been triggered by a particular event and be a relatively recent problem. Or it may be a problem that crops up in someone's life only occasionally. Sex addiction has many guises, but there are common denominators as we will see in the following chapter. But before we move on to diagnosis, this chapter will explore a variety of definitions and seek to understand why sex addiction causes such emotional, physical and social devastation in people's lives.

What is sex addiction?

The simplest and broadest definition of sex addiction would be that it's a term that describes any pattern of out-of-control sexual behaviour that causes problems in someone's life. Furthermore, it is a pattern of behaviour that cannot be stopped, or does not reliably stay stopped. The type of behaviour does not define addiction. The following is a list of common behaviours but it is by no means exhaustive.

Pornography	Sex cinemas	Fetish practices
Chat lines	BDSM [bondage,	Bestiality
Phone lines	discipline, sadism,	Child pornography
Prostitution	masochism]	Rape
Partner sex	Exhibitionism or	Web sex
Multiple affairs	voyeurism	

Almost any sexual behaviour or indeed, any behaviour at all, can become addictive, but it's not the behaviour itself that is the problem but the relationship to the behaviour. When we become dependent on something and can't stop doing it, in spite of all the problems it's causing in our lives, we're addicted.

Some professionals have argued that labelling a sexual behaviour as an addiction is pathologising that behaviour and therefore making a value judgement. For example, they might say that if someone has a pornography addiction then we're saying that pornography is wrong and dangerous. But this thinking completely misses the point. It is the relationship to pornography that is the problem, not the pornography itself. This is the same with alcohol. Most would agree that there is nothing wrong, per se, with red wine, but if you need a bottle every morning before you can get out of bed and then you follow it with three or four more over the course of every day, the chances are you're addicted to it. If your partner has also left you because of how much red wine you drink and your health is suffering and you're about to lose your job and consequently your home, then I think it's safe to conclude that your relationship to red wine is not healthy. It's a dependency, an addiction, a compulsion or whatever you want to call it. For that individual, red wine has become a problem, but there will undoubtedly continue to be many millions of other red wine drinkers who are not addicted and can continue to enjoy their tipple of choice.

This is equally true of sex. As said before, sex addiction is not a moral issue, it is a mental health issue. There are many millions of men and women who enjoy pornography, chat lines, prostitution, multiple sexual partners and a mind boggling number of other sexual practices who are not 'addicted' in any sense what so ever. They enjoy their sexual experiences and they are experiences that add to their sense of self and their enjoyment of life. This is a completely different scenario from someone who is addicted, whose sexual practises diminish their sense of self and wreak havoc on their lives. The bottom line is, if something is damaging your life but you can't stop doing it, you're an addict.

But is it really an addiction?

Historically the term 'addiction' was only used for chemical addictions – substances such as alcohol, tobacco, heroin and other drugs that cross the blood–brain barrier and alter the brain chemistry. More recently, psychological dependency has become recognised as a significant contributory factor to addiction (Miller, 2005), meaning that substances such as cannabis, which is considerably less chemically addictive than alcohol, can still be classed as an addictive substance. Furthermore, it's now known, as we will explore later in this chapter, that activities as well as substances directly affect our brain chemistry.

The notion of an activity being an addiction is a relatively new one but one that is becoming increasingly recognised (Courtwright, 1982; Dickson, Derevenksy and Gupta, 2002; Rosenthal, 1992; Taber et al., 1987). These are often referred to as 'behavioural', or 'process', addictions as opposed to 'chemical' addictions. But the term 'addiction' is still an issue for some and consequently you may find people referring instead to video game overuse, pathological gambling, compulsive debting, problem over-eating and so on. To be honest, the bottom line is that both sufferers and clinicians will use their own favoured term and it doesn't matter what that is as long as help can be offered. But it is precisely the provision of help and its socio-political implications that perpetuate the argument over its name.

How we classify a condition as a society is not just about health, it is most definitely also about money and politics. The *Diagnostic and Statistic Manual of the American Psychiatric Association*, or DSM for short, is the most widely used and accepted reference tool for recognised conditions. When something is in DSM, it formally exists. And if it formally exists, the public can rightly demand treatment for it. In the world of addictions, there might also be an argument that if a substance or a behaviour has been formally accepted as being 'addictive' then prevention strategies need to be put in place; perhaps there also needs to be controlled access and/or distribution, and compensation may need to be available for innocent sufferers. So if pornography addiction were to officially appear in DSM, just consider how much that could cost the government in treatment provision and policing the industry. Personally, I think as a society we should be taking much more responsibility for the porn industry as we increasingly are with gambling since 'pathological gambling' entered DSM, but the financial ramifications are enormous.

There are other controversies around DSM. If a condition is listed then it means it is a problem that needs to be treated or managed rather than a difference to be accepted. And the sufferer may then be saddled with a label that could potentially cause shame and discrimination. It's interesting to note that Asperger's Syndrome was only accepted by DSM in 1994 and homosexuality was not removed until the 70s. So up until relatively recently, anyone who was gay was considered to have a mental health problem and there was no support or funding available to help children with Asperger's. Being labelled with a condition or a problem can be both a blessing and a curse. For some it allows them to understand that what they're struggling with is something that's caused problems for many others. The stigma may be removed and energy can be focused on overcoming the problem rather than feeling to blame. But the flipside of this is that for some people, the label becomes a heavy burden under which they feel they have no power or escape. Therefore, the most important thing is to discern what the client wishes to call their problem and what that definition means to them.

While the medical and therapeutic communities continue to debate the best name for the problem, the term 'sex addiction' is becoming increasingly popular on the street and in the media, and many therapists rightly worry that it is also being overused, misused and misdiagnosed. According to my survey it seems that the term 'sex addiction' is favoured with 43 per cent of sufferers defining it thus, 22 per cent preferring love addiction, 17 per cent sexual compulsivity and only 10 per cent favouring hypersexuality (Hall, 2012). Whatever the problem is called, what really matters is its definition, not its name.

What sex addiction is not

One of the proposals going forward for the next edition of DSM is that sex addiction could fall under the heading of Hypersexual Disorder. If this happens, it is my belief that this could lead to a gross misunderstanding of sex addiction and many sufferers may continue to be misunderstood and not be able to find the help they need. Although the proposed definition is about preoccupation with thoughts of sexual behaviour not just acting out, and it must be experienced as a problem for the individual, there is still the risk that it will seem as though clinicians are defining 'hyper' as too much. In my clinical experience, sex addiction is not the same as a high sex drive. Many of the addicts I've worked with do not get sexual pleasure from what they're doing and it does not satiate their drive. In fact some would go so far as to say they consider themselves to have a very low sex drive. Consider the following two case examples.

Frank

Frank, a 52 year-old solicitor, arrived for help having been picked up by the police for curb crawling in a local red light district. He was ashamed and devastated. His habit of driving around looking for prostitutes had been part of his life for over 20 years and he would spend at least an hour most evenings following the same familiar route looking at the girls on offer. But in over 20 years he had only ever slept with six prostitutes – all of which he bitterly regretted. The last time had been nearly two years ago and he'd vowed never to do it again. He explained that he had absolutely no interest in sleeping with a prostitute again and had always had a good sex life with his wife. But for some reason that he could not fathom at all, he felt compelled to drive round and round and watch the women looking for business.

Julian

Julian was 32 and engaged to get married. He described his relationship as 'very happy' and was really looking forward to finally tying the knot after seven years of living together. His fiancée didn't know that he was coming for therapy and he hoped she'd never find out why. Julian's problem was pornography addiction, and he wanted to overcome it once and for all as all his previous efforts had failed. As far as his fiancée was concerned, Julian was a night owl who stayed up late most nights after she'd gone to bed playing computer games, but in reality what he was doing was downloading video clips of porn. Julian described how he would sometimes be up until four or five in the morning searching for the right sequences to piece together to make his perfect show reel. I asked him if he enjoyed masturbating to them once they were complete. 'You're joking,' he laughed in reply. 'I'm usually far too knackered by then and just go straight to bed.'

Neither Frank nor Julian would describe their sex drive as high and they're certainly not alone. Perhaps one of the biggest myths about sex addiction is that it's a condition suffered by men with high sex drives that they can't control. This is simply not the case. The acting out behaviour is sexual in some respect, but the primary motivation is not satiation of sex drive. It is not linked to the physical essence of libido but to the psychological need to satisfy a deeper subconscious urge.

In many ways, sex addiction has more in common with eating disorders than it does with other addictions (Goodman, 1993). In one study by Patrick Carnes (1991) 38 per cent of his sample had an eating disorder and in the UK 79 per cent of those with another addiction cited eating disorder (Hall, 2012). In the same way as bulimia, anorexia and compulsive over-eating are about an unhealthy relationship with food, sex addiction is an unhealthy relationship with sex. In healthy individuals, both sex and food satisfy a natural, innate and primitive drive, but when the relationship becomes corrupt, sex addiction has no more to do with sex drive than eating disorders do with hunger.

However, there are definitely some who suffer with sex addiction who say they have a very high sex drive and who would describe their initial motivation for acting out as being a way of meeting their sexual needs. But further investigation and exploration of their feelings often exposes this as untrue. In the same way as someone with an eating disorder might misinterpret feelings of hunger or fullness, so someone with sex addiction can misinterpret their sexual desire. When sex or food are used compulsively, to the point where it's causing significant problems in someone's life, the function is not to satiate a natural desire but to meet a deeper need. In sex addiction, the attempt to satiate the deeper need may also be accompanied by desire and therefore the two can become confused. For example, if someone masturbates every time they feel lonely or bored or angry or sad, after a while they will associate each of those emotions with desire. Like Pavlov's dogs who salivated every time they heard a bell whether there was food or not, the addict may seek sexual gratification every time they feel a negative emotion whether or not they feel desire.

Another common misconception about sex addiction is that it's an impulse control disorder. But consider again the case studies earlier. Both Frank and Julian may have experienced difficulty controlling an impulse at an earlier stage of their life or their addiction, but these behaviours are pre-conceived and pre-planned.

The function of addiction

To understand any kind of addiction, you need to recognise that it's much, much more than a bad habit that's been developed over a period of time. Addiction has a function, a psychological purpose (Dodes, 2002). Sex addiction is a coping mechanism, a way of managing life. It is a strategy used to alleviate negative emotions and create positive ones. Some people refer to addiction as an anaesthetising behaviour, a way of numbing out the world. Others refer to addictions as hedonistic behaviour; a way of seeking perpetual pleasure. Often it's both, or at least that's how it starts, but over time the drug of choice, be that sex, cocaine, alcohol or food creates the very problems you're trying to escape and provides very limited pleasure indeed.

In some respects you could argue that all of human behaviour is based on our desire to increase or elicit a positive feeling state and reduce or eliminate a negative one. We are pre-programmed to seek pleasure and avoid pain as a survival mechanism. Surely that's why there are magazines in the doctors' waiting room. Rather than focus on our illness, anxiety or boredom, we can distract ourselves with something more interesting. We all have a multitude of techniques and methods for cheering ourselves up and calming ourselves down. Hopefully most of them are healthy. People with addictions are no different except that their drug of choice has often become their only coping mechanism. For someone with sex addiction, rather than finding appropriate and healthy ways of regulating emotion, preparing for sex, thinking about sex or having sex has become their primary coping mechanism. It is the only method they have for managing life. Their addiction becomes a buffer between them and the world – a world that is often becoming increasingly unmanageable.

The organisation Sex Addicts Anonymous describe the experience of sexual acting out as The Bubble (SAA Publications). They say that the bubble provides a wall between you and the world and that whilst in it an addict can feel free and liberated, floating above normal life feeling as though nothing can touch them. They can see what's going on in the outside world but it feels detached and unreal, all they can really feel is inside the mystical world of the bubble. But the bubble is also a trap and when it bursts and you hit the ground, reality can be overwhelming.

Sex addiction can be viewed as a particularly powerful mood-altering drug because there is such a wide range of sexual experiences that can elicit a range of emotional responses. In the same way as some drug users will mix and choose between uppers, downers and hallucinogenics, the sex user can choose behaviours that will give a range of feeling states. And as science continues to advance, we increasingly understand that those emotions are not purely psychological but are direct products of our brain chemistry. People who are experienced in using sex to modulate emotion can unknowingly, but very effectively, create almost any emotion they wish.

The neurochemistry of addiction

Pleasure is not purely psychological; it's a physical process triggered by chemicals in the brain – primarily dopamine, endorphines (natural opiods) and adrenalin. These chemicals are all naturally occurring; someone with a chemical addiction is able to tinker with these chemicals by the addition of others and the process addict has developed a fast access root to the source of those pleasure chemicals through their behaviour. It's a bit like having a cocaine dispenser in your brain that you can activate at any time you like or need. You can activate it either by acting out or just by fantasising about acting out. Different sexual experiences trigger different chemicals in the brain (Crenshaw, 1996). Nearly all will trigger dopamine but others focus more specifically on adrenaline or testosterone or oxytocin or endorphins. So while all sex might be experienced as pleasurable, for some the addition of risk or pain or love will trigger additional chemically induced emotions.

The brain is made up of literally millions of neural pathways that carry the necessary messages that make us think, feel and act, and there are a specific set of pathways responsible for delivering the feelings of pleasure. If we always access those pathways in the same way, they will become stronger and other pathways that might have previously been used to access the pleasure chemicals become weaker. But while these pathways become more fixed they become less effective at delivering the desired effect and hence the addict finds they need more stimulation in order to get the same affect (Blum et al., 2000; Duvauchelle et al., 2000). This is what's known within the addiction field as 'tolerance and escalation'.

For a moment, compare sex to food and consider how it would be if the only food available to you was chocolate? Bliss you may think, but imagine eating nothing but your favourite bar week after week after week. It wouldn't take long before you'd become bored and when you do, you'll probably change brand or choose a bar with a higher cocoa count. But as the weeks pass you'll find the pleasure gradually diminishing again. Now imagine that someone offers you an apple and suggests that perhaps you'd enjoy that instead. You take it with keen anticipation, but unbeknown to you, your fruit pathways have become over-run with the pleasure-seeking chocolate pathways and the apple tastes completely bland and uninteresting. What would you do?

This is the dilemma of the addict. Their sexual acting out has created a fast track to dopamine and in the meantime their other pleasure pathways have begun to fade away. They may still enjoy listening to music or spending time with friends, but compared to the instant hit they can get from acting out, it's a poor substitute. But each time they access their reward system through sex, the weaker the other pathways become.

The neurobiology of addition encompasses more than the neurochemistry of reward. People with addiction experience difficulties with impulse control, deferring gratification and making judgements about harmful consequences – all processes that involve the frontal cortex of the brain and underlying white matter. These areas of the brain are altered by addiction and since they are still maturing in adolescence, this is why early exposure is believed to be a significant factor in the development of addiction (*Addiction Today*, December 2011).

Recently it has also been highlighted that the internet can impact our brain chemistry (Hudson Allez, 2009). It seems that when we're looking at the fast moving images of the internet we tap into a different part of the brain. That feeling of losing touch with time and space that many of us can experience as we waste hours on eBay or researching an interesting holiday destination is not purely psychological. It's the impact the internet has on the orientation of our brain. Hence when someone with sex addiction uses the internet for their sexual arousal, it seems the pleasure pathways are amplified and accelerated.

Addiction is a condition of the brain that disrupts the circuitry of the brain and challenges control. Continued chemical misuse or behavioural acting out changes the chemistry of the brain and the brain literally becomes dependent on the chosen drug or activity to feel pleasure and reduce pain.

There's more on neurochemistry in later chapters, but for now we'll conclude by looking at the consequences of sexual addiction.

The consequences of sex addiction

Sex addiction affects every area of a sufferer's life. Initially, the secrecy may seem to provide protection from harmful consequences, and the illusion that 'if no one knows, it won't matter' can perpetuate the behaviour for months or even years. But every choice we make in life comes at a cost and it's only a matter of time before an addict finds themselves bankrupt. The sense of loss and destruction that people with sex addiction feel is key to the definition. If there are no negative consequences, then the behaviour may simply be a lifestyle choice. But if life is becoming increasingly unmanageable and unbearable, then the behaviour is more likely to be experienced as a compulsion or an addiction than a choice that comes from free will.

The type of behaviour will dictate the level and extent of damaging consequences. Some may experience significant financial difficulties, others may have legal implications, and others create workplace difficulties or cause health concerns. A significant proportion have caught sexually-transmitted infections (STIs), suffered from anxiety and depression and had a serious desire to commit suicide as the table below indicates. Escalation can result in changes to the arousal threshold commonly resulting in physical dysfunction such as erectile and ejaculatory problems and also changes in sexual tastes. One very worrying side effect of sexual addiction is the growing link between addiction and sexual offending behaviour as the sexual template, or 'love map' as defined by Money (1989) becomes corrupted.

As well as physical and practical difficulties, all addicts are likely to experience growing problems in their personal relationships and their sense of self. As addiction escalates and an addict increasingly prioritises their acting out behaviour over their sexual and intimate relationships with a partner, distance and conflict can grow. These problems are further exacerbated by the secrecy and deceit required to maintain the behaviours and may explode exponentially if discovered or disclosed. Sex addiction is more damaging to relationships than any other addiction because for many, it breaches the contract of sexual fidelity and trust. As you can see from Table 1.1, 46.5 per cent had lost a relationship due to their behaviour.But by far the most damaging consequence of sexual addiction is the impact it has on self-esteem. This is another area where some choose to take sex addiction into the moral realm rather than mental health, assuming the impact on self-esteem is caused by the shame associated with their choice of sexual behaviours. This may indeed be the case for some, but many do

Table 1.1 Harmful consequences (Hall 2012)

Consequence	Actual	Potential
Feelings of shame	70.5%	48.8%
Low self-esteem	65.0%	45.6%
Losing a relationship	46.5%	71.4%
Loss of employment	4.1%	26.3%
Wasted time	62.7%	41.5%
Wasted money	41.9%	35.5%
Debt	14.7%	24.0%
Impaired parenting	14.7%	19.4%
Physical health problems	15.7%	19.8%
Catching an STI	19.4%	47.0%
Mental health problems	49.8%	43.3%
A serious desire to commit suicide	19.4%	–
Sexual dysfunctions	26.7%	22.6%
Legal actions against you	6.0%	17.5%
Press exposure	0.9%	17.5%

not necessarily consider their behaviour to be wrong or bad. What damages a person's self-esteem is often not the behaviour itself but their dependency on it. They may not see anything wrong with viewing pornography, but when they're spending 8 hours a day or choosing to be online rather than sleep with their wife or go to their child's nativity play, then their feelings of self respect and integrity are damaged. Similarly someone with sex addiction may not have any issues with the sex trade or prostitution and if, or when, they were single it may not have caused them a problem. But once in a committed relationship where they value fidelity and trust, it is the contradiction of their own values that they can't cope with. The dependency on some kind of sexual behaviour and the incessant pursuit of it in spite of all the damage it causes, is what kills self worth. Unfortunately the lower self worth plummets, the less resources someone has to fight addiction. Therefore, as we will see in later chapters, one of the key tasks of the therapist is to help to rebuild self-esteem.

In addition to the 'actual' consequences of sexual addiction, it's also important to remember the 'potential' consequences – in other words, the risks. Whilst some have been luckier than others in what they've had to suffer, living in constant fear and dread that the world could come tumbling down at any second is in itself, a very real negative consequence. Table 1.1 is from the UK survey undertaken in 2012.

Understanding the impact of sex addiction is key to recognising it as a 'real' problem in people's lives. Whatever you want to call it, however it is defined – it wrecks peoples lives and having listened to countless stories of waste and devastation, in my mind there can be no doubt. Below are what just a few people said in the survey when asked: 'What has been the worst consequence of your addiction?'

'I lost my wife and my daughter.'

'The ramifications have been far greater than I ever could have imagined. My marriage is still impacted, although I have a loving wife (same one!). I still struggle with shame and depression regarding this as I have still not achieved a healthy sexuality. I still struggle with occasional (fortunately relatively rare) relapses that also have effects on my life and marriage.'

'My addiction has robbed, and continues to rob me of my life. I have become the person I never wanted to be, I have hurt my wife and have a past which would destroy friendships and alienate me even further if it were to come out.'

'The hurt caused to my partner, the damage to her trust and love towards me, and almost losing 20 years of marriage.'

'Seeing the impact on my partner. Her life is greatly diminished since her trust has been shattered. I also now realise that my behaviour significantly undermined my ability to be a loving and caring partner over many years.'

'Wasted opportunities, a sense of hopelessness and being consumed culminating in near bankruptcy. Not very nice and it still haunts me.'

'Continual discovery of my behaviour has destroyed the deep love my wife had for me, undermined her self-esteem and stripped her life of joy for years.'

'Losing the only woman I've ever truly loved.'

'I was caught by my 11 year-old son viewing adult channels on TV which he kept secret for quite a while before being able to confide in his mother.'

'Unwanted pregnancy.'

'having been in a relationship for 13 years, married for 4, my sexual addiction got too much when i had an affair. my wife found out about it and a lot more stuff came out in the open. i then lost my marriage, causing my 2 children to go through a huge emotional phase in their young lives, which i don't think they will ever get over.'

'Nearly loosing my soul mate (and now husband) because I HAD to sleep with some guy who's name I didn't even know.'

'Being arrested.'

'i am a 30 year old virgin who has never had a girlfriend or dated. Porn has distorted my view of real women and i now think my natural libido is not what it should be. Porn has been a comfort blanket to my anxieties but has at the same time helped to increase them whilst stopping me from facing up to my problems and living my life to the full.'

'Clinical depression. My ex-husband finding out after 5 yrs I was having an affair. Frequent tearful visits to GUM [genitourinary medicine] clinics. I contracted an STI after being raped in my teens and I still put myself at risk sometimes.'

'Wanting to commit suicide.'

'Losing child.'

'Depression, isolation.'

'Police warning, self-loathing, terror of catching an STI if something has gone wrong and the absolute fear of losing those I love.'

'Shame ... risk of infections, inability to have a relationship.'

'Failure of two marriages, daughter in drug rehab, son who does not talk to me.'

2 Assessment and diagnosis

You cannot treat a problem until you know what it is. In every area of psychology and medicine, accurate assessment is essential and never more so than in sex addiction where confusion abounds. Misdiagnosis is common among people with sex addiction and the focus of the work often becomes the cause or the consequence, rather than the addiction itself. But this isn't necessarily the fault of the clinician.

Many people with sex addiction come for counselling because of the anxiety or depression that the problem is causing. Or because of the impact it is having on their relationship or on their sex life. Although the situation is beginning to change as sex addiction becomes more widely recognised, there are still many who will initially seek help for a secondary issue. For many people it's too painful or risky to talk about their sexual acting out so instead they will seek help for the consequences without openly acknowledging the cause. Others may be aware that their sexual behaviour has originated from a childhood wound and they come for help with this and only hint at the extent of their current addiction. While the cause and the consequence both need to be worked on, unfortunately the addiction is too often left to continue to thrive. In some cases it may become apparent that the compulsive sexual behaviour is a symptom of another mental health problem such as a personality disorder or post-traumatic stress disorder, in which case both need to be professionally addressed. As we will see in Part II of this book, it's essential that treating sex addiction is seen within the context of working with the whole person, and therefore the cause, effect and addiction need to be considered.

Assessment is also essential for breaking through denial. Accepting that you've got a problem with sex addiction is not easy for most and while some people may come for counselling with an inkling that they may have a problem, many will struggle to accept the severity. A formal assessment process can help clients to explore their situation in an objective way and come to a conclusion for themselves. It's essential that therapists do not try to force a diagnosis of sex addiction, as this can prevent someone seeking the help they need at a later date. Before any kind of assessment can begin, it's essential to understand to what extent someone is ready for and motivated to change.

Assessing motivation for change

Someone who has already defined them self as a sex addict is quite different from someone who is not yet aware that the term sex addiction even exists. A tool that can be helpful for considering this is the stages of change model, first developed by Prochaska and DiClemente (1982; see Figure 2.1). The model is a useful tool for considering motivation levels and can be used to pitch therapy at an appropriate level and set an appropriate pace. As you can see, the model starts in the pre-contemplation stage when someone may have no awareness of any need to change and then moves on through a variety of stages before the change is made permanent and the model is exited permanently. Here we will explore the first four stages of the cycle – namely, Pre-contemplation, Contemplation, Preparation and Action. If someone is already in the Maintenance or Relapse stage, assessment will almost always have been completed.

The pre-contemplative stage

Someone in the pre-contemplative stage generally arrives in therapy either presenting with a different problem or because they've been sent by a disgruntled partner. Typically they will know little or nothing about sex

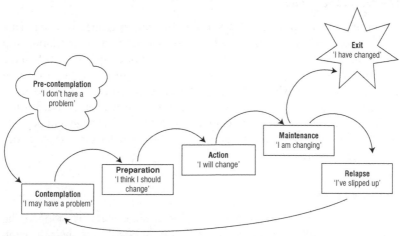

Figure 2.1 The stages of change

addiction and will be reluctant to consider it as a problem at all. The best therapeutic strategy for someone in this stage is to establish what they *would* like to work on and provide sufficient information on sex addiction to raise doubt. Questions such as 'How would you know if your sexual behaviour was causing you a problem?' or 'What has been the worst consequence of your behaviour?' and information about possible effects and consequences are much more effective than direct challenges, which may increase defensiveness and denial. An assessment tool, such as the one in this chapter or Patrick Carne's comprehensive Sex Addiction Screening Test (available at www.recoveryzone.com) may be offered, but should be given in the spirit of curiosity rather than necessity. Someone in the pre-contemplative stage may not be ready to face their behaviour head on and therefore the essential strategy is to ensure the therapy door is left firmly open.

The contemplative stage

A person in the contemplative stage will already be aware of the impact of their sexual behaviour though they may not have much information about the condition or have come across the term 'sexual addiction'. At this stage education is essential to help understand the problem more fully, and begin to accept the potential and actual consequences of continuing the behaviour. Providing optimism about the ability to change is also useful here, but space must be given to explore any feelings of ambivalence. The use of assessment tools, as mentioned earlier, can be particularly useful as they can provide essential food for thought.

The preparation stage

It is during the preparation stage that the decision to change is made. This may have come about due to a life change such as starting a new relationship or becoming a parent or receiving a career opportunity. Or it may have come from a near miss of discovery or simply out of exhaustion of living this way. Someone who seeks help during this stage is likely to have reasonable awareness of their problems and the consequences, but further work on assessment can help to cement the decision to change and provide the necessary motivation and awareness to work at underlying issues rather than simply 'trying to stop'.

The action stage

When someone has made the decision to change and has stopped the behaviour, they often attend therapy as a way of confirming their decision rather than seeking help. They may attend once they've hit rock bottom in one way or another, and the common refrain is 'I've had my wake up call – I will never, ever, ever do this again.' At that moment it can seem as if no further help is required, as someone in this position is often absolutely convinced they can break the addiction alone. Unfortunately relapse is common in addiction – in spite of the great tragedy that discovery can cause. Hence when someone presents in the 'action' stage, a formal assessment process can help to fully ascertain the size of the task ahead and provide an opportunity to discuss how therapy can be used to assist them on their journey into full recovery.

Before we move on to look at the assessment criteria, we'll explore the additional complications that may arise when people present with love addiction or sex-offending behaviours, and also additional considerations when assessing female addicts, adolescents, people from the LGBTQ community. Each of these client groups share more similarities with sex addiction than they do differences but it's worth being aware of some of the nuances that may present in the therapy room.

Variations of sex addiction

Love addiction

Love addiction, also known as romance or intimacy addiction, shares many similarities with sex addiction and may or may not include sexual behaviour. The key difference is that it is the process of attraction that creates the buzz rather than any overt sexual behaviour. In reality since many with sex addiction enjoy the chase just as much as the catch, the presentation in therapy may be identical but some clients may prefer the term 'love' addiction than 'sex' addiction as demonstrated by 22 per cent of survey respondents (Hall, 2012). Whatever the behaviour, whether serial affairs, endless flirtations or short-term relationships, the chosen behaviour becomes compulsive and a primary coping mechanism. A pattern soon develops that while they appear to be seeking a meaningful relationship where they feel loved, as soon as the relationship matures from the lust and attraction phase into deeper attachment, the love addict will move on. Some people with love addiction find themselves trapped in long-term abusive relationships where they continually seek love. Like someone with sex addiction, in spite of the harmful consequences to their self-esteem and often their safety, they're compulsively driven to gain their partner's affection and positive regard. Research in the field of love addiction is very limited, and hence there may be more confusion about definition and treatment than we are currently aware and clinicians should be careful to notice individual treatment requirements (Sussman, 2010).

Sex offending

It's estimated that 55 per cent of sex offenders are also sex addicts (Blanchard, 1990) and since escalation is a common feature of addiction, crossing a boundary into offending behaviour is a real risk for many addicts. In my survey 43 per cent had viewed either child or animal pornography and a further 18 per cent had engaged in exhibitionist or voyeuristic behaviours. All clinicians working in this field need to be aware and ready to work with, or refer, sex-offending behaviours and establish appropriate confidentiality contracts and supervision. Some clients will confess straying into illegal areas in the first session but others may spend many weeks or months gaining the trust of the therapist before hinting at the extent of their acting out. It's also important to be aware of the Sex Offences Act as there are significant variations in the classifications of pornography. This is particularly true when it comes to the viewing of underage images and while there continues to be so little understanding of sex addiction it's essential to understand where you may stand in terms of child protection issues. It is an unfortunate reality that many people with sex addiction have been erroneously labelled a risk to children and therapists who choose to work in this field can expect to find themselves drawn into complex ethical and legal dilemmas.

There is nothing you cannot view on the internet and, unfortunately, this means that sexual curiosity gets the better of many people and they find themselves increasingly drawn to the risk and excitement of the illegal unknown. Clever use of file-sharing and advertising pop-ups lure the user in while viewing statistics reassure them that their behaviour is normal and commonplace. Someone may view once and once only, but someone with an addiction may find a deeper unconscious need being met that draws them deeper in. Often that need is simply to reinforce the feelings of shame and disgust they feel at their own behaviour. Added to this, the shame that addiction creates, robs many people of the ability to follow their own moral compass. In terms of assessment and treatment, the goals of therapy are the same with the extra complication of ensuring that ethical standards and legal obligations are observed.

Special populations

Female sex addiction

Historically, research suggested that sex addiction was predominantly a male problem with only an estimated 8–20 per cent of people seeking help being women. It has often been argued that the prevalence is probably higher but women have more difficulty seeking help. Partly because of lack of specialist services and also due to the additional stigma that women may face admitting to 'out of control' sexual behaviours (Ferree, 2002). This is backed up by my UK survey where 25 per cent of the survey respondents were women but 60 per cent had never sought help compared to 42 per cent of men who had never sought help (Hall, 2012). The stigma might also explain why more women present as love addicts than sex addicts, preferring to focus attention on the relational side of sex than the act of sex 50 per cent in my survey compared to just 13 per cent of men (Hall, 2012). However, it's important not to make assumptions about the acting out behaviours of women, as much of it is similar to men. For example, watching pornography – 73 per cent women, 89 per cent men; fetish behaviours – 36 per cent women, 24 per cent men; stranger sex – 41 per cent women, 32 per cent men; and multiple affairs – 54 per cent women, 37 per cent men. In fact the only area where men differed considerably was in the use of sex workers with only 3.3 per cent of women compared to 30 per cent of men using their services. There are undoubtedly different opportunities for women to become addicted to sex than men with little female-focused pornography and a limited escort trade, but it may be that the female addict finds another arena for the addiction. I would hypothesise that the sex industry is the perfect hiding place for female sexual addiction. Not only can she get her unconscious needs met through sex but she can also get paid for it. In terms of treatment, there is little difference except in an awareness of differences in the social context of gender.

Adolescent sex addiction

Identifying sex addiction in adolescence poses a number of difficulties since many of the identifying factors might be described as 'normal' adolescent behaviours. Adolescence is a time of change and experimentation and hence many young people engage in sexual acts that are risky or that they later regret. And while hormones are raging and sex is a novelty, it's common for thoughts of sex and the pursuit of sex to feel all encompassing. Clinicians and concerned adults should also be aware of changing cultural norms and not jump to conclusions about behaviours that they find challenging. It's been suggested that diagnosing adolescent sex addiction requires a more detailed assessment, in particular about the role of masturbation and fantasies, and adults should suspend assumptions that young people cannot become addicted because the behaviour can't have existed for long enough (Griffin-Shelley, 2002).

Many clinicians confirm that sex addiction in adolescence is a problem, although it's often not recognised by their clients until later in life (Sussman,

2007). Within my survey 29 per cent reported that the problem began between the ages of 17 and 25, 31 per cent between 11 and 16, and 8.8 per cent under the age of 10. With the increasing access to the internet, more young people are able to intentionally seek pornography, although this does not necessarily mean they will develop a problem (Ybarra and Mitchell, 2005); however, it's clear that some are, and in a survey conducted by BBC Radio 1, 25 per cent of respondents said they were worried about their porn use. This is an area that needs considerably more research, both from the perspective of offering support and treatment for young people with sexual addiction, but also to provide education and preventative work.

LGBTQ sex addiction

Compared to heterosexuals, it's thought there is a greater incidence of sexual addiction among gay men; one proposed explanation for this is that gay men have more sexual outlets and hence someone with a predisposition to compulsive behaviours is more likely to develop the condition if they're gay (Grov et al., 2010). On the whole, sex addiction does not change among different groups but the differences in cultural norms and developmental backgrounds must be recognised and understood in order to provide appropriate treatment within gay communities (Weiss, 2002).

Lesbian, gay, bisexual, transgender and queer people have often come from a background of repressed gender orientation or identity issues, homophobic judgements, teasing, bullying and discrimination. Many people in the LGBTQ community also have complex issues relating to sexual shame, which is a common predisposition to sex addiction, but it's essential to understand the socio-political context of this shame and to provide a gay-affirmative therapeutic stance. Notions of sexual sobriety tend to come from a hetero-normative, monogamous viewpoint and it's important to recognise that many LGBTQ clients may not agree with these. Every person needs to recognise their individuality and be free to define which of their behaviours they feel are damaging and compulsive and which are not.

Classifications of sex addiction

In the same way as there is currently no formal definition and diagnosis criteria for sex addiction, there is also no clearly defined classification system. Although there are a significant number of characteristics that are common to all with sex addiction, there are differences in both the degree of addiction, also the cause and function of the addiction, and the presenting style. Broadly speaking, addiction is trauma-induced, attachment-induced or opportunity-induced or, in some cases, a combination of two or three.

Figure 2.2 The OAT classification model

As you can see in Figure 2.2, opportunity is present in each of the three classifications of addiction. In addition, a sufferer may have problems with attachment, trauma or attachment and trauma. In my experience it's essential to distinguish these differing presentations of sex addiction as the focus of treatment will vary considerably as will the skills required by a therapist. It also allows us to respect the growing diversity of people who struggle with sex addiction, who come from very different backgrounds. Many years ago it was believed that all addiction had its roots in either attachment or trauma, but as pornography becomes increasingly prevalent, so do the people who stumble into sex addiction with no prior pathology. This new classification of pure opportunity-induced sex addiction will require a different treatment approach from the intensive psychotherapeutic programmes offered in the past. We will look at the origination and treatment of these three types of addiction in depth in subsequent chapters, but for now I'll introduce the categories in order to provide a context for the assessment tool shown in Figure 2.2.

Beyond these three classifications, addiction may be assessed as mild, moderate or severe, and an additional category of people might be considered 'at risk' but not currently displaying classic signs of addiction. Someone might be considered 'severe' due to the degree of damage their addiction is causing in their lives or may potentially cause in their lives or because of the frequency. For example, someone who spends a minimum of six hours a day, every day, looking at pornography may be considered severe but if their behaviour has minimal impact on their life the client might prefer to gauge themselves as moderate, whereas someone who feels compelled to exhibit themselves in public but only gives in to the temptation two or three times a year might be considered severe due to the potential consequences if they were caught, especially if it was accompanied by regular intrusive fantasies.

Ultimately, only the individual can make the decision as to whether or not they believe their behaviour to be severe, moderate or mild, but the clinician's experience may be used as a helpful barometer.

Trauma-induced addiction

The link between trauma and addiction are well documented (Carruth, 2011). Addiction may on some occasions be directly triggered by a traumatic event, for example, bereavement, physical assault or sudden illness might instigate a habit of using masturbation for comfort that then leads to an addiction. Or sometimes a traumatic event, or events, occur in childhood, and sex becomes a way of coping with the subsequent emotional and physical fallout. Significant trauma can also have a direct impact on the structure of the brain and the repetitive nature of the compulsive behaviour can become a way of soothing a hyperactive amygdala and limbic system and reduce symptoms of hyper arousal and hypo arousal (Fowler, 2006; Fisher, 2007).

Someone with a trauma-induced addiction is most likely to use the behaviour to self soothe difficult emotions and the chosen behaviour may in some way replicate the initial trauma. For example, someone who's experienced significant physical abuse may become addicted to BDSM practices (Birchard, 2011). On the outside a trauma-induced addict may appear self controlled, calm and high functioning but inside there may be resonance of anxiety and stress. Someone with a trauma-induced addiction is also more likely than any other to experience powerful feelings of anxiety about giving up the behaviour.

It's possible that some people with a trauma-induced addiction may have never considered that their trauma may be linked to their addiction and may not mention anything about it in therapy. Assuming the trauma didn't happen within the family of origin, childhood may be otherwise happy, and adult relationships may be reasonably well balanced and functional. However, trauma that was experienced very early in life or was suffered at the hands of a primary care giver may present with attachment issues too. Indeed, early traumatisation may make it almost impossible for children to form healthy attachment bonds (Potter-Efron, 2006).

Attachment-induced addiction

'Addiction is an attachment disorder' is a common refrain among addiction specialists and this is undoubtedly true in a significant number of cases (Flores, 2004). But to assume that childhood attachment issues are always at the root of the problem is overly simplistic. We know that when a child forms a secure attachment with their primary care giver they are more likely to grow into an adult with positive self esteem who is able to tolerate and manage strong emotions and mild trauma (Potter-Efron, 2006). But if positive parenting has been unreliable or absent a child is more likely to fear negative feelings and turn to an addiction for comfort during times of trouble rather than to a person.

Someone with an attachment-induced addiction will be unconsciously using their behaviour as a way of soothing relational pain such as fears of rejection or suffocation, loneliness or low self-esteem. The behaviour may be a way of getting close to people in a controlled manner or alternatively a way of creating or maintaining distance from an otherwise committed relationship. For example, a happily married man with a history of attachment problems may use pornography or sex workers as a way of avoiding full commitment and intimacy with his wife. Or someone who has never been in a committed relationship may use their addiction as a way of experiencing physical intimacy.

Most people in the world have grown up with imperfect parents and most therapists would agree that some degree of attachment difficulties present in all clients, so why do only a few go on to develop addictions? And why do an increasing number choose 'sex' as their drug of choice? Attachment, like trauma, is certainly a common characteristic in sex addiction, but an element that is often overlooked in assessment is the power and significance of opportunity.

Opportunity-induced addiction

Whatever a client's history and individual circumstances, if there was no opportunity for sexual acting out, it would not happen. The reality of the Western world today is that 'opportunity' is everywhere and people, with or without a background of trauma and/or attachment difficulties, can now indulge their sexual desires and run the risk of becoming addicted.

The internet has turned pornography and cyber sex into what's known as Supernormal Stimuli. This term was first coined in the 1930s to describe the many different substances and situations that trigger our instinctive impulses beyond their original evolutionary purpose. One common example of this is sugar. Humans have a natural craving for sweet foods which, in hunter/ gatherer days, would have given us much-needed bursts of energy. But in our modern world, filled with an endless variety of sugary substances, that natural desire for sugar has resulted in a global obesity epidemic. Similarly, Mother Nature gave us a primal drive to seek out sexual partners and be aroused by visual cues – a drive required to survive. But the internet now floods our senses with visual stimuli and sexual opportunities, and hence pornography and cybersex, like sugar, have become Supernormal Stimuli and our brains must work harder to control and manage our primal appetite.

There appears to be common characteristics that predispose some people to be more easily influenced by the proliferation of sexual experience, mostly linked to healthy emotional regulation and adolescent sexual development, but it may be more a case of bad luck rather than bad judgement that leads so many down the road to addiction.

The profile of the 'typical' sex addict is changing. Fifty years ago it would only have been those with significantly dysfunctional backgrounds who would have been driven enough to pursue their sexual anaesthetic. But now there is an increasing number of clients with only minor historic difficulties who stumble upon the joys of sex and pornography and become hooked. In my survey, 44 per cent of respondents said they had no experience of childhood abuse or trauma and 26.5 per cent of respondents had never experienced any of the well-recognised attachment related issues. As clinicians it's important that we recognise this distinct client group and ensure we don't attempt to pathologise their past by trying to find trauma and attachment issues that either do not exist or are not relevant. There are few of us in life who have completely escaped trauma or a bit of negative parenting. And there are few of us who won't have used sex and relationships as an anaesthetic when life is hard. But someone with an addiction stays stuck in this pattern of behaviour and the reasons for this are often complex and ultimately the client must decide on whether or not their behaviour is out of control.

The assessment process

This assessment process includes three questionnaires that may be completed alone or with a therapist. The first questionnaire provides the necessary information to ascertain whether or not someone's sexual behaviour might be considered compulsive, while the second questionnaire assesses the severity. The third questionnaire may be used to solicit information about childhood and adolescence which can further inform whether the addiction was triggered by trauma, attachment or purely by opportunity.

Questionnaire 1: Do I have sex addiction?

1 Does your sexual behaviour have a negative impact on other areas of your life such as relationships, work, finances, health, professional status?
2 Does your sexual behaviour contradict your personal values and potentially limit your goals in life?

3 Have you tried to limit your sexual behaviour or stop it all together, but failed?

4 Are you more tempted to engage in sexual behaviour when you're experiencing difficult feelings such as stress, anxiety, anger, depression or sadness?

5 Are you secretive about your sexual behaviours and fearful of being discovered?

6 Do you feel dependent on your sexual behaviour and struggle to feel fulfilled with any alternative?

7 Have you noticed that you need more and more stimuli or risk in order to achieve the same level of arousal and excitement?

8 Do you find yourself struggling to concentrate on other areas of your life because of thoughts and feelings about your sexual behaviour?

9 Have you ever thought that there might be more you could do with your life right now if you weren't so driven by your sexual pursuits?

10 Do you feel as if your sexual behaviour is out of your control?

11 Do you currently, or have you in the past, struggled with any other addictions, compulsive behaviours or eating disorders? Such as drug, alcohol addiction, compulsive gambling, gaming, work or exercise, collecting?

12 Has anyone in your family currently, or in the past, struggled with any addictions, compulsive behaviours or eating disorders such as those listed above?

If the answer to more than half of these questions is 'Yes', then someone is likely to be struggling with sexual addiction. If there are strong feelings of ambivalence this may be because someone is still in denial of their problem or it may be that their difficulty is mild. The following questionnaire may help to clarify.

Questionnaire 2: Measuring severity

As mentioned previously, the severity of a behavioural addiction can only be measured by the person themselves. What one person might see as excessive sexuality may be normal to someone else. However, the tool shown in Figure 2.3 can help therapists and clients to explore the impact of the behaviour on someone's life and may be used to confront denial and as a motivation to commit to treatment.

This questionnaire should have given you an indication of the extent of the problem. If all the answers have been 'rarely' and 'mild', then no further action may be required at this stage beyond developing greater self awareness and careful monitoring that behaviour does not escalate.

	Frequently	Occasionally	Rarely
Over the past 6 months, how often have you engaged in compulsive sexual behaviour?	☐	☐	☐
Over the past month, how often have you fantasised about your sexual behaviour?	☐	☐	☐
Over the past month, how often have you struggled with intrusive thoughts and feelings about your sexual behaviour?	☐	☐	☐
	Severe	Moderate	Mild
What impact does your behaviour have on your every day life?	☐	☐	☐
What are the potential consequences of your sexual behaviour if it was public knowledge?	☐	☐	☐
What impact does your sexual behaviour have on your sense of self worth?	☐	☐	☐

Figure 2.3 Measuring severity

However, if the answers indicate that the problem is moderate or severe then it would be advisable to answer the following questionnaire to establish the category of sexual addiction being experienced.

Defining the type of sex addiction

The questions in this section can help you to begin to determine if an addiction is attachment-, trauma- or opportunity-induced. The questions are primarily about childhood and adolescence, a time when addiction is often set up. There is more about this in the next chapter.

Attachment-induced addiction

1   Were you separated from your parents or any other key people in your life when you were growing up, for example through adoption, fostering, bereavement, divorce/separation?
2   Did you experience any significant periods of separation from your family, for example through hospitalisation, a parent working away or attending boarding school?
3   Did you experience regular threats of separation, abandonment or rejection as a child?
4   Did you experience impaired parenting, for example as a result of family illness, disability, alcoholism, imprisonment, domestic abuse or extreme poverty?
5   Did you experience neglectful parenting, for example receiving little or no attention, affection or affirmation?

6 Did you and your family move home more often than you would perceive as 'average'?

Trauma-induced addiction

1 Did you experience any form of physical abuse in childhood, for example excessive physical punishment from your parents, carers, teachers, siblings or peers?
2 Did you experience any ongoing emotional abuse in childhood, for example aggression, threats, name calling or bullying?
3 Did you experience any sexual abuse in childhood, for example being touched inappropriately or being made to touch someone else inappropriately, or being made to touch yourself sexually and being watched or being forced to watch someone else being sexual or forced to watch sexually explicit material?
4 Were you ever sexually assaulted?
5 Were you ever physically assaulted?
6 Were there ever any incidents of domestic violence in your home?
7 Did you experience any traumatic losses in your childhood or adolescence, for example bereavement, sudden disability or illness of someone close to you?
8 Have you at any stage in your life witnessed disturbing scenes of violence, brutality, loss or suffering, or feared for your life or safety?

Opportunity-induced addiction

1 Did you have access to pornography from what you would describe as an 'early age'?
2 Did you experience encouragement or influence to be sexually active, either with others or through masturbation from parents or mentors?
3 Before the age of 16, were you able to access internet pornography, in private, almost any time you desired?
4 Has internet access and broadband significantly increased your unwanted sexual behaviours?
5 Did you use pornography more than 80 per cent of the time when you masturbated during adolescence?
6 Did you have easy and regular access to sexual partners, sex workers or other sexual activities, for example because of where you lived or worked, through travel or through a particular work culture?
7 Have you had the financial resources to pay for your sexual behaviours?
8 Has it been easy for you to keep your sexual behaviours hidden from others?

Understanding which category an addiction falls under is not simply a case of counting up the 'Yes's' because each statement does not necessarily carry the same weight. Someone may tick a lot of boxes in the 'attachment' category but self-awareness and subsequent healthy relationships may have dealt with many of those wounds. Therefore, childhood attachment difficulties may contribute to the addiction but the main activator may be a particularly traumatic event that happened in teens. Whenever questionnaires are used in assessment, it's essential to explore not just the facts revealed but also what they mean to the individual. The information elicited by assessment can then be used as a guide rather than a template.

3   How sex addiction starts

'Why am I a sex addict?' is perhaps one of the most common questions I'm asked when someone has recognised and acknowledged that they have a problem. The question is often asked in a state of confusion and with urgency as someone attempts to make sense of what can initially feel like an overwhelming and daunting diagnosis. 'Am I mentally ill?' 'Is it because of something I've done?' 'Is this because I was abused?' – the questions often come thick and fast and beneath the desperate desire to seek understanding is a simpler question – 'Can I change?' Before beginning to explore how sex addiction starts, it's important to offer reassurance that whatever the cause, the problem can be overcome. This is especially important when someone has suffered childhood abuse and has already made a link between that and their current behaviour. For someone with a trauma-induced addiction, it's easy to assume that the damage is already done. But whatever the category of addiction, developing a greater understanding of the underlying causes is essential as it allows any negative messages or behavioural patterns that may have been established to be challenged and healthier coping strategies can then be developed.

There is of course no single or simple answer to why someone develops sex addiction, whether it's attachment-induced, trauma-induced or purely opportunity-induced as outlined in the previous chapter. Understanding how something came to be is almost always a complex interweaving of many different factors whether that's understanding how you got into the job you do or why a car crash happened. There are always multiple factors to be taken into consideration, many of which are dependent on another.

For example, if you're an acclaimed violinist, chances are that your love of music started in early childhood, and from an early age you learned that you had an innate musical talent. Perhaps your parents encouraged you to listen to and play music, and your passion was nurtured and your efforts and accomplishments praised. Negative events may have played a role too. Perhaps your first violin was inherited from your late grandfather who you miss very much, but who inspired you to commit to the instrument. If you also had the financial resources to pay for lessons and perhaps go and see live concerts to feed your ambition, and your local secondary school happened to be known for its excellent music teaching, then your journey to success had an excellent start. However, changing just a few key factors or introducing a discriminating wild card such as illness or parental separation might have changed your direction and set you on a very different path. Understanding the fragility of a life path is important because it can help us to understand why people with an almost identical history might develop very differently. It can also help us not to place undue blame or regret on one single incident or circumstance, something that is especially important in sex addiction where shame can play such a crucial role.

When looking at the causes of sex addiction, it's important to ask two questions. The first is, 'why does someone become an addict?' and the second, 'why did they become addicted to sex'. The answers to the first question generally reside is childhood whereas the answer to the second is usually around the time of puberty and adolescence. There are a number of common patterns in the histories of people with addictions, whether that's to a chemical or a process, but the causes of choosing sex, rather than alcohol, drugs or gambling, are tied up with sexual development and also availability and accessibility.

Each of these causes is best explored through an integrative model that takes into account every area of a person's life. The BERSC model (see Figure 3.1) is an expansion on the biopsychosocial model first theorized by psychiatrist George Engel in 1977. This model allows a framework through which to consider someone's unique biological make-up, their emotional predispositions and scripts, relational experiences from childhood through to adult couple relationships, the societal factors that influence our lives and also any relevant cultural factors such as religion, ethnicity, sexual orientation, peer groups and work environments. This holistic framework is important for minimising shame and developing an accurate understanding of the factors that uniquely contribute to each person's addiction. The BERSC model also encourages a comprehensive treatment approach that focuses on the client's individual circumstances and needs rather than favouring any singular therapeutic approach.

The following pages in this chapter will explore the most common causes of sex addiction within the categories of attachment-, trauma- and opportunity-induced and will cover each element of the BERSC model. We will start with opportunity since, without this, sex addiction would not exist – in the same way as if our acclaimed violinist had never heard or owned a violin, he would never have got where he is today. Almost everyone will be familiar with the

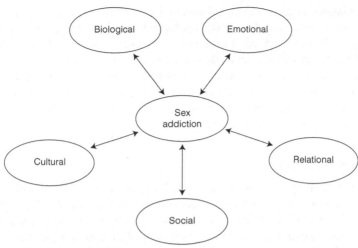

Figure 3.1 The BERSC Model

causes under the 'opportunity-induced' heading, while others will additionally identify with the causes under the headings of trauma and attachment.

Opportunity-induced addiction

Sex is available anywhere and everywhere. On the streets, in bars and clubs and in the privacy of your own home. The internet has allowed unlimited and anonymous access to any and every kind of sexual activity that our hearts and loins might desire. There are ample free online sexual activities to explore and there are no public health warnings or obvious negative consequences – until of course, you're hooked. Imagine how our world might be if heroin was available like this? How many more of us might follow our curiosity and sample the wares? If you had no idea that it could damage you or other areas of your life, what would stop occasional recreational use escalating into an addiction? In my survey, 1 in 5 people said not knowing sex could be addictive was the most influential factor in becoming addicted and 1 in 3 cited easy access to sexual opportunities.

No addiction can exist without opportunity, and in the absence of adequate education and advice, people will experiment, explore and take risks that they didn't know are there. It is the nature of humanity that we like new and pleasurable experiences and which ones we choose to follow and for how long is dependent on our temperament and our life experience. We will go on to explore these in a moment, but it's important to highlight that society is responsible for some of the causes of sexual addiction. I am not trying to suggest that we should enforce some kind of sexual prohibition, but in the same way as we teach and encourage healthy eating and responsible drinking, so we should establish appropriate public information for safe sexuality. Information that allows people to make informed choices rather than blindly stumbling into addiction as so many find they do. Sexual experimentation is natural, healthy and commonplace, but if you have a predisposition to develop addiction, and no internally or externally set boundaries, it's a quagmire. So with all these sexual opportunities available to us all, why is it that only some fall into addiction?

Brain development

It may be that some of us are biologically predisposed towards addiction, even before our birth. Addiction seems to run in families which supports a heredity factor as do twin studies and recent research showed that non drug users shared the same brain abnormalities as their siblings who were addicted to drugs (Ershe et al., 2012). We are still in the embryonic stages of understanding brain development both from a structural and from a bio-chemical perspective. The link between the brain and addiction has been researched and written about extensively over the years though research specific to sex addiction is still limited. However, there are a number of circulating hypothesises that are currently under investigation. It is beyond the scope of this book, and indeed beyond the capability of this author to explain all these hypotheses in depth, but here is a layman's guide to some of the latest thinking to mull over.

Dopamine dysregulation

It is now clinically understood that the common denominator in all addictions is dopamine (Robbins and Everitt, 2010). Dopamine is the neurochemical responsible for the experience of reward and pleasure and is naturally stimulated by eating, drinking and having sex. From an evolutionary point of view, dopamine is essential for our survival as it motivates us to continue to feed and reproduce. Dopamine is also heightened through anticipation and fantasy, which is perhaps why so many of us enjoy cookery programmes as well as pornography! Dopamine is also involved in memory processing, and it biases the brain towards events that will provide reward. These memories become stronger with repeated dopamine 'highs'. So the more you do something to increase your dopamine the more you'll want to do it (Berke and Hyman, 2000).

Low dopamine has been associated with ADHD, eating disorders and with addictions but there's a circular argument that, particularly within addiction and eating disorders, has yet to be resolved. Do low dopamine levels cause dependency on drugs, food and sex, or do excessive use of drugs, food and sex cause low dopamine? Or is it a bit of both? Evidence shows that drugs such as cocaine and heroin, flood the brain with up to 10 times more dopamine than the brain's usual base level and, over time, conditions it to expect artificially high amounts (Blum et al., 2000; Duvauchelle et al., 2000). With continued use, the brain requires more dopamine than it can naturally produce, and it becomes dependent on this external dopamine boost.

While the jury continue to debate this chicken and egg dilemma, there is also research underway to explore if early exposure to pornography may have a similar long term impact on dopamine regulation as happens with addictive dugs. There is ample evidence that early use of drugs, alcohol and nicotine creates a long-term dopamine imbalance (Manning et al., 2001); if sex has the potential to do the same then Patrick Carnes' prediction at the annual conference of the UK/European Symposium of Addictive Disorders (UKESAD) in May 2010 that we have a 'tsunami coming our way' will undoubtedly be right.

While research continues to be undertaken, there is one field in particular that appears to be supporting the hypothesis of dopamine involvement in sex addiction. Parkinson's patients are often prescribed dopamine agonists to improve motor and memory functions and one of the unwanted side effects of this is impulsive and compulsive sexual behaviours.

In addition to the debates already outlined, there is continuing research into the impact of trauma and attachment difficulties on dopamine and brain development – both of which will be explored later in this chapter.

Personality

The term 'addictive personality' is often used to describe a broad set of characteristics that many people with an addiction have in common. This term is not professionally recognised but many addiction specialists have noticed that there are common themes among both substance and process addictions. Examples of these common personality traits include:

- impulsiveness and difficulty delaying gratification
- risk taking and sensation seeking
- being a non-conformist
- difficulty managing stress and anxiety.

It's difficult to confirm if these traits are innate or learned behaviour but many parents would agree that these characteristics may be seen from early childhood. Someone suffering from addiction may find it helpful to reflect back on their childhood and consider how they were as a toddler and in their primary years. They might remember being a child who was always into something new and brave enough to climb the highest tree. And perhaps fitting in with friends didn't bother them much but they did prefer to sleep with the light on. The non-conformist personality trait often develops from a childhood where a child felt different from their peers. That might be because parents overtly said they were different in some way or because they knew for themselves that they did not conform to the norm.

It's worth flagging up here that there is increasing evidence of links between ADHD and addiction (Blankenship and Lasser, 2004), in part because of the role of dopamine but also because of the personality traits they share. A client may present having never received an official diagnosis, but if there has been an ongoing pattern throughout life of impulsivity, difficulty concentrating and sticking to tasks, then a formal diagnosis should be considered to ensure appropriate treatment. Similarly, someone who continues to struggle with ongoing anxiety may be suffering with Generalised Anxiety Disorder and should consider seeking concurrent help for this.

In addition to possible biological determinants and personality traits, there are common themes in the family histories of people with sex addiction – namely, a family environment where self-control was not taught, where there was no modelling of how to handle difficult emotions or experiences, and where there were secrets and shame.

Developing self-control

When we talk about self-control and its role in addiction, it's important not to reduce this simply to impulse control. It's true that many addicts struggle with impulse control, especially in the early days of their acting out behaviour, but maintaining a sex addiction usually takes meticulous planning and organisation. In the context of sex addiction, developing self-control means being able to make decisions and control one's behaviour based on sound judgement of your individual needs and any resulting consequences.

We begin to learn self-control in childhood and there are two ways in which parents can fail to teach this essential skill. The first, which is most common in sex addiction, is to have a strict and rigid home environment where a child is never allowed to make decisions for themselves (Carnes, 1991). In my survey 60 per cent of respondents described their family background as strict and controlling. There is either a spoken or unspoken dictate that the parents know what's best for the child. Subsequently it is the parents' will that is imposed, leaving no space for a child's will and willpower to develop. The consequence of over strict parenting is often an adolescent or adult who refuses to be controlled by anybody or anything other than the self, regardless of the consequences. This rebellious attitude might be overtly demonstrated in someone who breaks all the rules their parents held or it might be a quieter rebellion where the behaviour is acted out in secret.

The second way that parents may fail to teach control is by having a home with few or no boundaries, 26 per cent in my survey (Hall, 2012). A child who grows up with a sense that their parents never knew where they were or what they were up to, or that there were no rules to break, often grows up without ever knowing the benefits of moderating their behaviour.

Managing difficult feelings

Another essential lesson that parents need to teach is how to manage difficult emotions. None of us get through life without experiencing pain and hardship and therefore we all need to develop healthy coping mechanisms that will enable us to soothe the pain without creating further problems.

Many people with sexual addiction describe a family of origin where there was either no expression of emotion or emotions were expressed with such intensity that they were frightening or even dangerous. Seventy-seven per cent in the survey said they didn't learn how to manage their emotions and problems healthily. Either of these extremes can result in someone who has no model of how to healthily experience anger, sadness, frustration, loneliness, loss and so on and so on. Instead these emotions become buried and soothed with sex. And please note, sex can be a highly effective way of managing painful emotions, and consequently someone with an efficient addiction may truthfully say they never feel anything negative.

Secrets and shame

Many people with addictions learn to keep secrets from a very young age though, for many, the secret may be so deeply entrenched that at first it's hard to remember or acknowledge it. The secret may be something as serious as abuse or it might be a parent's alcoholism or infidelity. Or it may be a family secret such as an illegitimate child or domestic violence. Forty-one per cent of the survey were aware of secrets in their family. In these families there is often an outward projection of order and control and the child learns to keep up the public face of decency and respect and keep quiet about the things that are better left unknown. This sets up a pattern of behaviour in which secrets, double standards or even a double life are the norm.

Shame is another common denominator in the childhoods of people with sex addition. Fifty-two per cent in the survey said they felt shame in their childhood. For some of those, the shame may have been inflicted from outside of the family perhaps in some form of social discrimination for race or religious reasons. For others shame has been used by parents as a tool for control and punishment. Rather than chastising a child when they have done something wrong, they are made to feel bad and worthless as a person. This might be reflected in harsh or critical verbal statements or in behaviours such as humiliating punishments or silence.

Sex education

Understanding why sex, rather than a substance or other behaviour, became the drug of choice is often found within the messages someone learns about sex. Those messages pertain to gender, sexual attitudes and sexual behaviours. Many people with sex addiction were brought up to feel ashamed of their sexuality and therefore find it difficult to express it in a healthy way, 41 per cent in my survey. Sex may have been a taboo subject and masturbation, if acknowledged at all, was either sinful or perverted. Additional messages may have been that men were dangerous sexual predators and women don't like sex, resulting in illicit sexual encounters or paid-for sex. Conversely some are brought up with the belief that sex is a primary need that can be explored and exploited without emotional consideration for self or other. Sex without boundaries is encouraged and normalised.

Whether sex was vilified or glorified, many sex addicts had their first exposure to sexual material from an especially early age (Carnes, 1991); a surprising 41 per cent in my survey said they were using pornography before the age of 12. Of course, many young people grow up today having accessed pornography and not all will develop an addiction. However, I am seeing an increasing number of young men who have never masturbated without pornography and have never considered ever masturbating without it. Pornography used to be a masturbatory accessory, an extra treat, whereas now it is often seen as an essential foundation for it.

Sexual messages and experiences in adolescence can be particularly powerful and long lasting as this is when our sexual templates are becoming cemented in our brains (Money, 1989). While most would accept that masturbation is a natural and healthy way of discovering and enjoying one's sexuality, for someone with sex addiction it soon becomes a primary way of coping with the struggles of life. And while most adolescents slowly extend their sexuality towards partners, some lack the courage or the opportunity to do this. Therefore lone, secretive and often shame-filled sexual behaviours become the norm.

Adolescent loneliness

Adolescence is a time when 'fitting in' with your peers is at its most important. It is a developmental phase where self-identity begins to be laid down and the transition from child to adulthood requires looking more to peers for guidance and affirmation than parents. Most adolescents will have days when they say they feel like a freak. That might simply be because they don't have the right trainers or haircut, or it may be indicative of a much deeper sense of low self-esteem and separation. For someone with sex addiction, there are many more days when it is the latter.

A significant number of addicts report feeling different from their peers. Sixty-four per cent in my survey said they often felt left out and different, and 1 in 5 cited adolescent loneliness and isolation as the most influential factor in their addiction (Hall, 2012). The isolation may be because of something particular in their family such as following a particular religion or belief system, or it may be because of a difference in perceived social class or intelligence. Frequently moving home and changing school is another common reason that makes it difficult to make relationships that are anything more than transient. Another common factor is shyness – 74 per cent described themselves as shy and 43 per cent as very shy (Hall, 2012). It's hard to know if some people are born shy or if social difficulties make them shy. Either way, shyness can become a heavy burden that particularly impacts forming healthy relationships and developing support systems. These differences isolate the individual and make it easier to privately seek solace in porn and masturbation. Many clients have reported that while they enjoyed their private life of porn, it created a sense of shame that further alienated them from friends and potential partners. And so the stage is set for addiction.

Mike

Mike's addiction was induced by opportunity. He came to therapy for a pornography addiction which he'd struggled with for the past 12 years – since he was about 15. He spent at least 5 or 6 hours most days looking at online porn, visiting chat rooms or paying for webcam sex. He had always assumed he'd 'grow out of this' when he met the right girl. Three years earlier he had met the right girl and they were now living together. At first the sex was great but gradually he returned to his old habits and now they rarely had sex, which was a major issue for her. Mike was racked with guilt. He loved his girlfriend but she couldn't compete with his online sex life.

As with all addicts, there were multiple causes to his addiction. He'd been diagnosed with mild ADHD as a child so potentially there were some dopamine irregularities. His erratic behaviour had isolated him from peers and he described himself as growing up a bit of a loner

continued...

who found it difficult to fit in. His home was fairly stable. His parents were practising Christians, so rules were quite rigid and sex was never discussed. However, he remembered a brief period when his parents argued very loudly because his father had had an affair. It was obvious that he wasn't meant to know, but he overheard his mother's tirades on numerous occasions when she shouted and screamed about the dirty slut who was trying to break up their family. He couldn't remember how long the arguments went on for but they continued to blow up occasionally right up until he left home. When they did, both his parents would drink more, but the brave face was always maintained for the kids.

Mike first saw pornography when he started his secondary education at an all-boys school. Apparently it was part of the unofficial induction. He liked what he saw and being a very bright, IT-literate child he was soon accessing porn on the home computer. His parents assumed he was studying and he knew how to clear the history, so it was easy.

It was hard to pinpoint exactly when Mike became an addict. He began to use internet sex more and more, and he described it as becoming his 'closest and most reliable friend'. He knew some of the other lads from school used online porn too but they also talked about their sexual exploits with girls. He longed for that, but didn't have the courage, so he took further comfort from his secret best friend. It wasn't until he finally met his first and current girlfriend at the age of 24 that he realised how hooked he was.

Trauma-induced addiction

Traumas come in many different shapes and sizes. Some are very obvious such as violent assaults or childhood abuse, but others are more subtle. One writer suggests that anything experienced as a child as non-nurturing is a trauma. With that definition, I'm sure you'll agree there are few of us who have gone through life without experiencing trauma. However, what I'm referring to here are the more obvious traumas. The ones that clients are most likely to identify with, though some may need to dig deep into their memory banks to find them. They're what I would call capital T traumas – ones that the body can't forget.

These paragraphs are not intended to tell you everything you need to know about trauma, but rather how it links to sexual addiction. If you have experienced trauma or are working with a client who has, then further reading and study is essential to ensure the trauma can be accessed and worked with in a safe and supportive way.

Abuse

Abuse may be emotional, physical or sexual, and may come from within or outside of the family of origin. When abuse has happened within the family then there will almost definitely be attachment issues as well.

Emotional abuse is defined by the NSPCC as 'undermining a child's confidence and sense of self-worth – for example by ignoring them, giving degrading punishments, or constantly threatening or humiliating them'. When a child is denied the acceptance, love, encouragement, consistency and positive attention they deserve they often grow up thinking they are deficient in some way and not worthy of care or respect. Although it's most common to think of emotional abuse at the hands of parents, many of the clients I've seen have experienced this abuse either at the hands of older siblings, from bullies at school or by teachers or other carers. Emotional abuse often results in low self-esteem, shame and a reduced ability to healthily care for self or others. Sex may be used as a way of self-soothing or as a way of self-harming and reinforcing feelings of worthlessness and isolation.

Physical abuse refers to any intentional pain or injury inflicted on another. As with emotional abuse, this may happen at the hands of parents or others in a position of care, or in the form of bullying from peers or within the workplace. Ongoing physical abuse damages a child's ability to trust others and the energy required to learn about relationships is put into defending against possible risks of harm. Someone who has been physically abused may use sex as a way of forgetting the emotional pain as well as receiving much deserved and needed physical comfort. Conversely, some survivors of physical abuse use sex as an unconscious psychological way of getting their own back. There's more on this in the next chapter.

Sexual abuse is often one of the hardest areas for someone to identify, especially if it involved minimal or no physical contact. It's important to understand that any behaviour that coerces a child into sexual behaviour is abuse. For example, being made to view pornography or watch a sexual act or being used as an object for sexual arousal. Because sex addicts often feel so much shame about their own sexual behaviour they frequently minimize any inappropriate sexual behaviour in their childhood. But in reality, it is often within what they may perceive as being innocent or 'misunderstood' acts that the seeds of unhealthy sexual expression took root.

Research statistics vary in the amount of abuse present in the histories of people with sex addiction. In *Don't Call it Love* (1991), Carnes cites 97 per cent emotional abuse, 83 per cent sexual abuse and 71 per cent physical. In my survey, 38 per cent reported emotional abuse, 17 per cent sexual abuse and 16 per cent physical abuse. This may of course in part be dependent on the survey type and the clinical and subjective definition of abuse.

Interestingly those who had been through therapy in my survey reported higher incidences of abuse, which perhaps indicates that without therapy abuse is more likely to be normalised or denied.

Assault

An assault might best be described as a severe isolated incident of abuse, usually violent, that might be physical or sexual. As with abuse, that may happen within the home but more often it will be an attack by someone outside of the family. An assault may be physical, with or without a weapon, or be sexual, most commonly rape. In my survey 16 per cent had been physically or sexually assaulted. For most people, an assault will be terrifying but some, especially those with a history of abuse, may normalise the experience or explain it away by saying they were 'asking for it'. Someone who has survived an assault may use sex not only as a way of managing the emotional impact but also as a way of soothing the physical memories.

Other shocks to the system

We all have to come to terms with losing a loved one at some time in our life, but when it happens prematurely as happened for 21 per cent of survey respondents (Hall, 2012), losing a parent, sibling or young partner, can be experienced as a trauma. We don't expect people to die young; we expect our relationships to be secure and safe so when the un-thought of happens, it can rock our lives to the core. If, on top of the shock of loss, the death happens in a traumatic way – such as through sudden illness, an accident or because of crime – the trauma can be even greater.

Sudden illness or disability can also be experienced as a trauma, whether that's to oneself or a loved one. I have had a number of clients who became carers at a young age because of a parent's illness or disability, and this sudden responsibility and subsequent loss of childhood can have similar consequences to experiencing a deliberate act of trauma. Another trauma that's often forgotten is the impact on children of witnessing domestic violence. This had happened to over 1 in 10 of respondents in my survey.

Job loss, whether through redundancy or dismissal, is not a trauma to everyone but to some it is. Especially if the redundancy is unexpected and results in a sudden change of lifestyle. I remember one client in particular who lost his job just a few weeks after his wife had divorced him. This resulted in him losing his wife, his children, his home and his job with company car. He also lost his work colleagues, his routines, his status and his sense of purpose in life. He was traumatised.

The impact of trauma

The full impact of trauma can be hard to acknowledge, especially for someone who has successfully used their sex addiction to soothe their emotional pain. It may also be especially hard for men in our tough-guy culture to admit to themselves, let alone to others, how frightening or upsetting the experiences have been. One writer said that when a sex addict has experienced trauma, especially in childhood, the addiction is not necessarily a pleasure-seeking strategy but a survival strategy (Fisher, 2007). This is because letting go of the addiction may allow the devastating and terrifying feelings of trauma to resurface. Another common scar of trauma is anger. Anger at the aggressor, at the circumstances, at the lack of protection by others, at the inability to defend oneself. Sex can soothe this anger.

Trauma can also influence the choice of sexual behaviours. There has been increasing evidence that some compulsive fetish behaviours and paraphilias may be linked to previous trauma. 'The Opponent Process Theory of Acquired Motivation' (Soloman, 1980) describes how a negative emotion or experience can be reframed as a positive in order to re-write the script. For example, someone who was bullied and humiliated as a child might pay a dominatrix to sexually arouse them by doing likewise. Hence turning trauma into triumph (Birchard, 2011).

Like sex addiction, our understanding of trauma has changed significantly over the last few years, especially how trauma impacts the brain. It is now known that the imprint of the trauma is in the limbic system and in the brainstem; in other words, it is stored in our primitive animal brains, not in our thinking brain. And the part of the brain known as the amygdala, which is responsible for 'fight and flight', often remains hypersensitive long after the trauma has passed (Van der Kolk, 1996). This is why someone who's experienced trauma may remain mentally anxious and hypervigilant and have an overactive startle reflex long after any conscious memory of the trauma has passed. This hypersensitive amygdala may be triggered by any number of external sources throwing the body's sympathetic nervous system into what's known as hyperarousal, or the parasympathetic system into hypoarousal, and temporarily by-pass the thinking part of the brain. Sexual behaviour may become a way for a trauma sufferer to numb feelings of hyperarousal such as hyperactivity, obsessive thinking, rage and panic and also alleviate feelings of disassociation, numbness, depression and exhaustion experienced in hypoarousal. In short, it is thought that addictive behaviors can become an effective technique to regulate the nervous system (Fisher, 2007).

Peter

Peter had a trauma-induced addiction and came for therapy because he was terrified his partner of 10 years was going to find him out. He had a job that meant he was away in Europe 2 or 3 nights a week and whenever he was he would spend hours watching the hotel's pay for TV channels. Over the years he had learned where all the strip clubs, massage parlours and brothels were in most of the major cities around Europe – he joked that he could write a 'rough guide' on the subject.

He described his childhood as difficult but loving. He'd had a sister 5 years younger but she was run over and killed when he was 12. The whole family was obviously badly affected and his parents struggled for a while, but his grandparents were very close and always on hand if his parents weren't. His early teens were marred by the tragedy and he was aware that he never rebelled like some of his friends did. At 15 he started going steady with a girl at school and spent much of his time with her. They got engaged at 24 but at 26, after a few weeks of unexplained illness, she was diagnosed with leukaemia. She died 18 months later.

When I met Peter he was 48, a successful businessman, amicably divorced from his first wife and a father of 3 children. He had first started using porn when he was 26 while his girlfriend was having chemotherapy. He said it helped to take his mind off what she was going through. His addiction had slowly escalated but he'd had many, many months of abstinence at various points in his life. He explained that it had raised its ugly head again 18 months ago when he and his current partner had got engaged. As we worked through his history, he discovered that each time his addiction had returned, it had been when something had unconsciously reminded him of his painful past.

Attachment-induced addiction

Whatever a child experiences in life and whatever opportunities may be presented to them in adolescence, if there is a secure parental attachment they are likely to fair well. Where there is safe, reliable, supportive parenting it's possible for a child to make mistakes, learn from them and move on. It is also easier for them to consciously recover from trauma. But without that fundamental bedrock of what psychologists call 'healthy attachment', addiction has a greater chance to take root and flourish (Flores, 2004).

Healthy attachment starts from the moment we are born. A newborn baby 'attaches' to their primary care giver, usually mum, in order to survive.

As the child grows they continue to need that attachment in order to develop healthily. When a child feels nurtured and cared for they have the courage to explore their world, knowing that safety is just a cry away. This attachment is important for emotional as well as physical development. When a child is still in the pre-verbal stage, they need a parent who is empathically attuned to their needs. And as they learn to talk they need a parent who is encouraging and responsive to their efforts to communicate. Without this a child may not develop the necessary skills to recognise and communicate their needs to others appropriately or to recognise and respond to the needs of others – including sexual needs. But the effects are not just emotional, they are also biologically imprinted.

Attachment and the brain

There is growing evidence from neuroscience that insufficient empathic care in early childhood creates a growth-inhibiting environment that produces immature, physiologically undifferentiated orbitofrontal affect regulatory systems (Schore, 2003). In other words, a child who does not receive its needs for attention, soothing, stimulation, affection and validation may find the consequences structurally written into their developing brain. The altered prefrontal function is associated with high risk of drug and alcohol addiction (Bechara and Damasio, 2002; Franklin et al., 2002; Goldstein et al., 2001). One proposed explanation for this is that the insecure attachment template is not able to produce its own endogenous opiates and therefore individuals will reach for external opiates to stimulate dopamine reward centres (Hudson Allez, 2009). Additionally, for the insecurely attached individual, the orbitofrontal area of the cortex may no longer produce sufficient dopamine or noradrenaline to facilitate sexual excitation and inhibition, and therefore an external source may become increasingly relied upon for something that the brain has not learnt to manufacture for itself.

Parenting styles

There are a number of reasons why attachment may be damaged in childhood, either from absent, abusive, negligent or inadequate parenting. If a child is physically separated from a parent for adoption or fostering or through bereavement, then there will inevitably be at least a short period of time when good parenting is absent. And abusive parenting, as discussed under trauma, obviously doesn't provide the necessary environment for a child to thrive. Negligent and inadequate parenting are often harder to recognise and some people can understandably get defensive if a therapist is deemed to be blaming a parent who they believe did their best.

Negligent parenting, while not overtly abusive, leaves a child feeling fearful as they are never fully sure how a parent will respond. A negligent parent is inconsistent – caring and attentive one minute and absent, rejecting or cruel the next. Usually this is the result of a parent's own personal problems, and they may be aware of their inadequacies and be apologetic to the child. The term 'inadequate parenting' can be used to describe the childhood situation where parents were unavailable or unresponsive due to extenuating circumstances – for example, physical or emotional illness of themselves or another child, parental separation or divorce, victim of domestic violence, extreme poverty or simply because of naivety. It's important with both of these parenting situations not to blame the parents but to recognise that the consequences may have been a contributing factor to how sex addiction got started.

There are many different degrees of unhealthy attachment. Some people may have always known that their problems result from poor parenting and their addiction is primarily caused by these wounds, whereas others see it as a minor contributing factor. One way of establishing the significance of childhood attachment is to look at the ensuing adult attachment style.

Adult attachment styles

- The Anxious Attacher – someone who is an anxious attacher will frequently feel insecure in relationships. They may be jealous and needy of attention and require constant reassurance that their partner loves them. Someone with this attachment style may seek out many relationships in order to achieve the attention and validation they desire. (Also known as the anxious/pre-occupied; Zapf et al., 2008.)
- The Avoidant Attacher – people with an avoidant attachment style would probably describe themselves as someone who likes their own space. Although they enjoy relationships, they can easily feel suffocated and tend to withdraw in order to recharge their batteries. An avoidant sex addict may seek relationships and sexual encounters where there is little or no emotion or affection such as with sex workers and pornography. (Also known as fearful/avoidant; Zapf et al., 2008.)
- The Ambivalent Attacher – ambivalent attachers find themselves flitting between anxious and avoidant. They crave intimacy and affection but are also fearful of it and consequently may be somewhat erratic in their behaviour within a relationship. They may use sex addiction to gain what is perceived as safe intimacy since there is no commitment. Or they may seek additional partners to ward off fears of rejection or suffocation from their primary partner. (Also known as dismissing/avoidant; Zapf et al., 2008.)

The way that someone relates in adulthood can provide clues to what happened in childhood. By looking at current styles of relating, questions can be asked about where someone learnt to think and feel like this. For example, someone who recognises themselves as an avoidant attacher might recall learning to be strong and independent when they were sent away to boarding school, a factor for 1 in 10 of the survey respondents. Or someone who's an ambivalent attacher might remember becoming conflicted when their parents separated or when they discovered a parent's infidelity. Twenty-seven per cent of the survey respondents witnessed their parents' separation when they were a child and 19 per cent a parent's infidelity. Although events like these often don't result in losing a parent altogether, they can significantly impact the way a child views adult relationships and the amount of trust they are likely to later invest themselves.

Bill

Bill had an attachment-induced addiction. He came for therapy aged 42 having been to many other therapists for his problem. He had been married for 18 years, had 2 children and his wife had always known about his sex addiction and supported him in finding help. The problem was she didn't truly know its full extent. Bill had managed to keep hidden how often he acted out and the massive debt he'd run up as a consequence. Bill had first used prostitutes in his early 20s when he was working on a construction project in Soho. He described how everyone used prostitutes there; it was normal. Since then he had developed a penchant for the best, most expensive woman he could buy. 'It's my treat,' he explained.

Bill had an impoverished childhood. He had never known his dad and his mum brought him up alone in a high rise flat on benefits. He was an only child and spent much of his growing up trying to look after his mum. She struggled with depression and was reliant on major tranquilisers for most of his childhood. Bill learned to cook and clean from an early age and he never asked for anything for himself – that would not have been fair. He was ashamed to admit that he was embarrassed by his home and his mum, and on the rare occasions he went to a friend's house, he was consumed with envy. Life was unfair.

Bill became an ambivalent attacher. He loved his wife and he cared for her, but through his addiction, he ensured he had another outlet where his needs could be reliably met.

4   How addiction is maintained and reinforced

All of us will at some stage in our life, be attracted to an addictive substance or process. That may be drugs, alcohol, food, gambling or perhaps exercise. But most of us are able to pull back. We recognise within us a point where our indulgence is becoming problematic and we either curtail our habit or stop all together. We know that although we may be enjoying what we're doing, it's either already beginning to harm us or will do at some point in the future.

There are a number of reasons why this doesn't happen for people with an addiction. And like causes, these maintaining factors can be viewed through the BERSC model. As highlighted in the previous chapter, in part that is because of biological factors, brain development and brain chemistry. The more someone uses a chemical or a process to produce a dopamine high, the less able the brain is to produce sufficient through its own resources. And the more effective the high, the stronger the memory and the brain's orientation towards seeking it again. For a trauma survivor, the brain has become hyper sensitive to arousal and therefore more vulnerable to seeking external opioids for self-soothing.

There are also significant emotional, relational, societal and cultural influences that both maintain and reinforce the addictive behaviour. It is perhaps more important to understand these maintaining factors than it is to know what caused the addiction, since it is in breaking these patterns that recovery is found. In the same way as every person with an addiction has a unique history that has lead them to addiction, so each will also have a unique combination of factors that reinforce and maintain it.

In this chapter we will explore those influences as they relate to opportunity-induced, trauma-induced and attachment-induced addiction but first it's important to recognise and understand that all addictions operate within a cycle. A cycle that if not recognised can keep someone unknowingly, and indefinitely, trapped.

The cycles of addiction

There are many different cycles of addiction that have been offered over the years that can help us to understand why it's so difficult to break out of addiction. Here I would like to offer three – each of which demonstrates a different dimension of the addictive process.

The four-step cycle

The four-step cycle (see Figure 4.1) was developed by Patrick Carnes (2001) and explains how sexual addiction builds in intensity throughout each stage. The *preoccupation* step describes the trance-like state that many addicts go into as they begin their search for sexual stimulation. *Ritualisation* is the step where the addiction intensifies as individual routines are developed to increase the preoccupation, excitement and arousal. The resulting *compulsive sexual behaviour* is immediately followed by *despair* where shame and hopelessness over the behaviour is experienced. The pain caused by the *despair* step of the cycle is then anaesthetised by returning to the *preoccupation* stage.

Oscillating release/control cycle

The idea of this figure-of-eight model, which continually flows between *control* and *release*, was first offered by Fossum and Mason in 1986 (see Figure 4.2). Since then it has been adapted by a number of addiction professionals to explain how someone can swing between states of mind and behaviours that are rigid and controlled to release behaviours that may either be experienced as euphoric or despairing.

As you can see from Figure 4.2, there are many activities that can be classed as either *control* or *release* and, for people with an addiction, both are equally damaging, as they will eventually lead to the other side of the cycle. For example, although sexual avoidance accompanied by a harsh regime of work and exercise may at first seem like a sensible and healthy alternative

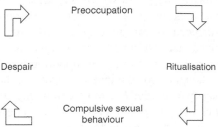

Preoccupation

Despair

Ritualisation

Compulsive sexual
behaviour

Figure 4.1 The four-step cycle (reprinted with permission of Gentle Path Press)

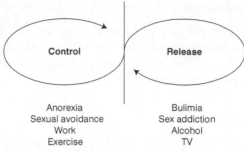

Anorexia
Sexual avoidance
Work
Exercise

Bulimia
Sex addiction
Alcohol
TV

Figure 4.2 Oscillating control/release cycle

to sexual addiction, in reality it will only be a matter of time before someone becomes exhausted and disheartened, and slips back into the *release* side of the cycle. The *release* behaviours are temporarily experienced as a welcome break from the *control*, but as guilt and shame gradually creep in so you're then thrown back into the *control* side of the cycle again.

The six-phase cycle

The six-phase cycle shown in Figure 4.3 is the cycle that I have developed over the years of my practice to help clients recognise how their addiction continues to maintain itself through their behaviours, thoughts and emotions. The length of each phase, and the length of time between each phase, varies from individual to individual, as does the content, but everyone I've worked with has been able to quickly identify with the model.

The shape of the model is also relevant as it demonstrates how intensity gradually builds from the *dormant* phase until a *trigger* speeds the build-up through the *preparation* phrase. The height of the cycle is *acting out* but this quickly drops to *regret* and *reconstitution* before gradually returning back to *dormant*. We will explore each of the six phases as they relate to opportunity-induced, trauma-induced and attachment-induced addiction in depth over the coming pages, but, in brief, they can be summarised as below.

1 Dormant – this is the phase where the addiction is temporarily in remission but underlying issues whether opportunity-, trauma- or attachment-induced, remain unresolved. Life may appear 'normal', but it's simply a matter of time before a trigger occurs.
2 Trigger – the trigger is an event, an opportunity, a bodily sensation, emotion or thought process that activates the behaviour. Almost anything may be a trigger but most commonly it will be a sexual opportunity or a negative emotion such as anxiety, anger, depression, sadness, boredom, loneliness or frustration.

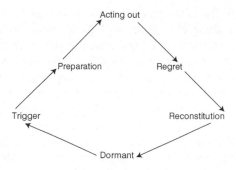

Figure 4.3 The six-phase cycle of addiction

3 Preparation – the preparation phase can vary in length considerably from just a few minutes to turn on a computer, to many weeks of planning an affair. This phase includes practical preparations such as the where, when and how as well as psychological strategies to create the environment where acting out can be tolerated and/or enjoyed.

4 Acting out – for some, acting out is a single event such as visiting a sex worker, which may last just a few minutes, whereas for others it may be a week-long binge of pornography use. Some describe it as a highpoint that brings euphoria and relief, but for others the accompanying relief is purely about getting the deed over and done with so they can finally begin their descent back to the comfort of the dormant phase.

5 Regret – depending on the consequences of acting out, the impact on personal values and someone's commitment to change, the regret phase may be experienced as little more than a momentary 'ooops' or weeks of despair, shame and self-loathing.

6 Reconstitution – during the reconstitution phase life is either consciously or unconsciously put back together again. It may be a time for rebuilding self-esteem, covering tracks and/or renewing resolutions not to act out again.

The dormant phase

The dormant phase is perhaps the hardest for anyone to recognise, especially for those who may stay dormant for weeks, months or even years at a time. Typically, a porn addiction may only be dormant for a relatively brief amount of time as there is ample opportunity to trigger the addictive behaviours, whereas other addictions may be dormant for much longer. During this dormant phase most people with sex addiction will be functioning perfectly adequately although some may have switched their addiction to something else. Some will use alcohol, work or exercise as an alternative way of self-soothing during this phase. But where no other addiction is used, it's tempting to assume that the sex addiction is under control or has gone away all together. What's important to recognise is that if the underlying causes of addiction have not been identified and resolved, the proverbial sword of Damocles is still hanging overhead.

For everyone, the opportunity-induced causes such as difficulties with self control and emotional regulation are still present as is a behavioural pattern of holding secrets and living a double life. In addition, many may continue to be working in a highly sexualised environment or have regular and easy access to the internet or sex workers.

For those with a trauma-induced addiction there will still be the scars of previous abuse or assault causing difficulties in regulating hyper and hypo arousal states. While nothing in the dormant phase is activating these states, a period of relative calm can be enjoyed. However, unless healthy strategies are learnt and adopted, the vulnerability to triggers continues to be high.

Attachment-induced addiction may stay dormant for an extended period of time, especially if a new relationship is found that can temporarily relieve feelings of loneliness and fears of rejection. It's common for an attachment-induced addict to feel that the new relationship has solved their problems, but the inevitable difficulties that arise in any relationship are likely to tip the balance at some point in the future.

The triggers

The dormant phase of the addiction cycle will, in time, be propelled by a trigger or series of triggers. For some people, triggers come out of the blue but for others there is either a conscious or unconscious building of tension, and an appropriate trigger may be awaited or even sought out.

For those with a pure opportunity-induced addiction, the trigger will almost always be an event or circumstance that creates the opportunity to act out. That might be the house being empty or a partner announcing they want an early night. It could be working at home for the day or a business meeting that will provide an easy opportunity to visit a sex worker. If multiple affairs are the drug of choice it might be a new person starting at the office or a business conference with an attractive colleague.

These opportunity triggers will be equally as powerful for all categories of addiction, but they are usually also accompanied by a negative emotional state. For someone with a trauma-induced addiction, emotional or physical feelings of anxiety or numbness, can trigger a desire to self soothe through sexual acting out. Whereas for people with an attachment-induced addiction there are more likely to be feelings of loneliness, isolation, rejection or suffocation that require soothing.

Sexual desire is another common trigger for each classification of addiction though its presentation may differ. Someone with a pure opportunity-induced addiction may describe their sexual desire as desperate and urgent, and this might be triggered by internal hormonal drive or by the sight of someone attractive. They may experience the desire for sexual satiation through their chosen behaviour as overwhelmingly powerful and almost physically painful. This may lead them to be hyper aware of any possible opportunity to act out and when that opportunity is found, this will heighten desire even further. Sexual desire in attachment-induced addiction may be experienced more as a desire for intimacy, affection and attention than sexual release and for someone with a trauma-induced addiction sexual desire may be absent or negligible until the acting out phase.

The preparation phase

Once triggered, the addiction enters the preparation phase of the cycle and the necessary practical and psychological arrangements are made to act out. This preparation stage is as much part of the addiction as the acting out phase. While in this place the trauma- and attachment-induced addictions are already escaping their emotional pain and all are increasing their arousal and anticipation. I have had clients who have spent months preparing themselves for the next time they'll see a sex worker. They have spent hours every day on meticulous research and planning, and often describe this phase of the cycle as being the most enjoyable. As explained in Chapter 1, sex addiction often has very little to do with sex.

Whatever type of addiction, most people will make at least some rudimentary plans to ensure they can act out without being caught. That might include changing their schedules or travel arrangements, creating an alibi for being online or being away from home, creating private email accounts and bank accounts, or any number of other things. Some people are not consciously aware of the preparations they are making because they are so caught up in the emotional bubble that it creates, or stuck in denial. This is a common phenomena in addictions and is often referred to as S.U.D.s – Seemingly Unimportant Decisions. An example of a SUD would be when someone says they 'just happened to be in Soho', without acknowledging that the business meeting was arranged weeks before, as was the hotel room and just enough untraceable cash to pay a sex worker.

The psychological strategies engaged during the preparation phase can be described as cognitive distortions. All of us experience cognitive distortions and will at times use them to our advantage. By consciously, or unconsciously,

Table 4.1 Common cognitive distortions

Rationalisation	If it was daytime I wouldn't park here, but it's late at night so I won't be causing an obstruction
Justification	It's raining and I don't have an umbrella
Minimisation	I'm only going to be two minutes
Magnifying	The only other place to park is absolutely miles away and it will take forever to walk from there
Blame	If my partner had remembered the milk I wouldn't be in this position
Entitlement	I've had a really hard day today, it wouldn't be fair to expect me to walk further than I have to
Uniqueness	It's ok for me to park here because I've lived here for over 20 years and I've always been very generous to the community
Mental filter	I'm not going to let myself remember the parking ticket I got last week
Victim stance	Typical – trust me to find the only shop without parking facilities, I'm not going to put up with it
Normalisation	Everyone parks on double yellow lines in this situation
Denial	It won't do any harm because no-one will know
Helplessness	I know I shouldn't, but I just can't help myself, I've always been bad with parking restrictions

thinking in a certain way, we can change how we feel about something and consequently change how we behave. It's a common strategy we all employ when we want to do something that we really know we shouldn't. For example, imagine it's late at night, it's raining and you desperately need milk. You drive to a local shop where you find double yellow lines outside and nowhere else to park. Now look at Table 4.1, which lists common cognitive distortions and see how they can be used to help you park illegally.

As you can see, there are many, many different ways to create the environment where we allow ourselves to do something that we don't think is right. Many people with sex addiction describe it as having two voices in their head. Or the devil on one shoulder and an angel on the other. One voice is saying 'Don't do it' but the other is constantly feeding messages that distort thinking until the other voice gives up.

For those who are in a relationship, cognitive distortions are also used to ease their conscience. Most commonly that will be by using 'denial' and saying 'what their partner doesn't know, can't hurt them', or 'blame' – 'if our sex life was better I wouldn't need to' or by creating a 'mental filter' that focuses on the bad aspects of the relationship or the partner to create sufficient emotional distance for acting out to occur.

Acting out

As explained in Chapter 1, all addictions serve a function – a function that is above and beyond pure sexual pleasure and fulfilment. That's not to deny the fact that most people enjoy what they do, but to understand why they continue to return to a behaviour that causes so much destruction in their lives, you need to understand the deeper need that it fulfils.

In a nutshell, all addiction is used to manage emotional pain. At the simplest level, it soothes the pain of not acting out, by ending the craving and preoccupation. Many people with sex addiction also report using sex addiction to manage anger and frustration, to relieve boredom, stress and anxiety, and to alleviate loneliness and feelings of low self-esteem. To an outsider, these may appear to be poor excuses for sexual addiction, but it's important to remember that most addicts have little or no other coping mechanisms. What's more, for those with a trauma-induced and/or an attachment-induced addiction, the feelings can be overwhelming.

Someone with a trauma-induced addiction may be using acting out as a way of regulating hyper- and hypoarousal states (Fisher, 2007). As you can see from Figure 4.4, the hyperarousal state is when our bodies are thrown into fight or flight; hypoarousal is when we are thrown into freeze. Both of these extremes are physically, emotionally and psychologically painful, and addiction can be used to alleviate the symptoms and bring the central nervous system back to its normal state. We may all experience these hyper- and hypoarousal states at some time in our lives but for a trauma sufferer, the window of tolerance is narrower and therefore they can be thrown into one of these states quickly and easily.

For someone with an attachment-induced addiction, the acting-out phase of the cycle will primarily be used to soothe relational pain. For example, an anxious attacher may use their addiction to soothe loneliness and to receive affection and attention. An avoidant attacher may use the behaviour as an intimacy regulator to stop themselves getting too emotionally involved

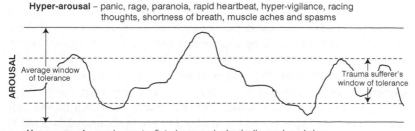

Hyper-arousal – panic, rage, paranoia, rapid heartbeat, hyper-vigilance, racing thoughts, shortness of breath, muscle aches and spasms

Hypo-arousal – numb, empty, flat, depressed, physically numb and slow

Figure 4.4 The window of tolerance (adapted with kind permission from Ogden, Minton and Pain 2006)

with one partner who might suffocate them. For the ambivalent attacher, the function of acting out may be to enjoy the attention and affection of someone while maintaining a safe emotional distance.

Achieving the required function may take minutes or days and it's important to remember part of this function will already be starting during the preparation phase. One person may achieve their need for affection or escape hyper arousal in a brief period of time, but others may need to binge on their chosen behaviour in order to gain the required result. Whatever the function, once achieved the addiction then enters the regret phase.

The regret phase

Some people with sex addiction immediately identify with the regret phase, whereas others say they feel little or no remorse. The reaction depends on two things: first, the negative consequences experienced; and second the amount of cognitive distortions employed to reduce those consequences. For example, if someone is instantly faced with financial loss, contracting an STI or an angry partner, they will feel more regret than someone who has 'got away with it' unscathed. And someone who feels great shame at their pornography use because it violates their personally held values will feel more self-loathing. However, if they're able to employ 'normalisation' to tell themselves that 'everyone does it', or 'minimisation' and say 'it wasn't that bad', their shame will reduce quickly and the regret phase may be brief.

Shame is by far the most common, and perhaps most devastating, consequence of sexual addiction, as we will explore further in Chapter 6. The shame may be the result of the actual behaviour contravening strongly held beliefs and values, such as not exploiting vulnerable people such as sex workers who may have been forced into the trade. Or it may be at living a double life and lying to loved ones. Or the shame may be a result of being too weak to break the cycle of addiction and having failed to live up to one's own intentions and expectations.

The regret phase can last for just a few minutes for some, to weeks and months for others. If the behaviour seriously contradicts someone's beliefs and values, then the resulting shame and damage to self-esteem can be immense to the point where the reconstitution stage is almost impossible and the shame becomes the trigger to act out again. Some people with a trauma-induced addiction can become so worried about the possible consequences of being discovered, that they create their own trauma that can trip them into hyper or hypo arousal states. For most, the regret phase is the most painful place in the cycle and some will have better resources than others to get themselves into reconstitution.

Reconstitution

Reconstitution is the phase where life is put back together again. What that means will depend on how much life has fallen apart during acting out. Some people with online addictions who binge spend the reconstitution phase looking after their physical needs. They may not have eaten, washed or slept properly for days, so this will be their first priority. Those who visit sex workers might be getting a health check at the GUM clinic, looking at how to replenish their finances and ensuring there is no traceable evidence for a partner or work colleague to discover. If the reconstitution phase is accompanied by a commitment to 'never act out again', then hard drives may be deleted, email accounts cancelled and future business trips changed.

For those whose addiction affects their work or social life, extra hours may be put in to make up for what's been lost. Partners often unknowingly benefit during this stage as more effort is put into relationships. Perhaps with thoughtful gifts and caring gestures, that to the unknowing partner, seem to come out of the blue or perhaps are seen as a welcome sign of reconciliation after an unexplained time of emotional distance.

Putting self-esteem back together can be a much tougher job than managing the practicalities. Cognitive distortions can help to minimise, normalise or excuse the behaviour, but most still find themselves battling with depression and anxiety until they can get themselves back on their feet again. Some may resort to another addiction such as alcohol, drugs or excessive work or exercise to take their mind off the pain of what they've done. Others go into therapy but never confess the true reason for their distress. In time, for some days, for others months, life does go back to normal again. But it's the false 'pretend normal' of the dormant phase, where the underlying issues remain unresolved and often unacknowledged, and the same vulnerability remains, waiting for the next trigger.

Tim

Tim came for therapy very aware of his addictive cycle though he didn't call it that. 'I'm trapped on the same old merry go round,' he explained. 'Over and over and over again, I do the same old thing. It's driving me crazy.'

Tim's addiction was to cyber chat and it was attachment-induced. He came from a very strict family where he was not allowed to mix with other children and he was constantly criticised for not being academically bright enough. He described his childhood as lonely and harsh. He could remain in the dormant phase of the cycle for

continued...

many weeks but would inevitably be triggered whenever he had an argument with his wife. At first he claimed that she always started the rows, but on reflection he acknowledged that there were some occasions when he deliberately provoked her.

The arguments, which often lasted for days, consisted of his wife criticising him for his inadequacies and insisting that he sleep in the spare room – where they kept the PC. Although he hated the arguments, it fuelled his cognitive distortions during the preparation phase. He felt justified in blaming her for his online diversions and would tell himself that he deserved a little TLC for putting up with her unreasonable tirades. While acting out he felt appreciated and valued by his online sexual companions, but when his wife finally apologised, which she always did after a day or two, he would feel guilty and ashamed of what he'd done. He would try to tell himself that no real harm was done, but he knew his secret online lovers made it much harder to make love to his wife, something she was always desperate to do in order to make up.

During the reconstitution phase, Tim would delete the history on the PC and delete all the contacts in his secret email account. He would throw himself into the relationship, promising his wife that he would be less irritating and promising himself that he would be more tolerant of the exacting standards that she imposed on him. Tim's guilt and shame prevented him from fully confronting his wife about their ongoing relationship issues, and he never considered alternative strategies for if it happened again. And it always did.

5 The partner's perspective

Partners are often the forgotten victims of sexual addiction. Most knew nothing about their partner's behaviour until discovery day and the news is devastating. A few may have known about occasional pornography use or may have known of an affair, but the extent of acting out is almost always a complete shock.

There is not space in this book to discuss all the issues that arise for partners of sex addicts, nor to offer the comprehensive advice and support they both need, and deserve. What's offered here is an overview of common reactions and how these impact on the treatment of sex addiction for the addict and an outline of the importance of recovery for the partner.

The impact of discovery

When sex addiction is either revealed or discovered the impact is twofold. Not only is there an intense feeling of betrayal, similar to that experienced by infidelity, but also there is the alarm of discovering a partner is an addict. In addition, some partners are also confronted with sexual behaviours that may cause them disbelief, confusion and perhaps disgust. Beneath the intense shock, there are other emotions that compete for dominance in the days and weeks that follow discovery. Some common emotional reactions are listed below.

Shock	Denial	Anger
Confusion	Isolation	Shame
Betrayal	Despair	Doubt
Fear	Sadness	Guilt
Disgust	Disbelief	Hopelessness
Grief	Depression	Numb
Anxiety	Relief	Stupid

Partners often describe themselves as being on an emotional rollercoaster, not knowing which way is up and struggling to believe what's happening to them. The partner who has most often been loved, trusted and respected for many years is no longer the person they thought they knew. This leaves them questioning not only their partner, but also themselves. Can they be a good judge of character? Do they know fact from fiction? Can they trust themselves? Their partner? The world they live in?

The cultural context of some gay and lesbian relationships can make the revelation of sex addiction especially confusing. If the relationship had been an open one, then deciding which boundaries have been crossed and where trust has been broken may be harder to establish. For some it is also more difficult to find support and empathy from within the community who may accept sexual variety as the norm and not understand the complexities of addiction.

In reality, their partner is still the same person they always were and there is no reason to doubt most of the qualities they'd enjoyed in their relationship. But now there is a critical extra piece of information. Information that will change both the partner and the future of the relationship forever.

The impact of the discovery is influenced by five key factors.

- The type of behaviour disclosed – Generally speaking it is easier for partners to cope with discovering a porn addiction (unless it includes underage pornography) and cyber/telephone sex than it is to manage physical infidelity. Ultimately it is the degree to which the behaviour contradicts a partner's personal value system that determines the reaction.
- The nature of the disclosure – Some discoveries are more traumatic than others, as one of the case examples in this chapter shows, but generally speaking a confession by the addict rather than accidental discovery is easier to manage.
- The degree of deceit revealed – When the acting-out behaviour has been continuing for many years and has been kept hidden through ongoing lies and dishonesty, this threatens a relationship more than when it's been short term and kept discreet. Similarly if disclosure has happened before but the addict had promised and reassured that it was over, a further discovery may be the last straw.
- The quality of the relationship – If a relationship has struggled before the revelation, then it will most likely be wrecked by sexual addiction. However, many couples are testament to the fact that a good relationship can survive and even become stronger once addiction has been revealed and confronted.
- The partners existing emotional and psychological state – Where there are pre-existing mental health problems or previous experiences of trauma, loss or betrayal, the impact can be especially devastating.

In the same way as everyone with a sexual addiction is unique and will present with a wide range of different emotional, psychological and environmental experiences, so are the partners. The following case studies give two very different experiences that we will return to throughout this chapter.

Lorna

Lorna had been married to Dave for 32 years and they had two grown-up children. Throughout most of their marriage they'd argued about how much time Dave spent at work, often to the point where Lorna would threaten divorce. Lorna discovered Dave's addiction problem when he forgot to turn off his laptop. Open on the page was a prostitution site, along with his booking of a girl in Lucerne where he was due to be on business that coming weekend. Lorna described herself as feeling numb as she went through his history bar and bank statements while he was away. When confronted with the evidence, Dave confessed to using prostitutes for the past 35 years. Lorna was confounded – Dave was the last person you'd ever suspect of that kind of behaviour. More than anything else she felt shock, anger and disgust. She also felt shame and isolation as she was sure none of her friends would believe what her loving husband had been up to. Mixed in with the anger at Dave, Lorna was also angry at herself, constantly telling herself she should have known what was really going on. She also struggled with self-doubt. Had she ever been enough for him sexually? Should she have made more effort to be adventurous and keep herself sexy? If she'd been a better wife, a sexier woman, would he have done this?

Nadine

Nadine and Simon had been married eight years and Nadine had always known that Simon sometimes watched pornography after she'd gone to bed. This had never bothered her much, as she believed he was entitled to his own 'private' time and she didn't feel it had a negative impact on their sex life. Nadine described her and Simon as soul mates. Both had been victims of childhood abuse, and Nadine believed this gave them a special bond and connection because they both knew where the other was 'coming from'. One evening, Simon

continued...

came home from work in tears explaining that he'd been sacked for using the company computer to watch pornography. He went on to say that his pornography use had been getting worse and worse over the previous ten years and he felt he was addicted. At first Nadine tried to comfort him that he was only doing what most blokes did, but as he described both the time and the material he was now viewing, she accepted that he definitely had a problem. Nadine was shocked and disturbed by some of what she'd heard, but most of all she was worried for Simon and also how they'd cope financially on one income. They googled 'sex addiction' to find out more about it and where they could get help, and Nadine resolved that they would get through this together. As far as she was concerned, they'd survived much worse so she wasn't going to let this beat them.

The pattern of disclosure

Evidence shows (Schneider et al., 1998) that disclosure of sex addiction is rarely a one-off event. Most often a partner will receive a gradual disclosure as more and more behaviour is either revealed or discovered. While it's easy to assume that this pattern of disclosure is a result of denial and dishonesty on the side of the addict, it is often more linked to a desire to protect the partner from being overwhelmed or making an irrevocable decision to end the relationship. There is more on disclosure in Chapter 11 but needless to say this gradual disclosure can feel to the partner like multiple betrayals and leave them worrying that they may never know the truth.

It is common for partners to endlessly interrogate and seek more and more information and details, a process that is exhausting for both. Partly as a way of ensuring everything is out in the open, but also in an unconscious attempt to feel a sense of control. Some feel that once they have all the facts, they'll know what they're facing and can make a decision about the future. In part this is true, but as many can testify, there are some things that are best left unknown. Particularly if it's information that leaves a visual image in the brain, such as looking at pictures of places where an addict has been or asking questions about sexual acts and people that then imprint themselves into the brain. Once an image is inside the brain it is very difficult to get out (as many addicts know for themselves) and in reality, these details are generally irrelevant and unnecessary and can cause more psychological harm for the partner.

Lorna

Lorna wanted to know everything – every single detail. And each time she questioned Dave, more was revealed. Not only had he visited prostitutes when away on business but he also visited massage parlours close to his office and had started going to sex cinemas where he had sex with men. Lorna's shock and disgust grew with each new revelation. Her determination to know everything got stronger and she would grill Dave for details day and night and insisted that he took her to see the places he frequented. Much to Dave's horror, Lorna wanted to go in and see the people Dave had slept with. With righteous indignation Lorna announced that she was Dave's wife and he would not be coming again. At that moment in time she felt powerful and in control but she didn't sleep for weeks as the haunting images of what she'd seen either kept her awake or appeared in her dreams.

Nadine

On the same evening that Simon was sacked, he told Nadine everything about what he'd been doing over the previous ten years. He explained that at first he only watched porn occasionally, when she had her period or when she was out. But as work had become increasingly stressful over the past four years he had started watching it every day – often for hours at a time. He wanted to tell her everything about the sites he'd visited but as he began to describe the things he'd seen on some of the hardcore BDSM sites she stopped him and said she didn't want to hear anymore. She could feel her anxiety rising as he detailed acts that were similar to the abuse she'd experienced as a child, and she told him she couldn't cope with the information and didn't see why she needed to know. Simon was clearly disgusted and traumatised by what he'd viewed and she didn't want to share that experience.

Coping with the fallout

Once sex addiction is revealed, most partners experience a desperate urgency to do something about it. First and foremost, most partners want to understand 'Why?'. 'Why did you do this?' and 'Why didn't you tell me?' are questions that demand an immediate answer. Unfortunately, most addicts – especially those who have not started recovery – are unable to give this much needed information. Most addicts don't know why they did it themselves and therefore explaining to a partner is impossible. They may come up with some thoughts and ideas but they rarely stand up under scrutiny as they have not been fully explored and understood by the addict. What a partner needs most during the fall out is to know who's to blame and whether or not it's over. Again, most addicts don't have the answers to these questions and while they might offer endless reassurance that they can stop, this is rarely believed. After all – if it's that easy to stop, 'why didn't you do so before now'? In addition to the 'whys' there are other urgent questions, covered in the text that follows.

Who should I tell?

Like addicts, many partners experience acute shame and that shame can keep them feeling isolated and alone. Most will feel shame not only about their partner's behaviours but also about it being out of control. In addition many will feel ashamed of themselves for being with an addict or for not seeing what may have been going on right under their nose. The best way to get support during this difficult time is undoubtedly to tell someone, but deciding who can be trusted can be challenging. Many partners do not want to be judged and told what to do and hence may avoid telling someone who they suspect will either tell them to 'stand by their man' or to 'leave him immediately'. They may also feel a duty to protect the reputation of their partner and not threaten the relationships he has with others, especially other family members and children.

Conversely, some partners want to tell everyone. In their understandable anger and quest for justice they may want to shout it from the rooftops, arguing: 'Why should I be the one to suffer in silence and why shouldn't everyone know what you're really like?' These feelings may be justified, especially for those who may have been deceived and manipulated for years, but the impact of such disclosures must be calculated, not just on how it will affect the addict, but also those who are told. It's especially important to make sure children are protected from information that they may not be emotionally mature enough to manage. No child wants to know about their parent's sex life, let alone any deviant sexual behaviours, and such information may be damaging. Similarly an aging or infirm parent may not have the resources to cope with such a painful disclosure.

What's most important to recognise when considering who to tell is that a partner can share as little or as much as they feel comfortable, with the people they most believe can offer support. Furthermore, there is no urgency. Perhaps it may help for other people such as close friends and family members to know at some stage in the future, but it does not have to be now.

Should I stay or leave?

Another question that feels urgent to answer after disclosure is whether or not to leave the relationship. This is a massive decision, especially if children are involved and therefore I always advise that it be considered carefully and over time. Deciding whether or not to end a relationship is always a painful decision and one that most people agonise over. Therefore it's best to postpone this process until the shock of discovery has passed and a full appraisal can be made of what will be lost and what might be gained by either course of action. The decision is also most wisely made when both the addiction and the process of recovery is better understood. This then allows partners to gain a more rational perspective of the extent of the problem that they are either committing to or walking away from.

Should we continue our sex life?

Many partners find it especially difficult to decide what to do about their sex life and to come to terms with the complex feelings that an ongoing sexual relationship can evoke. Some partners are shocked to find themselves wanting to be more sexual with their partner than ever before. This is a common response to infidelity and is understood in evolutionary psychology as an unconscious desire to re-establish the couple bond. By contrast some partners are repulsed at the thought of sexual contact and find themselves withdrawing from any kind of intimate physical touch. Others find themselves yo-yoing between both extremes. It's important to recognise that all these reactions are natural and commonplace and there is no right or wrong thing to do. Many partners worry that if they continue sex they are acting as if everything is ok and at the same time worry that denying sex will make the addiction worse. Most find sex difficult as they struggle to get thoughts and images of the acting behaviours out of their heads and worry that their partner may be fantasising about the same.

Another common problem is the devastating impact sex addiction can have on a partner's sexual self-confidence. It's essential that partners understand that they can not, and never could, compete with the sexual images in pornography or with the endless novelty of multiple sex workers or lovers. Sex within a relationship, especially when a couple have been together for many years, is completely different from sexual acting out. And the vast majority of addicts would never want their couple sex life to replicate their acting out behaviours. The only way to address these dilemmas is through frank and honest conversations between the couple, perhaps with the help of a therapist. This is explored further in Chapter 12.

How can I trust you?

Sexual addiction damages trust more than any other kind of betrayal and for most partners being able to believe what a partner says feels almost impossible. Even if a decision has been made to end the relationship or separate on a temporary basis, partners still want to know if acting out has stopped. For couples who stay living together, it's especially important for partners to know that nothing is continuing in the home. Unfortunately, it is never possible to prove innocence. There is never evidence to support that 'nothing' has happened, hence evidence is sought that something has.

It is very common for partners to want to check emails, mobile phones, bank account statements, travel plans and ask questions about any unaccounted for time. This can feel very uncomfortable for some who feel as though they are 'checking up' on their partner or being put in a position of acting like a parent figure. When this dilemma is reframed as establishing safety for the partner and accountability for the addict, both essential elements of recovery, then the situation can be more easily handled. Ideally couples should decide together how they will maintain accountability and openness in the relationship, agreeing appropriate boundaries and techniques for doing so. This is discussed further in Chapter 11.

What about me?

Many partners feel they get lost in the addicts recovery process. While he's attending therapy to explore his feelings and needs, the partner often feels abandoned to cope with hers alone. It's important that partners are encouraged to seek therapy for themselves. Not because there is something wrong with them, but because discovering sex addiction is a traumatic experience and they deserve the time and space to have their needs cared for.

In addition to a partner's emotional needs, there are many practical things to consider too. Sex addiction often comes at a financial cost and sometimes legal too. This means that some partners should consider getting professional help to explore these consequences. And perhaps most importantly, and often overlooked, some partners of addicts whose acting out has been physical should see a sexual health professional to ensure they have not contracted an STI. This is often something that partners do not want to face but it's essential that awareness is raised of the sexual health risks that had been hitherto unknown.

Lorna

Lorna was surprised to discover that as the weeks passed she began to feel more calm. Dave was obviously wracked with guilt over his behaviours and was committed to seeking help and overcoming his addiction. She had confided in a close friend who promised to support her in whatever decisions she made and in spite of the haunting images in her head she was embarrassed to confess that their sex life was better than it had been in years. Her self-esteem was still in shatters but she resolved to give herself time to get over the shock before making any decisions that would impact her future forever. She still had outbursts of rage, usually directed at Dave, but he continued to reassure her that even though he couldn't explain his behaviours, he was still very much in love with her and wanted their relationship to continue.

Nadine

Over the weeks that followed Simon's disclosure, Nadine became increasingly anxious. He had refused to put parental control software on their home computer saying it was unnecessary and she struggled to control the panic that welled up inside her whenever she wasn't in the house to see what he was up to. This was exacerbated by the fact that she couldn't bring herself to have sex with Simon and she was sure he must be finding other outlets to meet his needs. Nadine didn't tell anyone, as she thought they should be able to manage the situation together and although Simon had originally said he would definitely get help, he didn't seem to be doing anything about it. Nadine began to worry that she would never be able to get over what Simon had done and she would never trust him again. As a 32 year-old with no children, she wondered if it would be wiser for her to walk away now.

Understanding co-addiction and co-dependency

Many books written on sex addiction, and indeed on any addiction, refer to the partners as either a co-addict or co-dependent. Basically, these terms mean the same thing and both are broad headings that encompass a range of partner behaviours that may be deemed as supporting, or at least, colluding with the addicted partner. With their roots in chemical dependency it's perhaps easier to think that a partner who chooses to stay with someone who is drug or alcohol dependent has their own conscious, or unconscious, reasons for doing so. But since sex addiction is so often completely hidden from a partner, I believe these labels are at best unhelpful, and at worst damaging and stigmatising. Furthermore, close inspection of the diagnostic criteria for someone who is co-dependent is remarkably similar to the criteria used for someone suffering with post-traumatic stress disorder (Steffens and Means, 2009). And in my experience, many partners are 'traumatised' by the discovery of sex addiction and will understandably find themselves pre-occupied by their partner's past or current behaviours, struggling to function adequately in their daily lives and obsessed with checking up on their partners.

There are undoubtedly some situations where partners are collusive in the behaviour and this seems to be particularly apparent in partners of sex addicts with an attachment-induced addiction. In these cases, the couple relationship has often been impaired by attachment difficulties over many years and the original unconscious fit may have supported the addiction. As with addicts, all partners are different. And all couple relationships are different. There are commonalities as we discuss next, but there are many differences too. So while labels and lists of common reactions are helpful for some, it's essential that therapists, and those they work with, maintain an openness to the individuality of each situation.

Partners of opportunity-induced addiction

The partners of those with a pure opportunity-induced addiction are most likely to have some awareness of their partner's sexual behaviours. They may know that they sometimes watch porn and may be aware that their work brings them face to face with sexual opportunities. Be that a work culture where affairs are commonplace or a particular location such as Soho or frequent travelling abroad. These partners often have a comfortable and liberal attitude towards sex and will have been given no reason to assume their partner is straying outside of their agreed couple boundaries.

When sex addiction is disclosed or discovered, the opportunity partner may struggle more than any other to believe that sex addiction really exists. They are most likely to insist that a partner just 'gets a grip' on pornography use and if there's been infidelity they're more likely to see this as a sign of moral weakness than an addiction. Once sex addiction has been understood, these partners can suffer particularly harshly with thinking they should have seen it coming or recognised the signs. Trust can be especially difficult to re-establish if environmental opportunities are not removed.

Partners of attachment-induced addiction

Attachment-induced addiction has its roots in troubled childhood relationships. Unfortunately, these problems are often replicated in the couple relationship and consequently many partners of an attachment-induced addict may have experienced a number of relationship difficulties. Most often these relationships will either be highly conflictual or fall into a parent/child dynamic. This is explored further in Chapter 11, but in brief these partners often feel like they have always been the responsible one in the relationship. Many partners of an attachment-induced addiction had difficulties in their own family of origin such as feeling abandoned or neglected or experiencing parental infidelity and/or separation. Conversely, a few come from especially close family backgrounds and found themselves unconsciously drawn to the independence and autonomy that a partner who struggles with intimacy and commitment often displays.

The discovery of sex addiction, which often includes some element of infidelity, can evoke a huge amount of anger for these partners. Many feel they have always had to work hard at their relationship and have frequently been forced to take the parental role. Some feel they have never been a priority in their partner's life and the discovery of addiction is often the last straw. These are the relationships that most often need couple counselling to explore unconscious collusions, in addition to recovery work for the partner.

Partners of trauma-induced addiction

Partners of trauma-induced addicts are often similar to those of attachment-induced addicts since the two often go hand in hand. However, for the small number of addicts whose addiction is almost entirely induced by a significant trauma, there are differences. Most partners are aware of the trauma in their partner's background, though few will know the exact details. Many trauma survivors have never talked about their experiences, choosing instead to anaesthetise with addiction. Furthermore, clients have told me that they specifically do not want to talk to their partners about trauma because they want to protect the relationship from what feels like contamination, and keep it a safe refuge. However, many partners do have either a conscious or unconscious awareness that their partner frequently

Lorna

Lorna was married to an attachment-induced addict. She had always argued that Dave was more wedded to his work than he was to her and she was determined not to be like her mother who silently put up with her father's army career until he finally left her for another woman when Lorna was 12. Unlike her mum, Lorna was determined to ensure her husband lived up to his marital and parental responsibilities. She could not deny the painful similarities between her current situation and the one her mother had found herself in. Unlike her father who had always been a womaniser, Dave was a quiet and shy man who she was sure would never stray. She had fallen for his childlike charm, but over the years she'd decided it was just an excuse not to grow up. Since the disclosure, Dave was doing his best to be a 'good boy' and win back Lorna's love and trust. She couldn't imagine being without him, but neither could she imagine ever forgiving him.

Nadine

Simon's addiction was trauma-induced though opportunity had played a significant role. Nadine could not stop thinking about the kinds of behaviours Simon was into. She felt physically sick when she thought about it and couldn't begin to consider how, or if, she could live with knowing what turned him on. She knew that it was all linked to his childhood abuse and she wanted to do everything in her power to help him recover – but all she could feel was panic. She had to work extra hours to support them and her parents were asking questions but she wanted to protect Simon from their inevitable judgements if they knew the truth. Nadine decided to visit her GP, without telling Simon, for medication to help her cope. She didn't want to burden Simon any more than she had to as she was sure he was wrestling with enough. Although he appeared to be coping fine and her resentment of this was beginning to grow.

struggles with anxiety and restlessness. They may have an empathy that comes from having experienced their own traumas too and often take the role of care-giver within the relationship. Couple collusions around the victim/persecutor/rescuer drama triangle are common and are explored further in Chapter 11.

I don't know if it's coincidence or Karma, but in my clinical experience, the discovery of trauma-induced sex addiction is nearly always a traumatic experience in itself. The revelation may be accompanied by police intervention, disciplinary charges, being sacked, unwanted pregnancy, STIs or assault. What's more, partners are often shocked by the type of behaviours, which are more likely to include a fetish, pain and/or humiliation. Partners of trauma addicts are most likely to be traumatised by the discovery, especially if they're survivors themselves and consequently need extensive care to re-establish safe emotional ground.

Recovery for partners

As stated at the beginning of this chapter, unfortunately there is not room in this book to fully explore the needs of partners who find themselves the innocent victims of sexual addiction. Needless to say, those needs are extensive and important and partners must be allowed space to share their feelings openly. Knowing they won't be judged and trusting they'll receive the empathy, care and support they deserve. In brief, in order for partners to recover they need to do these things.

- Manage the shock – All partners experience shock, regardless of how much or little they previously knew. Finding healthy ways to manage the emotional, physical, psychological and practical impact of disclosure is essential.
- Establish support networks – Many partners feel hugely ashamed of what's happened and fear they will themselves be judged. Finding others to talk to can not only reduce shame but also provide essential ongoing support. Others might be friends, family members, partners of other addicts or a professional therapist.
- Set boundaries – Most partners are left feeling they have no control of their lives and consequently it's important that boundaries are set to create safety. Those boundaries are most often around accountability and honesty and also physical and emotional boundaries between the couple.
- Understand addiction – Like the addict, understanding addiction can help to reduce shame and blame. Furthermore by understanding the unique situation of the addicted partner, it's easier to make an informed and rational decision about whether to try and rebuild the relationship.
- Understand themselves – All partners question why they either consciously, or unconsciously, chose to be with an addict and what either staying or leaving the relationship may mean about them. Developing greater self-awareness and insight can provide much needed resources for both recovery and growth.

- Rebuild self-esteem – Most partners experience significant self-doubt when addiction is revealed and consequently self-esteem can be very low. Recovery for partners means reclaiming their sense of identity and self-worth, including themselves as a partner and as a sexual being.
- Plan a future – Life does and will go on and although there is no rush to decide the future of the relationship, at some stage this decision needs to be made. Whatever the decision, partners need a new sense of purpose and direction.

How partner reactions affect addiction recovery

There is no doubt that the loving support of a partner significantly increases the likelihood of recovery from sexual addiction. This is further assisted if the couple are able to work together to strengthen their commitment and intimacy and fight the addiction side by side. However, this is often far too much to expect from a partner who has not only been betrayed and deceived, but who might rightly claim that if they'd known the truth about their partner, they may never have loved them in the first place.

When a partner stays in shame and blame this can continue the cycle of addiction for the one with the addiction as they are continually reminded of the pain they have caused. Similarly if a partner is not able to find the necessary resources to cope for themselves, the addict is likely to put more energy into their partner's recovery than their own. There are some partners who seem to successfully take control of the situation and will endeavour to help in the recovery process. But where this involves infantilising and/or controlling the addict, their partner may never develop their own internal locus of control and establish their own coping strategies. If a partner leaves this can devastate the addict to the point where recovery seems pointless since they have already lost what was most important to them. Or it magnifies the trauma or attachment issues that are at the root of the addiction. Conversely, some addicts know that their relationship has been dysfunctional and is a contributing factor to their addiction. But in the wake of the discovery of addiction, they feel increasingly duty bound to work at the relationship.

When an addict is in a relationship, the impact on the partner and how they work through it, either together or apart, significantly affects the treatment process. Wherever possible, services need to be provided for both so each can recover and rebuild their lives.

Lorna

Lorna and Dave's marriage became increasingly acrimonious. Dave tried his best to please her, but Lorna would not let him forget the pain he had caused – lest he be tempted to do it again. In the course of his recovery, Dave realised he had always felt controlled by Lorna and one of the functions of his acting out, had been finding autonomy. He tried to talk to Lorna about his feelings and his need for independence but she said he had no right after what he'd done to her. Dave eventually ended the marriage, and Lorna found herself in exactly the same position as her mother had been.

Nadine

Eventually Nadine cracked and Simon was faced with the full impact of what his behaviour had done to his wife. She could no longer rescue him and be his caregiver, and Simon realised he had to begin to look after himself and take responsibility for his own recovery. Nadine went into therapy to explore her own childhood trauma and how Simon's behaviours had re-triggered the pain. Simon threw himself into his recovery and together they rebuilt their marriage into one where both of them were survivors of trauma and survivors of his addiction.

Part II

Breaking the chains of addiction

In Part II we will look at the essential treatment objectives for anyone who is serious about recovery and consider some of the treatment options currently available within the UK and Eire. In Chapter 7 we examine the importance of making a commitment to recovery that includes changing faulty core beliefs, reclaiming values and a vision for the future, and determining appropriate sexual boundaries. Guidelines on how to personalise the six-phase cycle of addiction are provided in Chapter 8, which may then be used as a tool for identifying changes required to secure recovery. The part concludes with suggestions on how to identify the unresolved issues and unmet needs that often underpin addiction and a brief exploration of a variety of therapeutic approaches that can be utilised to address them.

6 Treatment objectives and options

At the time of writing this book, our understanding of sex addiction is still very much in its infancy in the UK and, subsequently, so are many of the treatment options. There are still some medical and psychological professionals who doubt its existence and many more who have not yet grasped the complexity of the condition. Unfortunately, the consequence of this is that many people with sex addiction have to approach a number of different professionals before they get the help they both need and deserve.

In this chapter we will explore the basic treatment objectives that must be addressed and the therapeutic approaches that are currently available within the UK and Eire. There is no evidence that any particular approach is more successful than any other, as long as each treatment objective is achieved. It has been known for many years that successful treatment for any psychological condition is ultimately dependent on the relationship between the client and therapist and on the motivation of the client. Someone who is unable to feel comfortable and confident with their therapist, for whatever reason, is unlikely to benefit from the therapy that's offered, no matter how brilliant the treatment might be. And someone who doesn't want to change won't.

In a nutshell, when treating sex addiction, therapy needs to address both the underlying issues that form the function of the addition and provide practical relapse prevention strategies. In addition, treatment needs to explore healthier emotional management techniques and how a fulfilling life can be achieved, without the addictive behaviours. Overcoming sex addiction is long-term work, especially for those with attachment and/or trauma issues. As discussed previously, addiction affects the brain and synaptic change can take between three and five years (Cozolino, 2002). This means that some element of long-term work is essential for many, whether that's alone, in therapy or as part of a recovery or 12-step community.

Treatment objectives

In total there are six treatment objectives for overcoming sex addiction and they can be remembered by the rather cheesy acrostic 'UR-CURED'. Please let me assure you that it is purely co-incidental that the first letters of each objective spell out UR-CURED. I have tried to come up with an alternative but have failed. UR-CURED is not intended to be a trite sales claim or marketing gimmick, but something that will be easy to remember. Hopefully the naffness will make it especially memorable!

- **U**nderstand sex addiction
- **R**educe shame
- **C**ommit to recovery
- **U**nderstand and personalise the cycle of addiction
- **R**esolve underlying issues
- **E**stablish relapse prevention strategies
- **D**evelop a healthy life

Understand sex addiction

First and foremost it's essential that someone suffering with sex addiction 'understands' the problem they're facing. Education should be a pre-requisite for any treatment approach, especially in our current social climate where there continues to be so much misunderstanding. Until someone knows that sex addiction is a genuine health condition, not something invented to excuse poor impulse control, infidelity or an insatiable sex drive, they will be unable to move on to the next stage of treatment. Education may be done independently or with a therapist within an individual or group setting. Part I of this book should provide sufficient educational material, but do check out any new thinking and research which may have emerged since publication.

Reduce shame

It is said that shame is to addiction what oxygen is to fire. Shame leaves us feeling powerless, helpless and unworthy of receiving the help and support of others. Shame is perhaps one of the most painful emotions we can experience and consequently it perpetuates the cycle of addiction as a person acts out to alleviate the pain of shame only to find it creates more. While someone is trapped in shame, recovery is not possible and relapse is almost inevitable.

It's important to distinguish between shame and guilt. Shame can be described as a painfully negative emotion where the self is seen as bad and unworthy, whereas guilt is a negative judgement about a behaviour. Hence guilt says 'I have done something bad' whereas shame says 'I am bad'. Both have a long tradition as both causes and consequences of addiction but research has shown that whereas shame is likely to increase addictive behaviour, guilt can be a significant motivator to overcome it (Gilliland et al., 2011).

Contrary to the belief of some, the shame experienced by people with sex addiction is frequently not from any ethical or anti-sex perspective. On the contrary, most of the clients I work with have no moral objection to watching pornography or visiting sex workers. Their shame comes from prioritising these activities over and above their commitments to partners, children, friends, work, finances, health and career and personal development. Some people who are addicted to fetish behaviours, such as visiting dominatrix, BDSM, scatting or water sports, and some, who compulsively have same-sex experiences although they would define themselves as heterosexual, can experience overwhelming shame about their behaviours. When this occurs it's essential that this shame is dealt with in the same way as someone who enjoys such activities without compulsion. Overcoming sex addiction should never be about changing an individual's taste in sexual behaviours, but about changing their compulsive use of the behaviour – whatever that might be.

Shame can damage someone's sense of self to the point where they no longer see themselves as worthy of the love of a partner, or the respect of children, or the unconditional regard of friends, or the promotion from a boss. They may experience a sense of guilt at the number of times they have lied or let down others due to prioritising a secret sex life, but the shame can wound to the point where change feels impossible. To overcome any addiction, the behaviour must be empathically evaluating in order to reduce shame. With shame removed there is then freedom to either decide that the behaviour is not a problem, or by reframing to guilt they may be more empowered to change.

Reducing shame is one of the toughest therapeutic challenges in treating sex addiction and is an ongoing process throughout the work. It can be particularly challenging in individual therapy. No matter how much genuine support, empathy and acceptance is offered, there's no getting around the fact that 'it's a therapist's job' to make a client feel better. Hence, the reassurance may not be received. And ironically, the stronger the therapeutic alliance between client and therapist, the more a client may feel like a failure or a disappointment if they are not making adequate progress or must confess to another relapse. These feelings are often a projection from childhood or from a couple relationship but, nonetheless, they can fuel shame. In addition, a therapist may often find themselves in a 'one step forward, two steps back' dilemma, as each shame-reducing intervention is countered by shame inducing messages and events outside of the therapy room. For example, hurtful comments from an angry or betrayed partner, or the shame experienced by seeing how a much loved partner has been broken by the discovery. Others who know about the behaviour such as family members or work colleagues may belittle and deride and the latest media headline about perverts or love rats can pierce deep. There may be ongoing negative consequences even after acting out has ended such as STIs, financial problems, unemployment that continually fuel shame and if there's a slip or relapse, all the other sources of shame are disproportionally compounded.

Many people who've struggled with addiction are reluctant to let go of their shame, as they believe it to be part of their penance or proof that they've accepted responsibility. Many also falsely believe that continuing shame is a necessary reminder of the pain they've caused which will help them not to act out again. There is more about reducing shame in Chapter 7 and also in Chapter 14.

Commit to recovery

Back in Chapter 2 we looked at Prochaska and DiClementes' stages of change. Once someone understands sex addiction and has begun to reduce shame, most will have made their way through the Pre-contemplative and Contemplative stages and be entering the Preparation or Action phase. It's important to highlight that everybody's path is unique and some are longer and harder than others, but full recovery is possible. Commitment to recovery does not necessarily preclude doubt, and therefore it's vital to acknowledge that there will be times when either the desire or the ability to recover is questioned. Addressing these issues early in treatment and agreeing how to manage them can help to ensure that commitment is maintained.

In order to make a commitment to recovery, it's essential to know what recovery is going to look like. Many people first seek help because their world is falling apart and the key motivator is survival. But it's important to move beyond this and develop a positive and optimistic vision of the future. Therefore focus needs to not be on just what someone wants to give up, but also what they want to gain. The next chapter gives some suggestions on how to achieve this.

Another part of the commitment process is to agree a commitment to therapy. As we'll explore more later in this chapter, most people benefit from both individual and group therapy as well as couple therapy if they're in a relationship. Furthermore, evidence suggests that regular, ongoing attendance at a support group, such as a 12-step meeting, can significantly aid recovery (Krentzman, 2007).

Understand and personalise the cycle of addiction

Everybody is unique and therefore every addiction is unique. There are of course many commonalities as we've previously explored, but in order to overcome addiction, it's crucial to fully understand the unique elements that make up an individual's sex addiction cycle. Chapter 8 is dedicated to this topic but in brief it means understanding the unmet needs and unresolved issues of the Dormant phase; identifying Triggers; recognising the cognitive distortions that happen during the Preparation phase; understanding the function of the addiction in the Acting Out phase; and becoming aware of how the Regret and Reconstitution phases are experienced and managed.

Resolve underlying issues

Unless the underlying functions of addiction are identified and addressed, someone with an addiction will continue to act out. Relapse prevention strategies may help to stop and stay stopped for a while, but without resolving the deeper unmet needs and issues, recovery will be reduced to pure will power and the sufferer has no choice but to 'white-knuckle' it.

While acting out continues it is often difficult to get to the root of the problem. Sex addiction can be such a powerfully successful anaesthetic that many sufferers are unaware of the pain beneath the behaviour. Although a thorough assessment may highlight probable unresolved issues, these may not move from cognitive recognition to emotional reality until weeks or even months after the behaviour has ceased.

This stage of therapy may be the longest, the slowest and the most painful as the root of addiction is exposed, examined and pulled out. There is not space in this book to provide full treatment strategies and suggestions for this work, but you'll find an overview in Chapter 9.

Establish relapse prevention strategies

Relapse prevention strategies are a part of treatment that needs to be woven throughout the work. Some people arrive for therapy having already stopped their behaviour and their most urgent need and request is to establish strategies that will help them to remain stopped. Others may have experienced the shock of discovery as such a traumatic experience that they're convinced they will not relapse – at least not for many months. Others will still be acting out and want to work on other issues before beginning the painful process of withdrawal. Whatever the situation, it's important to highlight that relapse prevention is a part of the treatment programme and that the process of establishing these strategies will be an ongoing part of not just therapy, but of life.

Relapse prevention work needs to highlight not only the emotional and environmental triggers that reactivate behaviours, but also the thought patterns that have become automatic, and probably unnoticed over many years. Cognitive neural restructuring strategies should be part of any relapse prevention programme and is explored more in Part III.

Develop a healthy life

Someone once wisely said that 'recovery is not about learning to manage addiction, but learning to manage life'. For many people with an addiction, whether to drugs, alcohol, gambling or sex, their addiction has become an integral part of their lifestyle and therefore stopping means changing the way they live. Those changes will almost certainly include how they relate in primary relationships and within their families as well as how other nurturing relationships can be either created or strengthened, and also how to develop a positive view of their sexuality and a healthy way to express and enjoy it. Other areas of life also need to be explored to ensure that life is experienced as meaningful and fulfilling. Chapters 11, 12 and 13 are dedicated to these topics.

Treatment options

As long as both client and therapist have a good knowledge of sexual addiction and agree goals for treatment, there is no wrong way for it to be delivered. As already specified there are a number of objectives that need to be addressed, but there are countless different ways of achieving this. Deciding what 'works' is down to personal taste and choice – a therapist must feel comfortable and confident in the techniques and strategies they use, as must the client.

Unfortunately, there are currently limited services available within the NHS (National Health Service), but hopefully this will change as sex addiction becomes more widely accepted and understood. Here I will present the most common types of therapy available, followed by the modalities currently favoured to treat sex addiction within the private sector.

Individual therapy

Individual therapy is probably the most common first port of call for people struggling with sex addiction. Any individual therapist who chooses to work with sex addiction must have at least a thorough understanding of the complexity of the condition in order to ensure that every treatment objective is being addressed. Some therapists will have sufficient training to work through each objective while others will choose to focus on resolving underlying issues and refer to another specialist for other aspects of the work.

Individual therapy is probably the best option for exploring and overcoming the underlying issues, particularly those relating to attachment and trauma.

There is no particular modality that is known to work better than others though cognitive behavioural therapy (CBT) and motivational interviewing techniques may be particularly beneficial for managing cognitive distortions and relapse prevention work. Attachment issues are often best addressed through integrative or psychodynamic psychotherapy and eye movement desensitization and reprogramming (EMDR) or sensorimotor psychotherapy may be required to address trauma. Individual therapists working in sex addiction can be found on the ATSAC website listed in the resources section and also on the IITAP website.

Group therapy

Most addiction specialists agree that group work is an essential component of lifetime recovery (Nerenberg, 2002). Although most people baulk at the thought of joining a group, it is the most effective way of reducing shame, as people with an addiction find themselves amidst others who struggle with the same difficulty but, nonetheless, are kind, loving, respectable and responsible people. Being confronted face to face with the realisation that sex addiction does not define a person can break through shame and isolation in a way that individual therapy cannot replicate. In addition the sharing of relapse prevention techniques can boost the chance of ongoing success as can having an ongoing resource of people to be accountable to and turn to in times of need. Attachment issues can also be worked through within a group environment and many group members will testify to making the closest and most profound friendships within a group.

Couple therapy

Many couples do survive sex addiction, but it's hard and difficult work. Couple therapy with someone who is trained in couple dynamics can help the couple to talk openly about their feelings and explore how they can heal their relationship. Couple therapy cannot offer treatment for the addiction or for the partner, but it can be an invaluable resource for couples dealing with the fallout. Couples who choose to separate can also be helped to ensure they divorce in the healthiest possible way – something that is especially important if there are children.

Specialist sex addiction treatment approaches

There are a number of different approaches currently available within the UK and Ireland. You can find full details of training opportunities within these modalities as well as where treatment is available within the resources section at the end of this book.

The 30-task model

This model, based on extensive clinical research in the USA, was created by Dr Patrick Carnes and is now available from some private therapists within the UK. The task-centred approach provides a framework for recovery over 30 individual 'tasks' that have measurable activities. For example, Task 1 is 'Break through denial' and includes 8 activities to be completed. Examples of those activities include making a problem list, making a list of excuses and finding a therapist. Task 18 is 'Establishing healthy exercise and nutrition patterns', and its activities include completing a physical assessment form, taking regular exercise and managing weight.

The 30 tasks are broken down into 3 core segments. The first 7 tasks are grouped under the heading of the 'Recovery start kit' and are designed to establish sobriety. Tasks 8 through to 19, known as the 'Recovery zone', focus on personal recovery; tasks 20 to 30 in 'Recovery zone II' focus on creating family recovery. These tasks can be followed in individual therapy or within a group or residential context.

Integrative cognitive behavioural therapy

Integrative CBT incorporates the well-known scientific advantages of Cognitive Behavioural Therapy with other key therapeutic approaches such as Person-Centred Therapy, the Egan Model, Schema Therapy and Existential Psychotherapy. Pioneered by Eoin Stephens in Ireland, this approach to treating sex addiction covers five key areas: building a therapeutic relationship; taking problem-solving action; cognitive-emotional re-learning; schema change; and acceptance of the human condition. It is a comprehensive treatment approach that provides both practical and pragmatic change along with resolving negative core messages and developing a healthy relationship with both self and others. Services are available primarily within Ireland but a growing number of UK therapists are adopting its principles and approach.

Psycho-educational treatment groups

The psycho-educational treatment group was one of the first formal treatment options available within the UK and was started by Dr Thaddeus Birchard in 2001. The key advantage of this treatment approach is that it combines proven therapeutic interventions with the established benefits of group work. These groups are developing a proven track record and are increasingly offered by a number of therapists around the UK, including the Hall Recovery Course created by myself. The Hall Recovery Course follows the integrative BERSC Model and consists of four modules: 1. Understanding addiction; 2. Overcoming blocks to recovery; 3. Establishing relapse prevention strategies; and 4. Restoring a healthy lifestyle. Groups are limited to a maximum of 8 participants and run over a fixed number of between 16 and 20 weeks. The programme is also available as a 7-day residential. The Hall Recovery Course focuses on the three essential tasks of recovery, which bluntly boil down to: Face it; Understand it; and Fight It. You can find more details in the resource section.

In-patient programmes and treatment centres

In-patient programmes provide a thorough and multi-disciplinary approach to treating sex addiction that is tailored to each individual. After an initial assessment, most people also undergo thorough bio-psycho-social assessment to establish history and determine evidence of co-morbidity and any other addictive processes. A decision is then taken on an appropriate treatment plan, which is typically between four and six weeks. All inpatients are seen by a consultant psychiatrist throughout their time in treatment and have a dedicated keyworking counsellor.

A typical programme is based around daily group therapy and the groups include people experiencing difficulties with a variety of addictive substances and behaviours. There is an underlying theme of 12-step recovery and patients attend the relevant 12-step meetings while in treatment. Abstinence from all addictive substances and behaviours are an important foundation for the depth of emotional work that needs to take place so there are restrictions on electronic devices and mobile telephones.

Trauma reduction work may also be offered where appropriate and may be in the form of EMDR or a week-long experiential trauma reduction programme, which is highly effective in reducing shame. Some centres also provide workshops and complementary treatments such as yoga and meditation. Family work is a key element in helping the change process and may involve the family coming for a day's education and therapy. And after completion of the programme, many centres provide ongoing counselling and a free weekly aftercare group.

Online recovery programmes

There are many different online recovery programmes that come from a variety of different perspectives. The great advantage of online resources is their accessibility, but unfortunately some people who have been addicted to online pornography or cyber sex should probably be avoiding time online. The lack of face-to-face support can also be a drawback though many do have their own online communities. My personal favourite is one called Recovery Nation. Developed by Jonathan Marsh, a former addict himself as well as a therapist, it offers a health-based approach to treating sex addiction. What I particularly like about the site is that it provides practical tools as well as education for the person with the addiction, the partner and the couple.

The Kick Start Recovery programme is a free resource developed by myself that can be downloaded from the web to provide a starting point into recovery. As with the Hall Recovery Course, it covers the three essential tasks: Face it; Understand it; and Fight It. The programme includes self-assessment tools, psycho-educational material and relapse prevention strategies. People with a mild, opportunity-induced addiction may find the programme sufficient to overcome the problem, especially if they have access to a good support network or combine it with a 12-step programme. For others it provides an informed foundation from which to consider further treatment options.

12-step and other self-support groups

Self-support groups have been an invaluable source of help for all kinds of addictions and while there are a variety of options available, by far the best known is the 12-step programme first proposed by Alcoholics Anonymous in 1939. 12-step programmes have since been developed for almost every addiction imaginable and are available worldwide. The founding principle of 12 steps is to follow 12 clearly outlined recovery objectives within the supportive environment of other addicts. The most established groups within the UK are SAA (Sex Addicts Anonymous) and SLAA (Sex and Love Addicts Anonymous). The advantage of these groups is that they are free and can offer a lifetime of support. However, they are run by volunteers and while there is always a facilitator running the group there is no professional therapeutic input. This means that most people will need to have had at least some therapy during or before joining a group.

Partner therapy

Few things can devastate a partner more than the discovery of sex addiction as we briefly explored in Chapter 5. Most partners are completely unaware of their partner's behaviours until they're discovered. The shock of the discovery can leave a partner questioning not only their partner, but also their relationship, themselves and their world. Most partners can benefit from having a therapeutic space of their own to explore and resolve their feelings and consider future options. For some partners, the discovery also brings up other problems within the relationship and/or unresolved issues from childhood. Partner therapy can be within an individual counselling setting or within group work.

Finding a treatment approach that works is often a case of trial and error and as mentioned previously, ultimately the most important factors in success are the relationship with the therapist and the motivation of the client. What follows throughout the rest of this book is information, examples and suggested exercises that can begin the UR-CURED treatment objectives. They can be worked through independently, or within individual or group therapy.

Ultimately, getting over sex addiction is about realising you're not alone and committing to recovery – however long it takes. Below are just a few things that people said who took the sex addiction survey when asked: 'What has been the most important or helpful thing you've learnt during your treatment of sex addiction?'

'I'm not alone.'

'Connection is key – connection with others, with myself, with my past and with the world. Sexual addiction is a symptom of relationships gone wrong.'

'To stop feeling shame. And I must take responsibility to change, or nothing will ever change.'

'To understand your core values and believe that these better describe you than your behaviour and so to focus on these rather than escapism.'

'Tackling the underlying issue has helped self-esteem and taking back self-control, which has diminished the need to partake in such activities'

'The Group and the explanations into how the brain and addictions work.'

'That the cycle can be broken and that I'm not the only one.'

'The influence of my childhood on my actions as an adult.'

'That I cannot resolve this on my own; I need to talk to, and work with, people who understand the issue.'

'Probably that I was not alone and that there is light at end of tunnel. Also I learned a lot about my childhood stuff that had been pushed aside and forgotten but became very significant in the causes and reasons for my illness.' 'I can feel love and affection without sexual encounters.'

'That I have a choice to take a different more constructive path.'

'That I'm not some drooling, raincoated deviant, but that my problem with addiction is more common that generally realised. That I'm far from alone; there are people, otherwise good, wholesome individuals, who also suffer as I do. Exposing my behaviour to view has been excruciatingly embarrassing; after all, it was always supposed to be completely private, without involving anyone else.

'The most important has been understanding the cycle of addiction and how un-met needs and triggers play such a key role in maintaining the addictive cycle.'

'To discover my true values and live by them with all my heart, strength and life.'

'The most important thing that I've learned is that I'm not the only person suffering with sex addiction. Knowing that there are people who are going through very similar things to me, and that there are people who've come out at the other end has been inspiring and has offered me hope.'

'Working to find my authentic self and being true to that. Part of that has been about being more assertive about my real desires instead of always adapting to needs of maintaining a relationship.'

'I had to want to stop. Thinking you did because it was the right thing to do wasn't enough. Really really wanting to stop was the single most important factor.'

'Learning to love and take care of myself and my own emotional, physical, sexual and spiritual needs.'

7   Making a commitment to recovery

Once someone understands the concepts of sex addiction, the next step is to begin to reduce shame and commit to recovery. No one can beat a problem unless they believe they deserve to and they believe that they can.

Committing to recovery requires developing self-belief and a vision of a new, happier future. A future that is free of shame and offers fulfilment. There also needs to be an acceptance of what will be lost, namely the acting out behaviours and the rewards that they brought. Inevitably there will be a mourning period but as long as there is true hope for the future, the loss process can be made bearable.

In this chapter we will explore how to reduce shame and rebuild self-esteem by identifying and changing faulty core beliefs. Also how to build a vision for the future built on what's most important and set sexual boundaries that fit with that vision and personal values. And crucially, making a commitment to recovery also means stopping destructive sexual behaviours.

Identifying core beliefs

According to the great guru Patrick Carnes, sex addiction starts with faulty core beliefs (Carnes, 2001) and unless these beliefs can be re-written, the wheels of the addiction cycle will continue to turn. It is undoubtedly true that our individual belief systems form the cornerstones of how we think about ourselves, how we think about others and how we view our world. Our thoughts, feelings and behaviours are defined by our belief system, even though some of those beliefs may be outside of our conscious awareness. The problem with faulty core beliefs is that they tend to become a self-fulfilling prophecy. Someone who has grown up feeling unworthy of the respect of others is more likely to develop relationships and behaviours where they continue to be disrespected. And someone who doubts their intelligence and their ability to effectively communicate their needs is less likely to seek out the education and career options they both desire and deserve.

Most of our core beliefs are formed in early childhood and someone with an attachment or trauma-induced addiction will most likely have developed faulty core beliefs that need to be identified and changed. For example, someone with an attachment-induced addiction who was neglected and not praised as child may grow up believing they're not worthy of love. And someone with a trauma-induced addiction who was the victim of bullying or abuse may grow up feeling alienated from others and unable to protect themselves. These faulty core beliefs are then reinforced by the addictive behaviour as the multiple affairs of attachment-induced addiction leaves someone feeling increasingly unworthy of the love of their partner and people with a trauma-induced addiction feels isolated and ashamed of their addiction to dominatrix sex.

The picture is slightly different for someone with an addiction that was primarily induced by opportunity, who may have grown up with a relatively healthy set of core beliefs. But as they spiral into addictive behaviours their view of themselves may change as they no longer see themselves as an honest person who is in control of their life. In the past, sex addiction literature has seemed to assume that all addiction was caused by faulty core beliefs, but in my experience of working with an increasing number of opportunity-induced addictions, the feelings of low self-worth have been a consequence of the behaviour, not the cause.

As a society we don't generally talk about 'core belief's but instead focus on the impact of those beliefs on our self-esteem. If you ask someone about their self-esteem, many will at first say it is good but often what they're referring to is self-confidence. Self-confidence is the term we use to describe how we feel about the things that we 'do', whereas self-esteem is how we feel about who we 'are'. There are many people in the world with low self-esteem who have, nonetheless, gone on to have successful careers and build beautiful homes and families. Indeed becoming good at 'doing' can become a substitute for feeling good about who you are as a person. And a life focused on creating an external image that is respected, admired and perhaps coveted by others, may be used as a cover-up for internal feelings of inadequacy.

Before we can start changing our core beliefs, we need to recognise what they are. Figure 7.1 is a simple questionnaire that lists 20 healthy core beliefs. The first 11 are beliefs about the self and the following are beliefs about self in relation to others. Having worked through this exercise, it may become clear how a lack of healthy core beliefs has both created and maintained the sexual addiction – there's more about this in Chapter 8. But the first task is to ensure that negative core beliefs don't get in the way of change. Shame is rooted in negative self-belief, and as discussed in the

	Healthy Core Belief	Firmly believe	Partially believe	Don't believe
1	I am a good person			
2	I am a loving person			
3	I am an honest person			
4	I am an intelligent person			
5	I am a strong person			
6	I am a competent person			
7	I am safe			
8	I can look after myself			
9	I can manage my emotions			
10	I am in control of my future			
11	I can change and grow as a person			
12	I belong			
13	I deserve to be respected			
14	I deserve to be valued			
15	I deserve to be loved			
16	I deserve to have my needs met			
17	I can communicate my emotional needs			
18	I can communicate my physical needs			
19	I can trust others to meet my needs			
20	I can empathise with others needs			

Figure 7.1 Identifying core beliefs

last chapter, shame perpetuates the cycle of addiction. Therefore developing healthy core beliefs will reduce shame. What's more, with a healthy set of core beliefs, it's easier to believe that addiction can be overcome and a new life can be enjoyed, which means that commitment to recovery is a positive choice rather than an enforced obligation.

Changing core beliefs

Changing core beliefs takes time – especially if they've been firmly rooted in childhood. The easiest way to change them is simply to challenge their truth and reality. Motivational Interviewing techniques can be particularly useful for highlighting discrepancies in the belief – for example, noticing the times and circumstances when someone is a good person or highlighting that they have already changed and grown. Cognitive behavioural therapy can also be used to establish change through exercises such as writing the pro's and cons of maintaining a negative belief or writing flash cards of new positive beliefs along with the evidence to support it. I find Transactional Analysis a useful tool, too, as it is often the internal ego state of the Critical Parent who is keeping the negative belief alive. When someone is able to move to their Adult ego state they often find it easier to rationally challenge the belief and re-write it.

Reclaiming personal values

Closely aligned to our core belief system are the personal values that we hold. The things in life that we hold most dear, our sense of right and wrong. Values can be defined as the principles in our life from which we derive meaning and fulfilment. When we live a life that is in line with our personal values, we are able to feel good about ourselves. Those values can also be used to determine our priorities and our decision making. In every case that I have worked with, sex addiction contradicts the personal value system of the individual, leaving them feeling ashamed and out of control. Over time, personal values slowly erode and many people may have forgotten what's really important to them. As part of my survey I asked: 'In what way has your sex addiction contradicted your personal value system?' Here is what just a few people said.

'It made me a hypocrite. Everything I brought my children up to believe in I was doing the opposite.'

'I feel and think like a bully sometimes ... but I hate bullies!''I believe in monogamy and fidelity. I would never intentionally have hurt my partner. However, my sexual acting out completely contradicts this.'

'It's totally the opposite to the real me. It's like there is a part of me that relentlessly demands satisfaction causing absolute inner turmoil and conflict with the real me. Or is this real me? That's the thought that destroys my self-esteem and eats the soul.'

'I consider myself generally as a caring, sensitive person for whom family means everything, and I believe everyone should be treated with honesty and respect, yet I have abused the trust my wife had in me through repeatedly lying and continuing with my addictive behaviour.'

'It makes me question my capability to be a mother and a good friend.'

'I don't believe in hurting women. But my behaviour is contributing to the exploitation of women isn't it? Somewhere along the line someone is getting hurt, aren't they? Even if I don't see it. I'm not happy that I'm cheating on my partner either.'

'I probably would dislike and disapprove of me if I met me.'

'I devalue myself I destroy the gifts of my life I hurt others.'

'My addiction could only survive within a bubble of lies and deceit, which to someone who thinks of himself as an honest and truthful person is a complete contradiction of values.'

'I feel ashamed of violating my values … i am dirty and unworthy. i failed myself and feel sad … i thought i could never wipe the slate clean.'

'I believe in life and in creativity and love. Sex addiction kills all of that and leaves you spiritually, morally, emotionally, mentally and physically dead. You're like a living junkie, only the scars are hidden inside you – no one else can see.'

'Completely. Most people who know me well would never associate me with my behaviour. They know me as someone who devotes considerable time and effort to my public image which is one of a responsible and trustworthy leader. I am well regarded in my professional field and my family and friends regard me as a good person that can be relied on to help them in a difficulty. If they found out about my secret behaviour they would be shocked and horrified. I was living a lie – and talking about the importance of honesty.'

'I believed I was a moral person but I did the most immoral things.'

'I always thought of myself as an honest and kind person. My addiction and the behaviours required to maintain it have made me a liar, a pervert and someone who has hurt the ones I love more than I ever thought possible.'

By reclaiming and recommitting to our personal value system, we can get back in touch with the things that give meaning and purpose to life. What follows is an exercise to help consider some common personal values. The list is by no means exhaustive so working through it may trigger additional values that are of more importance.

Once work has begun on developing healthy core beliefs and reclaiming personal values, the next task in committing to recovery is to use this information to decide which sexual behaviours are acceptable and which need to be stopped.

Box 7.1 Reclaiming personal values

In my practice I recommend that clients tick the 10 or more values that are most important to them and then put them in order of importance and priority.

Values list

Living with integrity

Living with compassion

Sharing my true self with others

Strengthening my role as a partner

Strengthening my role as a parent

Being an inspiration to others

Showing appreciation to others

Being dedicated to my work

Being charitable and generous

Developing intellectual depth

Expressing my spirituality

Enhancing my spiritual awareness

Enjoying rest, relaxation and play

Staying healthy physically and emotionally

Being dependable

Being reliable and responsible

Being honest and trustworthy

Being considerate of others

Loving others

Being loved by others

Being challenged

Overcoming challenges

Developing emotional maturity

Developing and enjoying creativity

Developing sustained friendships

Being validated by others

Developing patience

Connecting to my own feelings

Appreciating natural beauty/ nature

Connecting to purpose and meaning

Having personal independence

Feeling in control

Being faithful

Communicating feelings without fear

Taking care of others in need

Feeling happy and content

Experiencing a sense of accomplishment

Being open-minded to the beliefs and values of others

Treating others with respect

Being financially secure

Being courageous

Acting with honour and being honourable

Being able to assert my personal needs and desires

Setting sexual boundaries

The biggest difference between sex addiction and other addictions is that total abstinence is not the goal. However, many treatment approaches and some 12-step groups recommend complete abstinence from any kind of sexual activity, alone or partnered, in the early stages of recovery. The reason given for this is that it may be helpful for down-regulating dopamine, and while there is no clinical evidence to support this there is ample clinical experience that many people benefit. A period of abstinence provides space to focus on the self and others in a non sexual way and allows previously anaesthetised emotions to come to the surface. Abstinence can also eliminate the anxiety that sex is an essential need and provide the opportunity to practise healthy self-soothing techniques. A period of between 30 and 90 days is often recommended but ultimately it's up to the individual to decide which behaviours are essential for sobriety and a timescale that works for them. We explore developing a satisfying sex life later in Chapter 12 and you may find it helpful to skip ahead and read parts of it now, but for this 'commitment' stage of recovery, the key task is to decide what's ok and what's not ok. That decision will be unique to every individual, but for it to be sustainable it needs to fit with core beliefs and personal values. The purpose of the circle exercise below is not to pass moral judgement on any sexual activities, but to decide what's right for you. (This exercise has been adapted from the three-circle exercise used by Sex Addicts Anonymous.)

Most people are more comfortable doing this exercise alone where it may be easier to be completely honest and open about sexual behaviours. However, once completed, it's beneficial to discuss the OK and IFFY areas with a therapist, 12-step sponsor, or trusted friend, who will challenge you if necessary.

Once this circle exercise has been completed and a decision has been made about what is OK and what is not OK, the next step, if it's not already been taken, is to stop. Some people like to set a day for when they will stop and make preparations beforehand such as those discussed in Part III, but most will already have stopped due to the crisis that brought them to this point. In my experience, it is better to stop immediately, as soon as the decision to change has been made. Not only does this protect against further damaging consequences, but it also allows the task of recovery to be fully acknowledged and understood.

Box 7.2 The circle exercise

On a sheet of paper, list every kind of sexual activity you have ever been involved in, alone and with other people. That might include masturbating with porn, masturbating without porn, having sex with a partner, engaging in cyber sex, telephone sex, viewing late night TV channels, voyeurism, visiting massage parlours, sex cinemas, sex workers, dogging sites, stranger sex, affairs, one night stands and so on and so on.

Once this has been done, the challenge is to separate the list into the appropriate areas in the circle below. The top OK circle is where you write all the behaviours that fit with your values and you are completely comfortable with. The bottom NOT OK circle is for the behaviours that are definitely outside of your value system. The overlap IFFY area is for those behaviours that you're currently unsure about. You might be unsure because you don't know how you feel about it or whether it would cause a problem for a partner. You should also list here any behaviours that, although OK in themselves, might lead to the NOT OK circle. For example, someone who's addiction has been to visiting sex workers may not have an addiction to internet pornography but they may put internet porn in their middle IFFY circle because they know they are much more likely to be tempted to visit sex worker sites when online.

Figure 7.2 The circle exercise

Creating a vision for life

We will end this chapter with an exercise that, in my clinical experience, can cement a commitment to recovery more than anything else – one that is particularly challenging, but can literally be life changing. This exercise requires looking at the inevitability of mortality and deciding what you want to do with the rest of your life. I have used this exercise as part of the Hall Recovery Course for many years and it has proven to be one of the most significant turning points for many people.

Box 7.3 Creating a vision

The following is adapted with kind permission from 'Lesson 2', Recovery Workshop at www.RecoveryNation.com

People who struggle to commit themselves to a vision for their life are really struggling with one of the most fundamental issues there is to struggle with: their own mortality. The realisation that they have only a finite amount of time on this earth and a finite number of experiences to be had. As a child, you were not bound by the awareness of mortality and were free to dream and experience to your heart's content. But as healthy people transition into adulthood, most recognise that there are limits to the life they can lead. They realise that to achieve fulfilment, their life must have purpose. That is when the process of 'settling down' begins and they choose those areas of their life that they will commit themselves to mastering. Those areas that they want to anchor their identities to. Being a parent. Being a partner. Achieving competency in their career. Helping others. Being physically fit. Being financially stable. Being a servant of God. That is not to suggest that these are the values that people *should* pursue; merely examples of what many *do* pursue. The choosing of these values does not guarantee fulfilment, but it does lay the foundation for learning how to derive fulfilment from one's life.

Pursue your vision with passion

Now, passion is a good thing. A life without passion is every bit as destructive as a life with. But in the mind of someone struggling with

continued...

Box 7.3 continued

addiction, passion can be a dangerous thing. Be careful. Just as this passion to enact your life's vision can provide you with the energy and focus needed, it can also zap you of that energy when your life is stressed and/or out of balance. In other words, pursue your vision with passion, but don't equate that passion as the validation for your life's vision. If you didn't understand that ... read it again. Eventually, pursuing your vision with passion will give way to developing true depth in your life. This depth will not replace your passion, it will merely supersede it as the primary force in maintaining your identity. When that happens, your life will no longer be vulnerable to emotional instability. In most addicts, passion is the primary driving force in decision-making ... and one of the goals of your transition to health is to develop depth, instead.

To achieve personal fulfilment as an adult, a vision must be formed as to how you want to define your identity. Of what legacy, if any, you wish to leave for others. This legacy can be as simple as the relationship between you and your partner (e.g. having shared yourself completely with another human being); or between you and your children (e.g. having laid the foundation for their generation's fulfilment); or between you and your community (e.g. knowing that the community is better because you were a part of it). It doesn't matter what you define as important ... what matters is that you now define it. There is no more room for 'I don't know what I want.' Make your choices. There is nothing wrong with looking back and saying, 'I was wrong about that choice ... and I want to change what I am pursuing', but to rest on indecision – when you are talking about something as valuable as the remaining years of your life – is unacceptable. Make your choices and then drive towards those choices with focus and confidence. Should you become aware that you have made the wrong choice somewhere along the line, adjust. It is no big deal. The big deal is never choosing to begin with. Those are the lives that are in constant motion without ever achieving depth and thus, never achieving their potential to derive value from their life.

But I really don't know what I want

This takes us back to the mortality issue. At this stage, you likely have another 10 to 50 years of active, quality life left. Within the concept of time, that is infinitesimal. But within our own egocentric existence, that is a lot of time. Forever, in fact. Think about that.

You now have 'forever' to develop depth from within your values. You have 'forever' to develop maturity and skill in managing your life. And, you have 'forever' to potentially waste to inaction, fear and non-commitment. It can't be argued that, as an adult, lacking a vision for one's life is tolerable. Any vision, even if it is the wrong one ... is better than having none at all. Why? Because it gives you something objective to work with. To evolve. Without this vision, the only way to manage one's life is by learning to manage emotions as they are experienced. Everything's reactive. This, as opposed to taking a proactive role in establishing emotions through stability and value competency. So what would keep someone from creating such a vision? The answer is the same answer that can be applied to why some are unable to fully commit themselves to ending their addiction: mortality. Not the fear of dying, but the fear of accepting that they are living a finite life. Because they cannot accept this, they tend to hold desperately to all options, to all potential. They don't want to limit themselves because that would mean closing off a part of themselves forever. Subconsciously, closing off certain life options is to acknowledge the finite qualities of one's life. It is to acknowledge that time and experience are no longer infinite.

An immature person sees closing off of certain options in their life (like addiction, or access to the stimuli that feed that addiction) as limiting themselves. It's the 'What if?' thought process. 'What if ... my soul mate is out there waiting?' 'What if ... I was destined for something great but never took the time to pursue it?' 'What if ... I can't recover?' A mature person sees the refinement of their values (aka their vision) not as a limiting aspect of their lives, but as an opportunity to develop and experience infinite depth within those values. Think about that. Think about the difference between being in a marriage as a man who is keeping all options open; and being in a marriage as a man who is committed to developing infinite depth within that marriage. The former is based on fear (of not losing out on things); the latter is based on a commitment to one's vision of being in a partnership.

The exercise

1 Take at least 20 minutes to be alone. If you have a family, ask them to respect this time that you are taking. Make sure that you leave your mobile phone off. That the dog is fed. That there

continued...

Box 7.3 continued

will be no distractions. Take a walk by yourself. Sit alone on the beach. Find somewhere secluded and then, think. Think about who you are, the life that you have led, and the life that you want to lead from this point forward. Think about your legacy. Create a vision that you would feel comfortable committing yourself to pursuing. One that, as you someday look back upon your life, will allow you to feel proud of the person that you developed into. Of the life that you led.

2 (OPTIONAL) If you have someone in your life to talk with about this vision, consider talking with them. You are not looking for validation, correction, guidance ... you are just moving one step closer to making this vision your reality. However, it is important that the person you choose to share this vision with, will not listen with a critical ear.

3 Write out your vision – it should be at least one page long and encompass your personal, practical values. Think about the following areas your life – relationship, family, career, hobbies, friends, spirituality, charity. As a general rule, the more personal, the better. Ensure that it is practical, not idealistic. And that it is a vision that is capable of sustaining a healthy life. Are there enough values identified that have the potential to generate fulfilment. To counter instability. To drive decision-making.

Creating a vision is just the start, a decision then must be made to intentionally live a life that pursues that vision. To turn the vision into achievable goals and give those goals the same level of passion and intensity that the addiction had previously consumed.

8 Understanding the cycle of addiction

In order to break the chains of addiction, once and for all, it's essential that each person understands their individual cycle of addiction and the unique factors that keep them trapped in their behaviour. Back in Chapter 4, I introduced you to the six-phase model that I use in my recovery courses and here we will explore that cycle in more depth. By going into each phase of the cycle and identifying the individual thoughts, feelings and behaviours that happen at each point, it becomes possible to establish ways to break the cycle.

For example, someone with a trauma-induced addiction might identify that feelings of anxiety 'trigger' acting out – once discovered, work can begin in therapy to find healthier ways to manage anxiety as well as making lifestyle changes that reduce it. Someone with a pure opportunity-induced addiction might identify that one of the cognitive distortions they use within the preparation phase is telling themselves 'I can't masturbate without pornography'. Having identified this they can then learn new masturbatory routines in addition to establishing if sexual desire is the motivator or another emotional need. An attachment-induced addict may recognise that during the regret phase when they feel huge guilt at betraying their partner this impacts them in the reconstitution phase as they find themselves being compliant to unreasonable demands rather than addressing underlying relationship issues.

As explained previously, each phase of the cycle is unique to each individual and will last for differing amounts of time depending on the person and on the circumstances. Some may spend months in the dormant phase while for others it may only be days. Others will spend weeks in preparation and for others it will be minutes. It's also important to note that the lines are blurred between each phase. Identifying exactly when the dormant phase has ended with a trigger or developed into preparation is almost impossible but fortunately it's not important. As long as the key features of the cycle are identified (see Figure 8.1), knowing precisely when they happen isn't significant.

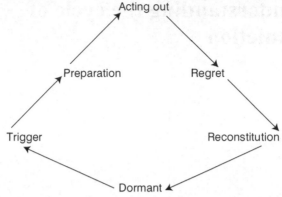

Figure 8.1 The six-phase cycle of addiction

Over the following pages of this chapter I will offer a number of tools and evaluation exercises that can be used either alone or in a treatment setting, to begin to identify the individual components of the addiction cycle. It doesn't matter whereabouts on the cycle you start, since the very nature of a cycle means it has no real beginning or end. Therefore it's usually easiest to start with a phase that seems the simplest to answer or is more consciously available. Most people find that a pattern soon begins to build as they work round. For example, having completed the exercises for the dormant phase and identifying that 'loneliness' is particularly difficult to manage and the quality of relationships is inadequate, it will then become easier to recognise that feeling lonely and being rejected by a partner is a common trigger.

Throughout this chapter we will use Craig as a case example and see how he completed his personalised cycle.

Craig

Craig is a 24-year-old who has struggled with pornography addiction and escalated use of webcam sex for nearly 10 years. He always assumed he would stop when he met the 'right' girl but now, in spite of being 2 years into a loving relationship, the problem is still there. His addiction was primarily opportunity-induced with some attachment issues too.

The dormant phase

The dormant phase of the addiction cycle is where the addiction may appear to be temporarily in remission and life has returned to 'normal'. But 'normal' for someone with an addiction is a place where underlying needs continue to be unmet, core beliefs are still unchallenged and issues relating to opportunity, trauma and attachment remain unresolved. The exercises in Box 8.1 provide a start point to begin to consider what some of those underlying causes and unmet needs may be.

Box 8.1 Evaluating unmet needs

Evaluating emotional regulation

How good are you at 'healthily' managing the following feelings?

	Good	Average	Poor
Loneliness			
Feeling I don't belong			
Boredom			
Sadness			
Anxiety			
Anger and frustration			
Stress			
Feeling overwhelmed			
Shame			
Sexual frustration			

Evaluating relationship quality

How would you rate the quality of your relationships with the following people?

	Good	Average	Poor
Partner			
Children			
Parents			
Brothers and/or Sisters			
Friends			
Work colleagues			

continued...

Box 8.1 continued

Evaluating life balance

How would you rate your overall satisfaction with the following areas of your life?

	Good	Average	Poor
Couple relationship			
Family time			
Work (paid or unpaid)			
Hobbies and interests			
Relaxation and leisure time			
Personal growth and development			
A sense of purpose and meaning in life			
How is my general sense of self esteem?			

Craig's cycle

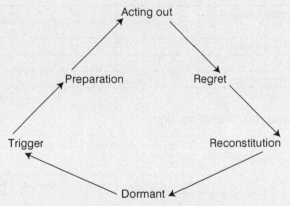

Feelings: Loneliness, boredom, shame, frustration
Relationships: Partner good, parents poor, friends average
Life: Couple time good, work poor, self-esteem poor

The trigger phase

Some people recognise one or two common triggers that propel them out of dormancy towards acting out. But for many others there is a series of triggers, each quietly building upon the other until sufficient momentum is built to go into the preparation phase.

Identifying triggers is a crucial part of addiction recovery since without it, it's impossible to learn how to avoid and/or manage those triggers. But until there has been a period of abstinence from acting out, as we explored in the last chapter, triggers may be hard to identify. Many people with addiction find it difficult to notice triggers because they experience their behaviour as being 'habit'. When an opportunity arises, such as being alone in the house or away on a business trip, acting out is something they automatically do because they always have. Although this is undoubtedly true, making note of those trigger environments enables hidden issues to be uncovered and successful relapse prevention techniques to be developed. The exercise in Box 8.2 can be used to identify triggers.

Box 8.2 Identifying triggers

Opportunity-related triggers

These are the triggers that are most likely to occur for each category of addiction and relate to lifestyle and general emotional management. Tick as many as appropriate.

Environmental	Emotional
Empty house	Feeling bored
Unprotected internet	Feeling stressed
Having time on your hands	Feeling angry
Having money in your pocket	Feeling sorry for yourself
Being abroad	Feeling ill or tired
Being in cities or certain places	Feeling unfulfilled
Being away from home	Feeling entitled
Seeing an attractive person	Feeling ashamed
Being flattered or flirted with	Feeling sexually aroused
Being with certain people	
When using alcohol or drugs	

Other_____

continued...

Box 8.2 continued

Attachment-related triggers

Someone with an attachment-induced addiction is likely to identify with many of the following triggers that all relate to feelings generated within relationship to others. Tick as many as appropriate.

Getting into an argument with a loved one
Feeling overwhelmed by responsibility and/or duty
Feeling trapped by another's needs
Feeling unable to confront a loved one
Feeling unable to communicate your needs and/or views
Not having enough time for yourself
Feeling rejected
Feeling lonely
Feeling left out
Feeling unvalued
Feeling attacked and/or defensive
Other _____

Trauma-related triggers

These triggers will be most relevant to those with a trauma-induced addiction and connect to how external stresses and anxieties are managed. Tick as many as appropriate.

When life is particularly stressful
When life feels out of control
When life feels empty and meaningless
Feeling fearful
Feeling powerless
Feeling anxious
Feeling depressed
Feeling empty or dead inside
Feeling agitated and restless
When you feel vulnerable
When you feel you must be strong and/or fight
When your body feels tense
When your body feels numb
Other _____

Craig's cycle

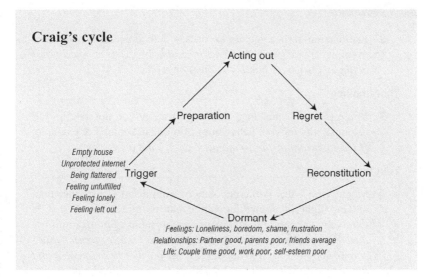

The preparation phase

Once a trigger, or series of triggers, has been experienced, someone with an addiction moves into the preparation phase where the emotions they wish to anaesthetise against gradually begin to disappear amidst the practical and psychological activities of preparing to act out. These preparations may be both conscious and unconscious but by making them fully conscious the work can then begin on stopping the cycle by eliminating them.

As discussed in Chapter 4, the activities of the preparation phase broadly fall under the headings of cognitive distortions (CDs) and SUDS. The exercises in Box 8.3 can help these to be identified.

Box 8.3 Recognising cognitive distortions

Recognising cognitive distortions

Below is a list of the 12 most common cognitive distortions that allow the addiction cycle to continue. Read the examples and then write down the thinking pattern that you most commonly use.

1   Rationalisation – this is when you make excuses for your behaviour using logic and reason. For example, '*Acting out is ok because I haven't done it for ages which proves it isn't an addiction*' or '*It's not possible to masturbate without pornography*'.

Your thinking _____

continued...

Box 8.3 continued

2   Justification – when you use excuses to defend your behaviour. For example, '*I can't help it when I'm drunk*' or '*No one could resist acting out when it's handed to them on a plate*'.

Your thinking _____

3   Minimisation – this is a thinking strategy for not taking full responsibility for your behaviour or staying in denial. For example, '*I'll only be online for 10 minutes*' or '*It's not as bad as ...*'

Your thinking _____

4   Magnifying – this is the opposite of minimisation so rather than making light of something, an event or circumstance that is relatively unimportant is given greater status. For example, '*I have had an absolutely horrendous day and I am so stressed that I cannot cope so I need to act out*' or '*My partner has ridiculed and abused me and therefore it's ok for me to soothe how I feel*'.

Your thinking _____

5   Blame – this is when someone else is blamed for your behaviour. For example, '*If my wife was more into sex I wouldn't need to do this*' or '*If my work was more fulfilling I wouldn't act out*'.

Your thinking _____

6   Entitlement – this kind of thinking often comes either from grandiosity or from self-pity and is when you find reasons to tell yourself you deserve to act out. For example '*I need to act out because I didn't have much sexual experience when I was younger*' or '*I work extremely hard to support my family and deserve the occasional treat*'.

Your thinking _____

7   Uniqueness – this is similar to entitlement but is more about focusing on what you perceive as being unique about yourself or about your personal circumstances. For example, '*I'm a very successful person and people would expect me to enjoy sexual variety*' or '*I was born with a particular fetish and this is the only way to satisfy it*'.

Your thinking _____

8   Mental Filter – this strategy is used to filter out any thoughts that might stop acting out from happening. For example, '*Last time*

I acted out was fantastic and I didn't have any regrets' or *'My partner is totally unreasonable all the time and so I need to act out'*.

Your thinking _____

9 Victim stance – this is when you make excuses for your behaviour by putting yourself in the role of victim. For example, *'It's not my fault I act out I was abused as a child'* or *'I have to act out when everyone is picking on me'*.

Your thinking _____

10 Normalisation – this is often used with generalisation to make acting out seem like 'the norm'. For example, *'All men look at pornography'* or *'It's instinctive to want to sleep with a beautiful woman'*.

Your thinking _____

11 Denial – this is perhaps the most common cognitive distortion and simply involves blocking out reality. For example, *'If my partner never finds out there will be no problem'* or *'There is nothing wrong with acting out'*.

Your thinking _____

12 Helplessness – this can be a particularly powerful cognitive distortion, especially for those with low self-esteem. For example: *'I can't help acting out, I have never had any will power'* or *'I can't help it, I'm a sex addict'*.

Your thinking _____

Identifying SUDs

Many clients have said that identifying their SUDs (seemingly unimportant decisions) has been a key element of their recovery. Even when they've not been able to identify many triggers or cognitive distortions, they have been able to recognise their behavioural actions and by bringing these into conscious awareness they are then better able to stop them.

One of the most effective ways of identifying SUDs is to create what's known as a behaviour chain. This involves thinking about the last time you acted out, or the last few times if they were very different, and working backwards to identify the events that led up to it. Box 8.4 is an example of Craig's behaviour chain.

Box 8.4 Identifying SUDs

Acting out event: Monday – masturbated to live web sex show

☙ I was checking out which girls were live on the web sex site, but told myself I was only looking out of curiosity

☙ I felt really stressed and decided 10 minutes of porn would help me calm down and get to sleep

☙ I was looking at jobs online that I wish I was qualified to do

☙ I didn't go to bed with my girlfriend because I said I was too stressed to sleep and was going to go online to look at jobs

☙ I was moody all evening and pissed off about work

☙ I had a really bad day at work and drove home stressing about how much I hate my job and deserve better.

If this exercise is repeated over a number of acting-out events, then a pattern soon begins to emerge. For example, another client who had a problem with sleeping with sex workers noticed that the start of his behaviour chain was almost always making a decision to have a meeting in London rather than at another location. Inevitably this resulted in him telling his wife there was a social after the meeting and surreptitiously putting cash aside to pay for his behaviour.

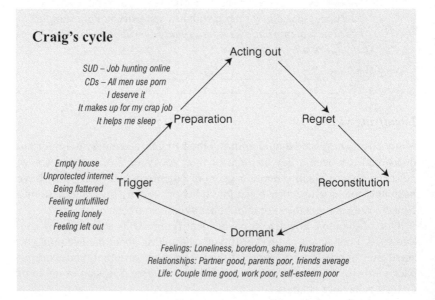

Craig's cycle

Acting out

SUD – Job hunting online
CDs – All men use porn
I deserve it
It makes up for my crap job
It helps me sleep   Preparation   Regret

Empty house
Unprotected internet
Being flattered   Trigger   Reconstitution
Feeling unfulfilled
Feeling lonely
Feeling left out

Dormant

Feelings: Loneliness, boredom, shame, frustration
Relationships: Partner good, parents poor, friends average
Life: Couple time good, work poor, self-esteem poor

The acting out phase

The acting out phase of the addiction cycle always serves multiple functions. The most obvious ones are sexual arousal, stimulation and usually satiation, but there are emotional outcomes as well. By identifying these it becomes easier to understand which deeper needs are being satisfied and then work can begin on finding healthier ways of meeting those needs.

The exercise in Box 8.5 provides an opportunity to analyse what is gained by acting out and therefore what the additional functions of the addiction may be.

Please note that while most people experience many negative emotions such as shame and guilt as a result of their behaviour, the purpose of this exercise is to identify the positive feelings that the behaviour elicits.

Box 8.5 Identifying the positives of acting out

Acting out behaviours

List acting out behaviours along here adding more space if required					
Emotions experienced	Powerful				
	Affirmed				
	Wanted				
	Valued				
	Desired				
	Calm				
	Relaxed				
	Excited				
	Cared for				
	Invigorated				
	Relieved				
	Independent				
	In control				
	Other				

Craig's cycle

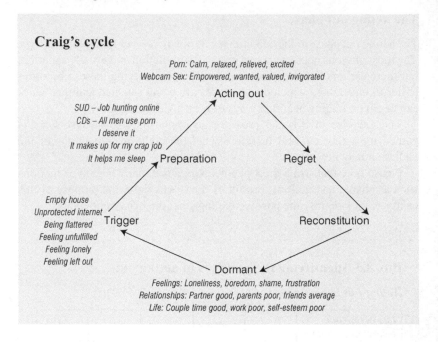

Porn: Calm, relaxed, relieved, excited
Webcam Sex: Empowered, wanted, valued, invigorated

Acting out

SUD – Job hunting online
CDs – All men use porn
I deserve it
It makes up for my crap job
It helps me sleep   Preparation   Regret

Empty house
Unprotected internet
Being flattered   Trigger   Reconstitution
Feeling unfulfilled
Feeling lonely
Feeling left out

Dormant

Feelings: Loneliness, boredom, shame, frustration
Relationships: Partner good, parents poor, friends average
Life: Couple time good, work poor, self-esteem poor

The regret phase

Both the regret and the reconstitution phases of the cycle provide the opportunity for the true cost of sex addiction to be realised. During the other phases, it may be easier to forget or minimise the negative consequences, but now they can hit hard. Having said that, some people experience little regret, especially if they're able to minimise or avoid the harmful effects, while others find themselves racked with guilt and shame. The regret phase may last just a few hours or it may last for weeks or even months before someone is able to pick themselves up and move on to the reconstitution phase.

Identifying the impact of acting out on thoughts, feelings and behaviours can become a helpful disincentive to acting out again. But as many will testify, in spite of the intense feelings of remorse, the behaviour does reoccur until the deeper causes have been resolved. Personalising this phase of the addictive cycle is perhaps the easiest since the anaesthetising behaviours have subsided and the brain now has the cognitive capacity to interpret thoughts and feelings. The exercise I use is shown in Box 8.6.

Box 8.6 Identifying regrets

After acting out, how do you feel about the following:

- Yourself? _____
- Your relationship? _____
- Your life? _____

Craig's cycle

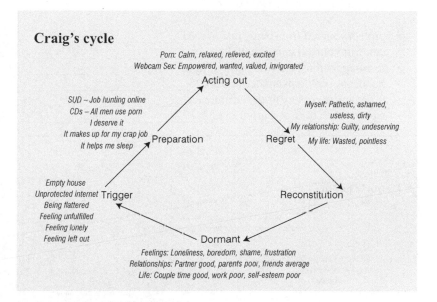

Porn: Calm, relaxed, relieved, excited
Webcam Sex: Empowered, wanted, valued, invigorated

Acting out

SUD – Job hunting online
CDs – All men use porn
I deserve it
It makes up for my crap job
It helps me sleep

Preparation

Myself: Pathetic, ashamed, useless, dirty
My relationship: Guilty, undeserving
Regret My life: Wasted, pointless

Empty house
Unprotected internet **Trigger**
Being flattered
Feeling unfulfilled
Feeling lonely
Feeling left out

Reconstitution

Dormant

Feelings: Loneliness, boredom, shame, frustration
Relationships: Partner good, parents poor, friends average
Life: Couple time good, work poor, self-esteem poor

The reconstitution phase

Like the regret phase, the thoughts, emotions and events of the reconstitution phase are often easier to recognise. Some people who've been round the addiction cycle many times find themselves longing for this phase. As they go through the preparation phase they may be eager to act out, to get it over and done with, so they can begin to get their life back together and return to dormant.

The actions undertaken during this phase are almost always done with the best intention of making amends, alleviating guilt and striving to not act out again. But often they perpetuate the cycle by feeding into the unmet needs. For example, someone with an attachment-induced addiction might put extra effort into not complaining about the relationship, when what they really need to do is become more assertive about their needs. And someone with a trauma-induced addiction may begin to drink more to alleviate their anxiety rather than developing healthier stress management techniques. Like the regret phase, identifying what happens during reconstitution can help someone calculate the true cost of their behaviours, and provide further motivation to change. The questions in the exercise below can help to elicit the common elements of this phase.

Box 8.7 Identifying behaviours in the reconstitution phase

After acting out, what do you do to:

- protect yourself from being discovered? _____
- comfort yourself emotionally? _____
- restore relationships with partner, family, friends? _____
- repair any problems created at work? _____
- make any necessary financial amends? _____
- stop yourself from acting out again? _____

Craig's cycle

Porn: Calm, relaxed, relieved, excited
Webcam Sex: Empowered, wanted, valued, invigorated

Acting out

SUD – Job hunting online
CDs – All men use porn
I deserve it
It makes up for my crap job
It helps me sleep

Preparation

Myself: Pathetic, ashamed, useless, dirty
My relationship: Guilty, undeserving
My life: Wasted, pointless

Regret

Empty house
Unprotected internet
Being flattered
Feeling unfulfilled
Feeling lonely
Feeling left out

Trigger

Reconstitution

Delete history, drink
Be the perfect husband
Throw myself into work

Dormant

Feelings: Loneliness, boredom, shame, frustration
Relationships: Partner good, parents poor, friends average
Life: Couple time good, work poor, self-esteem poor

Personalising the cycle of addiction is not a one-off task; it's a process of ongoing understanding that can continue throughout therapy and beyond. Although at the end of these exercises it's likely that someone will have a much better idea of their individual cycle, it's important to keep adding to it as new information and/or experience comes to mind.

As Craig personalised his cycle he began to see how it linked to his low self-esteem and poor relationships. Craig's parents had never praised him as a child and were cold and distant except on the rare occasions when he managed to meet their high academic standards. Throughout adolescence Craig worked hard to try and win his parents approval, often to the detriment of making and maintaining friendships. He would spend hours alone in his bedroom and whenever study got difficult, he would turn to online porn. Craig never felt good enough and as his self-esteem worsened, so his use of pornography increased. He dropped out of education completely at 16 and met his first and current girlfriend at 22. Technically he was virgin when they first slept together, but as a connoisseur of cybersex, he hoped she wouldn't know. Now at 24 he hated his job in a call centre and struggled to believe his girlfriend really loved him as much as she said. And he was convinced she wouldn't love him if she knew about his online sex life.

Until completing his cycle of addiction, Craig had never realised his addiction was a symptom of other issues in his life. Not only did the exercise help him to highlight areas of work for therapy, but he was also able to identify where relapse prevention work needed to be focused.

9 Identifying unresolved issues and unmet needs

All addictions serve the function of controlling emotion. For example, some recreational drug users take drugs to create a positive emotion of euphoria, while others use their drug of choice to anesthetise against negative feelings. Or of course, many do both. The same is true of sex addiction. Hence engaging in cyber sex or having multiple affairs may create a positive emotion of feeling wanted and affirmed, while losing yourself for hours in pornography might drown feelings of loneliness and low self-esteem. In order to overcome any addiction permanently, these deeper emotional needs must be identified and, if possible, resolved. It's important to remember that negative emotions are a part of life. We will all experience loneliness, boredom, frustration and a whole host of other difficult emotions at some stage in our lives. The key to permanent addiction recovery is to develop healthy strategies to manage these emotions rather than turning to a toxic behaviour that frequently creates the very emotions that the person is striving to avoid.

In this chapter we will explore how to identify and manage the common underlying issues that affect so many people with sex addiction. I must highlight that this can be long term work. Some people find they need extensive personal therapy for this part of the recovery process, therefore this chapter simply provides an overview and additional resources will be required to provide appropriate treatment. This is especially true in the case of working with both trauma and attachment-induced addictions (further reading is suggested at the end of this book).

Exploring childhood issues

All of us carry baggage from our childhood and some is heavier than others. Our early childhood experiences influence how we feel about ourselves, how we relate to others, and how we interact with our world. It is likely that everyone with sex addiction picked up unhelpful messages about how to healthily regulate their emotions and meet their deepest needs. And people with an attachment-induced addiction may find their adult relationships are continually impacted by the messages they learnt in childhood about how to love and be loved. Those with a trauma-induced addiction who experienced abuse as a child are likely to have the deepest and most painful scars.

Some people come for addiction treatment already aware of the impact of their childhood, while others may describe their childhood as 'happy' and 'normal' until further exploration reveals hidden wounds. Some of the previous exercises in this book may have highlighted difficulties in childhood or problems that may have originated there. For example, if the assessment questionnaires in Chapter 2 have already been completed, then you may already know if the addiction is opportunity-, trauma- or attachment-induced. In addition the core beliefs inventory in Chapter 7 may have highlighted areas of low self-esteem that had their roots in early childhood and the exercises in Chapter 8 will also provide essential information on areas of unmet needs that probably originated in family life. A useful way of identifying the childhood source of some of these difficulties, and a tool that may illuminate more, is drawing a life line.

Drawing a life line, from birth to late adolescence, that charts the key events of childhood, can often be an effective way of crystallising key childhood events and difficulties and can provide a framework for future therapeutic work. The exercise is described in Box 9.1.

Figure 9.1 is an example of how one client, Ali, completed his lifeline and we will use his story throughout this chapter to highlight how childhood issues can inadvertently create the environment where sex addiction develops. As you can see from Ali's example, his mum's illness, moving home, starting a new school where he was bullied, and being dumped by his first girlfriend were all identified as significant negative events. This information provided an opportunity to explore the impact those events had

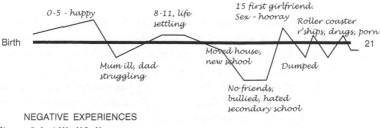

Figure 9.1 Ali's life line

Box 9.1 The life line exercise

This exercise requires a large piece of paper, a pen and a good chunk of time. People who struggle to remember their childhood might also find it helpful to have some photographs handy to jog their memories of key childhood moments. The objective is not to list every negative and positive event of childhood, but rather to provide an overview of key moments and to begin to get in touch with the times that may have contributed to developing sex addiction. Those key moments are likely to include times of loneliness and isolation, any events that were traumatic, abusive or particularly hurtful, and any other periods of strong emotion.

The following questions can be helpful.

1 What you were told about your birth? Was it a happy event? A surprise? Or a time of difficulty?
2 How was your relationship throughout childhood with mum, dad, siblings, grandparents and any other significant people? Were there any key moments that define those relationships?
3 Were there any significant losses or painful memories within the family? Include such things as divorce or separation, illness or disability, parental infidelity, moving house.
4 Were there any experiences of abuse or misuse of power/authority? Any times when you were made to feel ashamed or not nurtured?
5 How was your experience of school? How were relationships with peers and teachers at school? How did you feel about your education?
6 During adolescence, were there any significant events with friends, boyfriends or girlfriends that were difficult or affected your self-esteem?

on developing sex addiction. In particular, how his mum's breast cancer had impacted the whole family and how his father's increasing dependence on alcohol during that time had set up a pattern of seeking comfort from external sources. Ali felt he did not fit in at his new school, especially as he needed to spend a lot of time at home supporting his mum and dad. Getting a girlfriend at 15 had been a highlight, but when she dumped him a few months later, he became increasingly self-reliant and turned to drugs, and porn on his bedroom laptop, for comfort.

Managing negative emotions

In addition to exploring key childhood events, it's important to look at other significant emotions and how these were managed within the family of origin. Asking how key emotions such anger, sadness and fear were expressed in the family can give important clues as can asking what happened if you showed that you were angry, sad or fearful? Ali remembered that anger and fear were not expressed in his family at all – something he realised must have been around in abundance during his mum's illness. He went on to recall the time when he and his older sister were told of their mother's illness. His sister, who was only seven at the time, began to cry and their father's response was to shout at her and tell her she must be strong for her mum and that crying was a very selfish thing to do. He went on to remember other occasions when either he or his sister would express their fears or frustrations – each time their father told them they were selfish.

This example demonstrates another negative emotion that is very common in the childhoods of people with sex addiction – shame. When a child is brought up to feel shame, especially about something that is difficult to control, they are left feeling bad about themselves. In Ali's case it was perfectly natural that as children they would feel fearful, sad and angry. But their father's reaction told them that these emotions were wrong and that they were bad to feel them. Consequently Ali grew up trying to deny those feelings when they inevitably arose. Since sex is something that our society so often links with shame, when those 'natural' feelings of desire arise, a child who has been made to feel shame about other emotions, will more likely attach shame to their sexuality as well. And in a home where it's not possible to healthily express and talk about negative emotions, it's often impossible to talk about the complex, and often difficult, emotions around sex.

For many people with sex addiction, individual, or sometimes group therapy, may provide the first safe opportunity for negative emotions to be expressed. Emotions that may have been suppressed or repressed for a lifetime. Furthermore there is space to consider how these emotions can be accepted and integrated into self-identity and shared with others in a positive way.

Decision making, boundaries and self-control

As discussed in Chapter 3, many people with addiction come from backgrounds where there was either a rigid system of control or none at all. When children are not taught how to control themselves, they often grow up finding it difficult to make decisions that are based on an accurate assessment of their needs while considering the consequences. This then results in problems maintaining personal and relational boundaries.

Ali's parents were very strict and he and his sister were brought up to do whatever they were told. Ali's opinions and views, when he dared to voice them, were either shouted down or ignored, and consequently he never learnt how to use his own judgement to make decisions. He remembered times in adolescence when he wanted to rebel, as so many of his peers had done, but with his mother's illness, he didn't think this would be fair on the family.

During therapy, Ali was able to see how he learned to suppress both his emotions and his needs, often to the greater needs of his family. He recognised that he had few skills when it came to decision making and self-control and that was why his pornography use had escalated so fast. It was important for Ali not to feel that he was blaming his parents, as he felt they had brought him up the best they could, under very difficult circumstances. But having seen how the messages from his childhood had contributed to his sex addiction, he could now re-write them and choose a future that fitted with what he wanted for himself.

Identifying sexual messages

In addition to identifying key childhood events, it's also important to explore what's been learnt about sex and relationships – because the key to why sex was chosen as the 'drug of choice' is often found within these messages. We learn about sex from a variety of sources. Initially it is within the family home and later from peers and partners. We also learn from our communities, our culture and from society. There are often different sexual messages for men and for women, and different messages if you're straight or gay. Typically in Western society men are brought up to believe that sex is a powerful sex drive that they must learn to manage through will, and emotions have little to do with it. Conversely, women are the bastions of sexual safety who must protect their bodies, hearts and souls from men's desires while denying any lust of their own. There are perhaps more mixed messages about sex today than there has ever been at any other time in history. While some strive for greater sexual liberation, others use statistics of sexual crime and abuse, and indeed sex addiction, as evidence that we should become more conservative. Defining our sexual beliefs and boundaries is challenging in a world that advocates freedom and diversity – but it is a task that each of us must embrace. Ideally, the tools for the job are provided in childhood, but unfortunately there are some family belief systems that do not support healthy sexual decision making.

Broadly speaking there are four sexual belief systems that families adopt and pass on to their children, each of which can have a negative impact on healthy sexual development. These are listed below.

- Sex is the problem – The overriding message that this family imparts is that sex is bad and dangerous. A child brought up in this environment will grow up hearing that sex is the root of all evil, something shameful that should be approached with extreme caution. If a child grows up adopting this message, they may struggle to fully enjoy sex within a loving relationship, and seek fulfilment elsewhere. Or if the message is strongly opposed any negative experiences or consequences of sex may be denied.
- Sex is the answer – This is the type of family that promotes sex as the panacea for all of the world's ills. Sex is healthy, fun and natural. This is of course true, but this family lives in denial of any potential sexual difficulties or dangers and consequently someone brought up with this message may feel ashamed when sex does not live up to their expectations or when their reliance on sex damages other areas of their life.
- Sex is complicated – Many families send out mixed messages. On the one hand they may be saying sex is a problem when they give firm warnings about unwanted pregnancy and STIs and when they complain about our increasingly sexualised society. But on the other hand a poorly hidden porn stash or infidelity tells another story. People brought up in this environment have no clear boundaries or guidelines and may struggle to find a balance.
- Sex does not exist – In this family sex is never spoken of or hinted at. Parents may present as asexual and any budding sexuality in children is studiously ignored. There will be no sex education of any kind and children grow up either trying to deny their own sexuality or becoming secretive and ashamed.

It's an unfortunate reality that many families struggle to talk openly about sex and therefore many of the messages we receive are through our parents' behaviours, rather than through what they have overtly said. The following questions can help to illuminate the family's sexual belief system and also any other messages that developed through adolescence.

1 How was nudity dealt with at home? Were you a 'cover up' family, or was it ok to be seen naked?
2 Did you have any awareness of your parents' sexual relationship? Or of them as sexual people?
3 What happened if a sexual scene came on the television? How did parents react?
4 How did the family react to your puberty? Was becoming a man or a woman welcomed and celebrated? Was it met with warnings? Or was it ignored?

5 What messages did you pick up about men and women? In particular, what did you learn about male and female sexuality? Were there significant gender differences? How did that make you feel about your gender?
6 When you began to touch your genitals, either sexually or simply through curiosity, as all children do, how was this managed?
7 How did you feel about your budding sexuality during adolescence? Did you fit in with peers? How did you feel about boys/girls? Did you have any particularly painful or embarrassing early sexual experiences?
8 How was your experience of sex in early relationships? How did this fit with the messages you'd received about sex in childhood?
9 How did you first discover pornography? Was this a positive or negative experience?
10 While you were growing up, did anyone ever touch you or treat you in a sexual way that left you feeling uncomfortable, used or abused?

Ali recognised that he had come from a family where 'sex does not exist'. He had never seen his parents naked and had no awareness of any sexual contact between them. He was also aware that his mother's breast cancer was difficult to talk about, largely because it was located in such an intimate place. He received very little sex education at his secondary school and since he felt so separate from his peers, he felt he never had the opportunity to discuss sexuality even on a casual basis. He remembered a group of lads that bragged about their sexual conquests and realised his early sexual experience with his girlfriend was motivated primarily by a desire to feel 'one of the lads'. He felt a huge amount of shame about the fact that he'd never really taken his girlfriend's feelings into consideration and felt he 'deserved' to be dumped. Talking through these issues in therapy gave Ali an opportunity to look at what he wanted to think and feel about sex and begin to re-write the negative messages he'd heard.

Working with trauma

When an initial assessment, or work exploring childhood issues, reveals trauma, then it is essential that this is directly addressed in individual therapy. While previous trauma remains unresolved, the addiction will continue to both persecute and rescue – maintaining the addict in the role of victim. Over the past few years we have learnt more and more about the complexities of working with trauma and consequently treatment has become an increasingly specialised field. Trauma, whether as a result of childhood abuse, assault, or an extended period of stress and anxiety, has a direct impact on the brain. The earlier the trauma, the more significant the effect on the brain seems to be. But whatever the age, it's now known that the amygdala of the brain becomes hypersensitive to both actual and potential threat, as explained in Chapter 3. And as discussed in Chapter 4, sex addiction may be used to manage the resulting hyper- and hypoarousal states that the body is thrown into. The objective of resolving underlying trauma is to widen the 'window of tolerance' shown in Chapter 4 and provide healthier strategies for dealing with feelings of hyper- and hypoarousal.

Working with trauma, especially when it has been significant, requires specialist skills and knowledge in bodywork, and there is not space in this chapter to explain all the principles and strategies required. Needless to say, wherever and whenever trauma work is undertaken, the key priority is to create a safe therapeutic space where the past can be put in perspective and the 'here and now' can be separated both physically and psychologically from the 'then and there'. Below are three golden rules for overcoming trauma.

1 First and foremost, establish practical strategies and resources for support outside of the therapy room. For example, friends that can be a support, activities that can help to self-soothe, medication if required.
2 Ensure both client and therapist is confident in how to apply the brake, before starting to accelerate. This excellent analogy used by Babette Rothschild in her book *The Body Remembers* reminds us that when we're learning to drive, it's more important to know how to brake than it is to accelerate if we want to avoid an accident. When working with trauma, it is equally true that it's essential to know how to slow down or stop the work in order to ensure the old trauma is not reawakened.
3 Remember that any defences employed to manage trauma are also resources. It's essential that old coping strategies are not removed until new ones are available to take their place – this may include acting out behaviour. When working with trauma-induced addiction it may be necessary to postpone complete abstinence until healthier options are fully in place.

Working with attachment issues

People with an attachment-induced addiction will most commonly present with problems relating to others. The function of the addiction is primarily to regulate feelings of isolation and/or suffocation which may be experienced within a couple relationship or within other relationships. As with trauma,

Joe

Joe came for therapy because his porn addiction had got out of control and his wife was threatening to leave him if he didn't sort it out. Like his father, Joe had chosen an army career and his porn use had started whenever he was away on tour. But since he'd been signed off suffering from anxiety after a tour of Afghanistan, he had regularly started using porn at home. An exploration of his childhood revealed many incidents of physical abuse from his father and he shamefully confessed that he lived in terror of him. Up until now his unconscious way of managing his childhood trauma had been to soothe feelings of hyper-arousal with pornography. In addition, he had chosen a career where he regularly faced traumatic situations which he endeavoured to conquer and where he hoped he might finally gain his father's approval. In addition to joining a group programme to overcome his addiction I also worked with Joe individually to help him make sense of his childhood experiences. I also referred him to a trauma specialist who specialised in EMDR and sensorimotor work where he was able to talk through his latest experience in Afghanistan and learn practical techniques for recognising and improving his ability to cope with hyper-arousal.

there is not sufficient space here to explore working with attachment in depth, but broadly speaking work should focus on identifying the adult attachment style and the relational needs that are being neglected.

Attachment styles are based on two factors: how we perceive others; and how we perceive ourselves (Bartholomew and Horowitz, 1991). When we are comfortable with ourselves and others, we are likely to develop a secure attachment that results in healthy, fulfilling relationships. Many addicts have either an anxious attachment style that constantly seeks intimacy while being fearful of hurt; or an avoidant attachment style that is mistrustful of others and strongly independent; or an ambivalent attachment style which fears intimacy but also fears being alone. Having identified which style is favoured and where in childhood it may have begun, work can start on developing a secure attachment style that is comfortable both with intimacy and with independence.

An unhealthy attachment style often results in a number of relational needs becoming neglected and it is often these needs that are sought out in acting out behaviours. For some, the primary relationship is too risky a place to ask for those needs to be met since being rejected would be too painful. For others, a sense of safe independence can only be felt if some needs are kept outside of the primary relationship. Once these needs have been identified, work can begin to explore how they may be met within either a couple relationship, or other relationships that support addiction recovery.

Identifying relational needs

The term 'relational needs' came from the school of integrative psychotherapy where eight foundational needs were established as the essential building blocks for healthy mental health and relationship functioning (Erskine, 1999). Those needs are listed below.

1   Security – our need to feel safe in our relationships to others, knowing that we're free from threats of shame, attack, abandonment and engulfment.
2   Validation – knowing our feelings and identity are unconditionally accepted by another, including having our relational needs accepted and affirmed.
3   Acceptance by a stable, dependable and protective other person – this is about our need to have someone in our lives who we can trust and who we know is looking out for us.
4   Confirmation of personal experience – this defines our need to have someone who is similar to us. Someone who has been through similar experiences.
5   Self-definition – our need to feel separate, autonomous and unique.
6   The need to have an impact on other people – in order for us to feel satisfied in our relationships, we need to know that what we do and who we are can influence another in a positive way.
7   The need to have another initiate – to know that someone else will reach out to us and want to make contact, rather than always being the person who makes the first move.
8   The need to give love – we all have an inbuilt need to love and to be able to show our love for another.

Relationship psychotherapy is often an essential part of recovery for someone with an attachment-induced addiction. This is especially important if they are in a current relationship which may continue to trigger acting out behaviour. Couple work is usually also required to identify and overcome any unconscious processes that may be feeding the addictive system.

Eryk

Eryk was addicted to multiple affairs and although he loved his wife very much, he felt he was incapable of maintaining monogamy which he felt was essential for their relationship. He had come from a poor Polish background and was one of seven children. His father had died when he was five and his mother had taken on additional night work to try and support the family. He had no recollections of his mother ever being able to spend time with him and from an early age had multiple relationships with girls where he got the affection and attention that he longed for. Now at 45, happily married with three children, he continued to seek the company of as many women as he could. Eryk's was an avoidant attacher. His self-confidence was generally very good but he had little confidence in others and quickly identified that his relational need for security and knowing that he made an impact in his relationships was lacking. Through individual therapy and couple therapy he became able to develop greater assertiveness and confidence in getting his needs met within relationships that supported his recovery.

Part III

Establishing relapse prevention strategies for life

In Part III we will explore a range of strategies for both avoiding and managing the emotional and environmental triggers that can threaten relapse prevention, including the crucial role of re-wiring the brain. Chapter 11 explores the importance of creating healthy relationships and provides an overview of exercises to help strengthen couple relationships. Chapter 12 looks at what satisfying sexuality really means and how a positive sex life that fits with values can support recovery. Developing a healthy lifestyle that can replace the addictive lifestyle is explored in Chapter 13 and includes practical techniques for improving emotional intelligence, building assertiveness and maintaining a balanced life. This part concludes with an overview of the most common blocks to recovery such as breaking through denial, addressing unresolved shame, cross addictions and concurrent mental health difficulties such as anxiety, depression and personality disorders.

10 Avoiding and managing triggers

A trigger is any thought, feeling or sensation that generates the desire to act out. Or indeed, a series of thoughts, feelings or sensations that build, one on top of another, until acting out feels impossible to avoid. In Chapter 8, we explored how those triggers can be identified; here we look at how they can be avoided, and if they can't be avoided, how they can be managed healthily.

Broadly speaking, triggers are either environmental or emotional and some are predictable, and therefore avoidable, whereas others can hit you like a steam train when you least expect it. Once triggers have been identified, and as new ones are inevitably discovered, practical strategies must be developed, to stop them. The longer a trigger is ignored, the greater the snowball effect. In other words, it will build and build into an avalanche that may become impossible to stop.

Later in this chapter we will explore a range of practical techniques for both emotional and environmental triggers. But first it's important to understand how these triggers can become wired into our brains and how re-wiring can minimise their impact.

How triggers affect the brain

Controlling the thoughts, feelings and sensations that we experience when there's a trigger is not purely a psychological or emotional process. Especially when addictive substances or behaviours are involved. For example, if you've had a stressful day at work and you regularly and habitually reach for a glass of wine, a neural pathway to the pleasure chemicals in your brain will gradually be created. And as you continue to reach for that glass of wine, the neural pathway becomes stronger and stronger to the point where you will unconsciously link a glass of wine to a stressful day. Similarly, if you always restock on wine when you pass a particular wine store or you always have a drink of wine when you meet a particular friend, you will soon unconsciously link both the place and the person to wine. This process is also known as classical conditioning and was famously highlighted by Pavlov's dogs. If a certain set of stimuli is continually present before a rewarding event, those stimuli become increasingly associated with the behaviour at an unconscious and neurological level.

In terms of sex addiction, this means that over time the brain will have created neural pathways that respond automatically to certain triggers, with no conscious thought. For example, the sight of an attractive woman, or a day working home alone, or a business meeting in London might automatically trigger a desire to act out without any awareness of any cognitive thought. Similarly, an emotional trigger such as feeling angry, bored or lonely might instantaneously translate to sexual desire. Therefore to overcome sex addiction, the brain needs to re-wire. This re-wiring requires two components. First, re-programming the brain with positive, affirming statements that encourage and support change, and secondly maintaining sobriety to allow the unhealthy neural pathways to die off. This process is now commonly referred to as cognitive-neural restructuring.

Re-wiring the brain

Like the brain, the field of neuroscience is constantly changing and growing, and one of the more recent developments has been discovering how our brains can become re-wired through a process known as neurogenesis (Seigel, 2007). Neurogenesis is best achieved when there is consistency, frequency, intensity and duration. In layman's terms that means practise, practise, practise. In addition it's known that novelty, exercise and focused attention can facilitate neurogenesis. In other words, the very system that took place to create the addiction in the brain can be used to reprogramme it. Hence the habit of consistently and frequently watching intense pornography over a long period of time created the neural pathways, but by consistently and frequently repeating what's known as the 'pillars', new, healthier pathways can be formed. The pillars are part of a practise known as cognitive neural restructuring and consist of 10 statements that elicit a willingness and desire to change at a neuro-cognitive level.

It's recommended that the pillars are repeated three times a day for a month each. They may be practised alone, but when used in therapy, along with both active and passive relaxation techniques that encompass novelty, physical exercise and mindfulness, their effectiveness can be even greater. Many clients have found it helpful to carry their pillars with them, either in their wallet or on a phone, to read whenever they experience a trigger. Used in this way the positive messages contained within the pillar may become anchored to the stimuli.

Pillar 1: I am ready to change

I am ready to change. I have lived the way I have for too long. When I began this journey long ago my choices were just that; choices. Now they have grown into an addiction that controls me to the point that I feel I have no control. This process has affected my thinking, my feelings and my being. Those that I love have also been impacted, some have been devastated.

But now, I am ready to change and I commit to pay whatever price is necessary to accomplish this. I have already seen the power of bad choices in my addiction. Now I employ that same power but for positive choices. I will use the power of positive choice for the purpose of recovery and growth. I will begin the change now and I will recover from my addiction.

Pillar 2: My brain can change

My brain can change. My brain can be my best friend. It can also be my worst enemy. If I do positive things in my life it is because of the neural circuitry that exists in my brain. If I do negative things in my life it is because of the neural circuitry that exists in my brain. Although my brain does not exist in a vacuum, it does work systemically with my body, my emotions, and my spirituality.

I have allowed my brain to develop an addiction and my brain has taken control over me. Now I am taking the control back. I will form better and healthier neural pathways in my brain. A neural pathway is a network of neurons that are responsible for behaviour throughout my brain and body. Now I take control to develop healthier pathways in my brain and body. As I learn more about my brain I will become more and more in control. My brain is changing even as I read this pillar. My brain can change and I will recover.

Pillar 3: Empathy

In the past my actions have not always been empathic. I have hurt those I love, and most of all I have hurt myself. From this moment I commit to live, feel and express empathy in all that I do. I will think of how, in the past, my addictive and acting out behaviours have impacted those I love. From this point on, as I am compelled to engage in any form of acting out I will stop and feel how this action would impact those around me, and also myself, and then I will act in an empathic manner. I will also identify how my behaviours may impact those who do not know me. As I am empathic to others and myself my life will change.

Pillar 4: Consistency

Consistency is a friend of unhealthy behaviours. It can also be a friend of healthy behaviours. Through consistently engaging in unhealthy thinking and behaviours I have developed a pattern of acting out. This pattern has become a mechanism for coping and so unhealthy patterns have come to control my life. Just as consistency has been an enemy, it can also become a friend. From this point forward I will act consistent with my values and what I believe. I know that with each consistent choice greater learning takes place. As I consistently make healthy choices and avoid acting out, I will move closer to freedom and emotional health. Healthy choices made consistently will facilitate change at a cellular level of my being. As these cellular changes take place my entire physiology is changing and improving. I will act consistently and I will recover.

Pillar 5: Frequency

Good choices made frequently lead to lifelong positive changes. From this point on, I will not only make wise choices but I will make them frequently. With each choice that I make, the choice becomes more natural to me. Therefore, I will choose not to make unhealthy choices any more. I will choose to make wise and healthy choices on a frequent basis. This helps these decisions to become a natural part of my very being. With each healthy choice made frequently I will increase my freedom. The more often I choose healthy choices, the stronger I become. I will remember that as I choose healthy actions frequently, my brain continues to change and I become more free and more healthy.

Pillar 6: Duration

I will lengthen the duration of my healthy choices. I will choose wise choices over an extended period of time. I have started to make healthy choices on a daily basis. I will continue to do this but I will extend the days into weeks and weeks into months, the months into years, and the years into a lifetime. I alone am responsible for these choices being made. As I lengthen the duration of my choices my confidence will increase and I will recover. From now on I will no longer hold others responsible for my thoughts, my feelings, my actions, or my life. I can choose my future and I will do this by making healthy choices for the duration of my life.

Pillar 7: Intensity

Intensity has been one of my worst enemies. The more intense a stimulus is, the greater the impact it has upon my brain and body. The negative things I have experienced and chosen to take in have been intense and they have shaped my being. From this point forward I will remember the principle of intensity and I will never willingly allow such an intense and negative experience to come into my life. If I do allow such a thing, I am making a choice not to recover. Healthy changes can be made without intensity so long as I practice and apply the principles of consistency, frequency and duration.

Pillar 8: Reflection

When I started my journey I committed to pay whatever price was necessary in order to get well. To this point I have done that but I recognise this is only the beginning. I commit at this time to continue to pay whatever price is necessary and I will make that same commitment every day. As I continue to make that commitment I will continue to become more healthy. Life is worth living and living means more than simply surviving. Living means growing and I have now started the process of growing. I will continue to pay the price of growing and make positive decisions to keep myself safe from relapse.

Pillar 9: Maintenance

I now know the importance of avoiding unhealthy stimuli and choices. I will avoid unhealthy choices. I will avoid unhealthy stimuli. My choices to not avoid these things in the past have contributed to my current place in life. From this point on, as I have the desire to act out I will remember my values and my vision of a better life. I will act accordingly and I will avoid all unhealthy stimuli. I will pay whatever physical, emotional, psychological, spiritual and financial price is necessary to avoid this stimuli and get well. I will do this because I am making an investment in one of the most important creations in the universe – me. I would choose to walk a thousand miles many times over before I will allow unhealthy stimuli to come into my life again. I will avoid unhealthy stimuli and I will stay well.

Pillar 10: Gratitude

I have now begun to feel free and experienced living with honesty and integrity and for this I feel gratitude. I will allow gratitude to be a guide in my life. My life is better today than it was several months ago when I began this journey and I feel gratitude. I have learned to healthily accept and experience both pain and joy with dignity, and for this I am grateful. This learning has also allowed me to feel more grounded in my day-to-day life. As I stay grounded I think more clearly and as I think clearly I make rational choices. As I make rational choices I make the conscious choice to stay healthy. Hence I will continue to feel gratitude. I will find someone or something for which I am grateful, every day. No matter how painful a certain day may be I will find something to express gratitude for, even if the thing I express gratitude for is the ability to healthily experience pain. For the same mechanism that allows me to feel pain also allows me to feel joy. I will feel and express gratitude and I will continue to stay healthy.

(Source: Adapted to accommodate cultural differences between the USA and UK with kind permission of *Cognitive Neural Restructuring Therapy for the Treatment of Sexually Compulsive Disorders* (2010) by Matthew Hedelius, Psy.D., LCSW and A. Todd Freestone, Psy.D., LCSW.)

Cognitive neural restructuring can be an effective strategy for beginning to build new neural pathways but they take time and commitment. While that process is underway it's essential that there is no acting out behaviour so that the old neural pathways can weaken. Over the rest of this chapter we will explore the importance of avoiding both environmental and emotional triggers, and more importantly, how to manage those triggers that are often an every day part of life.

Avoiding environmental and emotional triggers

Many people with addiction feel as though they're surrounded by triggers and avoiding them is almost impossible. This is certainly true on some occasions, but the vast majority can be avoided if thought through in advance. The old cliché 'Failing to prepare is preparing to fail' is particularly true in addiction and therefore a key element of relapse prevention is planning. Below are a few examples of the kinds of strategies that might be useful but since everyone's circumstances are unique it's important to take time and brainstorm all the possible scenarios and develop personal strategies that will work for the individual. Once this is done, it can be really helpful to put the information and strategies into a single 'dos and don'ts' document that can be kept handy at all times.

People and places

Certain places, people and activities can become triggers to addictive behaviours – most commonly these will be things that have provided the opportunity to act out or have served as some kind of encouragement – for example, being in an environment where sex is easily available such as in certain districts of certain towns and cities, or being alone in the house with unrestricted access to pornography. For some, environmental triggers also include people, such as being with friends or work colleagues who regularly go to strip clubs or who talk openly about their porn use. In most circumstances, environmental triggers can be avoided, but that takes rigorous self-honesty and discipline. And it might sometimes mean letting someone else down. So if an invitation comes to a stag party in Amsterdam, the answer is no. If a partner is going away for the weekend then an addict needs to ensure either they go to visit a friend or relative or that their time is filled with healthy pursuits. For some, the only way to avoid work-related triggers is to change job. That can be a difficult decision to make that might involve financial losses. But those losses need to be weighed up against what would be lost if the addiction is not conquered.

Time and money

Too much time and surplus cash are common triggers that can often be avoided through developing practical strategies. Firstly ensure any spare time is usefully filled and made accountable. Free time not only provides opportunity for people with addictions but if not usefully used it can also be a painful experience as the urge to act out grows. But with a bit of pre-planning this can be avoided, or at least minimised. For example if a meeting finishes early, phone home or a friend immediately and say that you are en route home and then call them again when you arrive. Or if you have an evening alone, at home or perhaps in a hotel, arrange to meet a friend, go to the cinema or take a book to read. Spare cash can be another strong temptation. One way to manage this is to ensure that all money is accountable between the couple and that only a minimum amount of cash is ever carried around. For people who are single, it can be helpful to ensure that any excess funds that are not required for daily living are put into a savings account that is hard to access.

Porn protection

As technology spreads ever wider, pornography can be accessed almost anywhere and everywhere. At this moment in time there are no standard parental controls that come with hardware but there are a number of options for protecting most devices.

Parental control software can be put directly onto the router to ensure adult material cannot be accessed from any wired or wireless device or can be downloaded onto each PC, laptop or tablet. Currently, the most popular options are Net Nanny, kids.getnetwise and Safe Eyes. A good router will also provide options to set time limits for online access to prevent late night surfing or being online for more than an allotted amount of time.

Blocking adult content on mobile devices is currently much harder. Although you can block individual ISPs, there is no system for filtering all adult content nor for stopping the downloading of adult apps. Hopefully, this is a situation that will soon be resolved. However, there are a growing number of apps for sex addiction recovery that can be downloaded which could help as a deterrent. Adult channels on televisions can be removed or blocked via the operator's parental controls and if you call in advance to a hotel, adult channels in the room can be removed before arrival.

Another option is to download spy software, which can either record every page visited for another designated person to check or send an email to allocated email addresses. One version of this is X3watch which allows you to designate what they call 'accountability partners'. An option that is favoured by one of my clients, who is himself a technical wizkid, is a cloud based internet security package from www.opendns.com. Rather than loading onto the server or the device, this security package is stored on the internet and forces all the user's internet activity through its filter, which makes it almost impossible to evade. It also allows you to customise the 'block' page with a message to yourself or perhaps a picture of loved one, which can serve as a much-needed reminder of why you're blocking sites in the first place. But as my client said in a personal communication: 'No security system is entirely fool proof to a trained IT professional, so in such cases other means may be necessary, like handing Wi-Fi access at home over to someone else to manage. The safest approach is always going to be abstention from the devices usage, either entirely for a period, or at least avoiding using them at vulnerable times or only using them in publicly safe surroundings at good times.' He also pointed out that 'keeping up to date IS the catch'. As our society continues to provide easier and easier access to pornography, people who are committed to recovery, and those who wish to help them, will need to ensure that security and accountability is continually maintained.

Emotions

Emotional triggers are perhaps the hardest to avoid because it's often difficult to predict how we will feel. However, by developing self-awareness and emotional intelligence, through individual or group therapy, it can become easier to notice the warning signs of an emotional trigger and take evasive action. Through personalising the cycle of addiction back in Chapter 8, particular emotions will have been highlighted as triggers and that list can be used to consider how to avoid, or at least minimise, these emotions. For example, if someone has put anger as a trigger then certain situations that are known to provoke anger can be avoided, such as ensuring there is always plenty of time for travel to avoid feelings of road rage, or learning to become more assertive to get personal needs met. If loneliness is a trigger then developing a wider social network as well as deepening existing relationships may help to minimise this. One of the best ways of avoiding emotional extremes is to develop a balanced and healthy lifestyle, which we explore further in Chapter 13 and to learn to manage conflict and difference within relationships, which we cover in our next chapter.

Physical urges

One of the most challenging triggers for many addicts is their sex drive, especially during the early days of recovery and during abstinence. Although acting out is not primarily about satiating desire, there's no doubt that feeling sexually aroused can be a significant aggravating factor to managing triggers. For this reason it's imperative that the circle exercise described in Chapter 7 (see Figure 7.2) has been completed so that firm boundaries have been established. Furthermore, focusing on healthy relationships and positive sexuality, as we'll explore in the next chapter, can strengthen this resolve. There are a number of techniques for managing physical urges that can be helpful, most of which are based on some kind of physical diversion – for example, going for a run, playing sport, taking a walk in nature, laughing with friends, taking a cold shower or even sucking on a lemon! The most important thing to do is not to dwell on the physical urge or allow your mind to entertain thoughts of satiation, but rather to immediately do something that will distract your body and your mind.

Managing unavoidable triggers

Unfortunately, some triggers are unavoidable. For many people, seeing an attractive woman or sexual image on the street or in the media, being flirted with or being confronted with an easy opportunity such as an unprotected PC or unexpected time alone can be difficult times to negotiate. Someone with an attachment-induced addiction may inevitably experience times when they can't avoid difficult feelings within relationships, and for those whose addiction was trauma-induced may find periods of significant anxiety or loss challenging. There are two psychological techniques that can be learned and employed to help manage unavoidable triggers – namely, externalisation and mindfulness. Each of these can be learnt in therapy but there are also some excellent self-help books, especially on mindfulness to enable the skill to be learned at home. In brief, the techniques are as follows.

- Externalisation – This is a common feature of narrative therapy and can be a powerful tool for separating the addiction from the person. Essentially it allows someone to create a dialogue with the problem that is located outside of the self rather than being an integral part of it. In other words, when a trigger is experienced, rather than beating the self up with negative self talk or splitting the self into good cop/bad cop, the dialogue is aimed at the external problem – the addiction. So rather than saying 'I want to act out', externalisation would say 'The addiction wants me to act out'. By projecting the problem outside of the self a new relationship can be created with the problem, which can empower change while protecting the self.
- Mindfulness – This practice has its roots in Buddhist meditation but is now widely used to treat and manage a range of emotional, physical and psychological difficulties. It's a difficult concept to accurately summarise in a paragraph but, simply speaking, it means consciously bringing one's full attention to the present moment. Not only does this work to bring about a grounded and peaceful sense of conscious awareness, but it also assists neuroplasticy and allows new neural pathways to be developed. In practical terms, mindfulness teaches someone to notice the thoughts, feelings and sensations that a trigger evokes, but rather than act out, or dwell on them anxiously, replace them with calm, positive feelings and a different behaviour.

Learning to RUN

In addition to the psychological techniques discussed above there is one additional, very practical strategy that can be employed – RUN. Quite literally this means get out of the situation, and get out fast. Whether that means leaving the house, the office, the hotel or whatever it is. Get away from the opportunity immediately. In addition, it can be a useful acrostic to remember.

- **R**emove yourself immediately from the situation – don't let yourself flirt with temptation for even a second more than you have to – get out *now*.
- **U**ndistort your thinking – this will *not* make you feel better, one more time *does* matter, you do *not* deserve this, you do *not* want to have to lie again.
- **N**ever forget what you have to lose – you made the decision to stop being a sex addict because it was ruining your life – that fact has *not* changed.

Learning to RUN is perhaps the single most important relapse prevention technique there is. I have heard countless stories of relapse when this simple principle had been unheeded. If a trigger is ignored, minimised, flirted with or indulged, it will become stronger and stronger. Immediate action is always the best policy.

Once out of the danger zone it can be helpful, either alone or in therapy, to think back over the trigger and consider if better planning might have avoided the situation. Similarly it can be helpful to explore if there were additional circumstances that increased vulnerability, such as unresolved issues or unmet needs that could be further addressed. Or perhaps more work could be done to strengthen couple relationships or develop greater emotional control and resilience?

Although triggers can be painful and difficult to manage, it's important to recognise that they can provide essential clues to the underlying function of the addiction Furthermore, successfully managing triggers can create positive self-esteem and deepen commitment to recovery. Someone who has never been tempted often has less self-confidence than someone who has survived temptation.

Emergency stops

Many of my clients have found it useful to either carry with them, or have close to hand, some items that will ground them quickly and make them stop. Items include things like photos of loved ones or cherished gifts. Or on a mobile device they'll carry a particularly pertinent piece of music, perhaps the song that was the first dance at their wedding, or a piece of religious or inspirational music. Others transfer their values list and vision statement to their phone or e-reader to ensure they're always to hand as well as phone numbers of support people. Another powerful strategy is to have at hand 'the letter to self' – a frank and blunt reminder of what needs to be heard when triggered. The details of how to create the letter follow.

Box 10.1 The letter to self

This is a letter from you, to you, that will tell you what you need to hear when you're tempted to act out. The person who knows you best is yourself and this letter gives you the opportunity to let the best and wisest part of you speak directly to the you that is struggling with temptation. When you write your letter, consider the following.

1 Empathise with the circumstances under which you're likely to be reading this.
2 What are the consequences if you ignore this letter?

continued...

Box 10.1 continued

3 What challenges do you need to hear to help you address your deeper needs?
4 What encouragement do you need to hear?
5 What do you need to do NOW to stop the cycle?

Dear Tom

If you're reading this letter it probably means you're about to do something you shouldn't. Something has triggered the cravings again and you want to act on them. You're remembering the old days, the thrill and excitement. You may already be trying to work out how to create the opportunity to act out and distorting your thinking to suit your goal.

Each time is the same. There's the thought, the promise of pleasure. And the feelings underneath – anger? Loneliness? Entitlement? But every time ends up the same, you'll bitterly regret the thing you now think you want to do.

You'll worry about being caught, of losing Jenny. You'll despair over your broken commitments not just to Jenny, but to yourself as well. You'll feel embarrassed and ashamed with the kids, with friends, with colleagues. You'll feel bad about the people you've used. You'll have to lie – always there are lies, lies and more lies. You'll feel like shit. You'll beat yourself up for days and lose any pleasure in the things you've come to enjoy. You'll feel more trapped and alone. Acting out will make life worse, not better.

Right now your addict self is trying to seduce you with promises that don't work. What do you really need? Are you angry? Feeling unloved? Feeling unimportant? What do you need to take care of? Find out what you need and take care of it. Don't do the one that that will make all of the above worse.

The question is, if everybody could see what you are about to do, would you still do it? You are lovable and worthwhile. You deserve better than this. You deserve to get your needs met in a way that will make you feel good about yourself and comfortable and confident about who you are.

Please listen to yourself. Remember how far you've come, how hard you've worked. Think about the people you love. The people who love you. The people who care about you. Don't kid yourself that one more time will be ok. Instead, love yourself and R.U.N.

Tom

(Source: Adapted with permission from
Facing the Shadow, Carnes 2005)

When it didn't work

It's an unfortunate reality that most people with addiction will at times 'slip up' or experience a full relapse. Distinguishing between the two is important as it's much easier to recover from a slip up than a relapse and it prevents a momentary lapse of judgement or self-discipline getting worse. In other words, if someone addicted to pornography goes online for 15 minutes after weeks without, this would be a slip up. Similarly, if someone hasn't visited a sex worker in months but then makes an appointment but leaves before using their services, this would also be a slip up. Although this is obviously not good for recovery, it would be a mistake to categorise it as a relapse since doing so can so easily invite the cognitive distortion 'I've already blown it, so I might as well go all the way'.

Whether someone experiences a slip up or a relapse, the most important thing is to manage the associated shame, recommit to recovery and get back on track again. When relapse prevention techniques don't work, then it's time to revisit them and see what lessons need to be learnt. Then they can be reconstructed and strengthened.

11 Creating healthy couple relationships

When recovering from sex addiction, having a fulfilling and stable couple relationship can be both a support and an incentive. For many people, a happy couple relationship is one of the most important things in their lives. A place where they can love and be loved. Where they can find peace, comfort and support as well as stimulation and pleasure. A place that provides a refuge from the struggles of life. Therefore it's perhaps not surprising that the quality of the couple relationship is a key influencer of successful lifelong recovery. When a relationship is not happy, as most aren't after the discovery of addiction, a huge strain can be put on every area of life. This is especially true when there is pain, conflict or threats of separation – all of which are commonplace after the disclosure of sex addiction. Improving couple relationships needs to be a key focus for relapse prevention, since failure to do so will continue to trigger the addict in a myriad of ways.

For those who come for treatment while single, the desire to find a relationship is often a recent priority that has initiated the recovery process. A significant number of people, 46 per cent in my survey, found themselves forced into singleness as a result of their addiction and while reconciliation may not be an option, it's still important to explore what a healthy couple relationship might look like in the future.

This chapter explores the immediate issues most couples experience when faced with sex addiction and how the relationship can be supported and enhanced. Unfortunately, there is not enough space to fully explore relationships or sexuality in this section but there are many other excellent books available on the market, a selection of which are listed in the resources section at the end of this book.

Managing disclosure

D day, or 'disclosure day' is a commonly recognised phrase within the sex addiction community. D day is the day when a partner either discovers, or is told about the addiction and it is usually a traumatic event that's remembered for life. Unfortunately disclosure is rarely a single occurrence (Schneider et al., 1998) and therefore the trauma may be extended over a period of time. There are a number of reasons for this partial or gradual disclosure. First, it may be that information is only revealed as and when, discovery is imminent. Or some information may have been withheld in a genuine attempt to protect the partner and the relationship from destruction. Another common reason is that some behaviour may at first be deemed as unnecessary to disclose. This is particularly true of pornography use and cyber sex which some may feel is not adultery. However, while it may be true that only flesh on flesh sexual encounters can be described as adultery, any breach of trust within the relationship may be described as infidelity. If it's known that a sexual behaviour, be it in the flesh or online, has breached a partner's trust, then disclosure needs to be considered.

If possible, the disclosure should always be managed in a way that will minimise harm to both partners and this is often most helpfully done either in the presence of, or in consultation with, a therapist. Although some, or all, acting out may have been disclosed prior to attending therapy, it is still highly beneficial to conduct what is known as a 'therapeutic disclosure'. For many couples, the gradual release of information happens over a series of traumatic and turbulent days, weeks or even months. The conversations are frequently accompanied by high emotion and often fuelled by alcohol and consequently it's not uncommon for both partners to forget what has, and has not been, said. A therapeutic disclosure session can ensure that all the necessary facts are on the table and agreed. The process can serve as drawing a line beneath disclosure and providing a clear depiction of the damage that needs to be addressed.

Whether the disclosure is alone, or with a therapist, it is advisable for each member of the couple to be emotionally and physically prepared. Ensuring they have sufficient time and the right environment, and avoiding times when there may be interruptions or when either partner is feeling especially angry or vulnerable. The partner with the addiction needs to plan what they're going to say while the other needs to prepare themselves for what may be shattering news. Both need to consider what they will do after disclosure in terms of looking after their emotional needs. That might mean spending time with a close friend, attendance at a 12-step meeting, or booking an appointment with a therapist. Disclosure can be a traumatic experience and therefore preparation for the potential aftermath is essential.

How much to share

Of course, there is no golden rule on how much information should be shared, as each couple is different. However, many partners find they sorely regret hearing too many details. For example, knowing the exact number of other sexual partners may be overwhelming, as might the exact number of hours spent viewing pornography. Similarly, knowing the genre of pornography viewed or the sexual activities preferred on webcam may generate unwanted feelings of disgust. This type of graphic information can build visual images in the brain that are hard to erase and more often than not, these details are less important than knowing the broad facts.

Most couples find it useful to share the following.

- When the acting out behaviours started.
- The ways in which the behaviour escalated and when.
- A broad outline of the behaviours and whether or not physical adultery took place.
- Whether or not infidelity happened with anybody the partner knows.
- Whether infidelity happened within the home or any other locations that the partner frequents.

The latter two enquiries are particularly important to allow couples to feel safe within their home and local environments and within the company of friends. Where an infidelity included someone known then couples can agree together how to put boundaries around that relationship.

In the USA it is commonplace to use a polygraph as part of the disclosure process. This may be considered controversial by some, but with growing availability in the UK it's something that's worth considering. A polygraph can give partners a security of truth that is not available by any other means. And in fact, even the suggestion or discussion of using a polygraph can often be very revealing.

Rebuilding trust

Little damages relational trust more than sex addiction. Many partners will have experienced multiple infidelities as well as countless broken promises not to act out again. 'I don't know if I can believe anything he says anymore' is a common refrain of partners whose trust has been continually betrayed. It's an unfortunate reality that trust can take many years to build, but be broken in an instant. And once trust has gone, there are no fast ways to get it back. Couples can be helped to understand the process of trust building by recognising that trust is a gift that is given from one to the other and it's a gift that has to be earned. The task of the partner with the addiction is to make themselves trustworthy, while the other partner must become courageous and generous enough to begin to offer ever-growing tokens of trust.

Becoming trustworthy means being consistent, reliable, congruent, taking responsibility and admitting to mistakes and weaknesses. Someone with an addiction can begin to demonstrate these characteristics in every area of their life, for example by remembering to honour couple agreements – however small. I've heard many stories of massive arguments blowing up over forgotten phone calls, lost property and misplaced assumptions. While in isolation these may seem insignificant, to partners they represent feeling unheard, unrespected and uncared for. They can inadvertently remind the partner of underlying faulty thinking and possible character faults and hence building trust in these areas is often a prerequisite to finding faith in recovery.

All couples need to agree their rules around honesty and accountability. Most treatment programmes recommend 'rigorous' honesty and while this may seem imperative, it needs to be qualified by the couple. For example, will 'slip-ups' always be shared? Most partners do not want to know every time their partner is tempted, nor the occasions when they have a minor slip up such as clicking online for just a few minutes or going into a massage parlour but then instantly walking out. This is because they know it will trigger them to worry and panic when it's unnecessary. It's important to agree at what point a slip up does become something that needs to be disclosed and each couple must come to their own individual decision about this. Similarly, appropriate boundaries need to be established around therapy. Some partners want to know everything that is going on in therapy but this can put undue pressure on the partner with the addiction and seriously undermine the therapeutic process. It's important to understand that for many partners this is not about control, but rather about wanting security. Many will blame ignorance and naivety for ending up where they are today and hence may go to extreme lengths to avoid being ignorant again. However, it's essential that partners understand that knowledge will not protect them and if trust is truly to grow, it must happen in an environment where their partner maintains adult independence and autonomy.

Establishing accountability is another essential tool for rebuilding trust. The specifics must always be agreed by the couple and should serve two functions. Firstly accountability should support relapse prevention strategies by providing specific boundaries and guidelines for behaviour. And secondly, accountability should provide the partner with a greater sense of security on a day to day basis. Some couples confuse accountability with control – the key to clarity is that its purpose is to benefit both partners and provide boundaries and security. Many couples find it useful to write an accountability contract, either alone or in therapy, to clarify the expectations of each party – such as the following example.

Box 11.1 The Accountability Contract

Mike will …
- Clear all pornography off computers.
- Never delete history on computer.
- Leave mobile phone accessible at all times and on ring.
- Telephone from a landline whenever he arrives at and leaves the office.
- Provide Jean with a weekly work schedule.
- Make no purchase over £30 without discussion.
- Attend therapy regularly.
- Only use Facebook with Jean present.

Jean will …
- Put parental controls on all computers.
- Put password protection on adult content on television.
- Check email and mobile phone messages when feeling insecure and tell Mike.
- Telephone the office if feeling insecure.
- Take over managing all finances.
- Check any home TV/DVD viewing for triggering content.
- Attend therapy regularly.

Building better relationships

A happy and fulfilling couple relationship is built on a foundation of shared values, common goals, mutual respect and love. The discovery of sex addiction can shatter the very bedrock of a relationship to the point where some feel there is nothing left to rescue. For others it is the last straw in a relationship that was already fraught with difficulties and well past its demolition date. For those that are left, the relationship is often lying crumbled on the floor and the challenge is to see if there's enough raw material left for a rebuild. For all with an addiction, including those that are single, understanding why previous relationships failed and recognising the building blocks of a successful relationship is essential for recovery.

Bad relationships fuel addiction, especially for the attachment-induced addict who both craves and fears intimacy. For all categories of addiction, an unhealthy relationship can fuel feelings of low self-esteem, loneliness, anger and fear as well taking away a valuable possible resource for comfort and support. It's common for people with addiction to find themselves in dysfunctional relationships, but knowing whether this is a cause or a symptom of their problem is hard to recognise. In most cases it's a chicken and egg scenario where the addiction fuels the dysfunction and the dysfunction fuels the addiction. Many couples find that they fall into a familiar pattern of relating, that may inadvertently fuel the addiction and hinder couple recovery. The two most common patterns are explored below.

Identifying unconscious couple collusions

The drama triangle, with its positions of victim, persecutor and rescuer, was first identified by Dr Stephen Karpman in the field of transactional analysis in 1968 (see Figure 11.1). This unconscious collusion is a common pattern that's particularly prevalent in couples with a trauma-induced addiction where the addict, and sometimes the partner too, have childhood experiences of being in the victim role. The principle is that the couple get caught up in each of the three roles that are played out in their couple relationship. Most often one partner will unknowingly favour the victim role, which can often be recognised in language that denotes helplessness and self-pity. The other partner may then be left with no conscious choice but to play either the rescuer or the persecutor – both of which keep the other in victim role.

This couple collusion is particularly damaging for addiction recovery as it maintains each partner in a dysfunctional role that contradicts self-responsibility. Once the roles have been identified, couples can learn to break the cycle and accept healthy alternatives. Namely the victim accepts and owns their vulnerability without blaming the other or expecting to be rescued. The persecutor learns to assert their needs and express their feelings without coercion or aggression. And the rescuer adopts a caring role that allows the vulnerable person to develop their own coping strategies rather than doing the work for them.

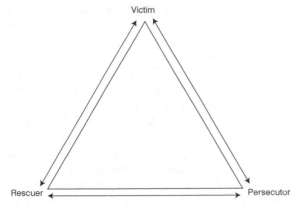

Figure 11.1 The drama triangle

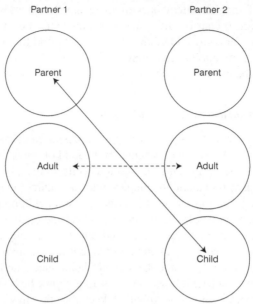

Partner 1   Partner 2

Figure 11.2 The PAC model

Another common collusion, especially for those with an attachment-induced addiction is the parent/child relationship, as described by Eric Berne in his development of transactional analysis. In this scenario, rather than both partners operating primarily from the adult ego state, one regularly adopts the parent position and the other the child (see Figure 11.2). The parent role is typified by a partner who feels they are the responsible one in the relationship who must look after and control the other. Language is full of shoulds and shouldn'ts and they feel they are the mature one in the relationship. The partner in the child role is then left feeling controlled and either rebels or relinquishes control to the other. Since the partner in the child role hasn't developed the adult ego state within the relationship, their behaviour is often child-like and hence perpetuates the collusion

As with the drama triangle (see Figure 11.1 earlier), the solution is for each partner to recognise that they play these roles and that each is losing out by doing so. Often the parent is tired of taking all the responsibility and is missing out on their healthy desire for child-like play and freedom. While the partner in the child role craves the opportunity to demonstrate their responsibility and be independent. While all couples inevitably go into these roles at times, for the couple relationship to be rebuilt, they need to learn to communicate with each other predominantly in the adult ego state.

More information and resources on both of these common couple collusions can be found in *Games People Play* by Eric Berne and *I'm OK, You're OK* by Thomas Harris – more details in the further reading section at the end of this book.

Strengthening intimacy

Intimacy can be a difficult thing to define but for most couples this is the aspect of their relationship that can bring most fulfilment. Intimacy is built on communication and can be broken down into six broad categories, listed below.

- Emotional intimacy – Being similar in emotional expression. For example, crying or shouting at the same sorts of things or both being alike when it comes to sensitivity or emotional resilience.
- Physical intimacy – Being close physically and sharing similar needs for affection, sensuality and sexual pleasure.
- Intellectual intimacy – Being on the same mental wavelength. Sharing thoughts and ideas with each other, and feeling able to understand each other's thought processes.
- Spiritual intimacy – Being able to share the things that are really important in our lives with the same levels of passion, such as personal values, commitment to family, religion, politics, human rights, environmental issues.
- Lifestyle intimacy – Having similar needs for day-to-day balanced living as well as sharing goals and ambitions for the future.
- Recreational intimacy – Being able to relax, laugh and have fun together.

Most couples who have chosen to stay together will continue to have, or have experienced in the past, good levels of intimacy in at least some of these areas. Working to identify what is good in a relationship as well as the areas where improvement is required is helpful for maintaining motivation for rebuilding the relationship, as well as providing focus for areas of growth.

Improving communication

Once addiction has been revealed emotions almost always run higher than at any other point within the relationship. Typically partners are angry and confused while addicts feel ashamed and fearful of losing the relationship. This combination frequently results in either bitter arguments or soul wrenching talks – often both. Learning to manage these difficult conversations, without causing further pain and damage, is important for both.

If a couple have had problems with communication and resolving conflict before sex addiction was revealed, it is likely to become worse. Exploring past patterns of communication can be helpful to ensure that the addiction isn't blamed for problems that have always been around. Entrenched communication problems are best addressed in couple therapy where the dynamics can be observed, explored, highlighted and worked through, but for less difficult situations, heightening awareness of good communication skills may suffice.

The key to effective communication is first and foremost to ensure that conversations happen within the right environment. The right environment includes not only the physical surroundings but also the emotional atmosphere between the couple. With regard to physical surroundings, the most important thing is comfort and sufficient uninterrupted time, and couple environment refers to appropriate timing, motivation and agreed objectives. If at all possible, times of extreme stress and tiredness should be avoided, as should occasions when too much alcohol may have been consumed. Conversations can also be eased if the objective is clearly stated. For example, a partner may specifically state that they want time to let off steam or the addict may say they want space to share what's happening in their therapy. When this is stated as the objective it then becomes clear that this is not a time for seeking resolution to specific problems, but is about hearing the other speak. When the conversation is about setting boundaries or discussing a particular event, this should also be clearly stated so both can focus their attention on the aim. There are often many conversations that need to be had once addiction is revealed, but trying to do everything at once can be both exhausting, futile and potentially destructive. Many couples benefit from agreeing certain times when they will talk about the addiction and then start those sessions with an agreed topic and objective. Each can then feel relaxed outside of these times, knowing they won't be ambushed with a difficult conversation and some sense of normality in the relationship can prevail.

Box 11.2 shows a checklist that can be used as a memory jogger for improving communication.

Managing conflict

Conflict is an inevitable part of every relationship and some couples struggle more than others to control and manage the accompanying difficult emotions. When addiction has been revealed it's common for all disagreements to escalate faster than before, as emotional and physical tolerance is lower. When arguments regularly escalate to the point where one or both partners feel they're destructive, or where children are negatively impacted, it's important that boundaries are put into place to ensure safety for all.

Box 11.2 Ten rules of effective communication

1 Be clear on the objective of the conversation.
2 Choose your timing and stick to the matter in hand.
3 Be clear about what you want to say, and own your thoughts and feelings by starting sentences with 'I think/feel ...' rather than 'You made me ...'.
4 Express your feelings as well your thoughts.
5 Don't use provocative language such as 'always', 'never', 'should' or 'shouldn't'.
6 Listen attentively and check you've understood what's been said.
7 Don't block conversation by interrupting, expecting mindreading, making assumptions, minimising the others feelings or becoming silent.
8 Don't rake up history unless you're talking about the past.
9 Don't generalise or use other people's opinions to back up your own argument.
10 If tempers begin to rise, postpone the conversation.

One of the most effective strategies for minimising conflict is to help couples view the addiction as the enemy, rather than each other. In this way the couple share a common adversary who they can join arms against and fight, rather than fighting each other. When emotions are running high, especially soon after disclosure, this can be difficult to achieve, but over time most couples find this a useful viewpoint. What's more, by externalising the addiction, a partner may be helped to stop blaming the spouse for having an addiction, but rather to hold them responsible and accountable for what they do with it.

Contrary to popular belief, the best way to reduce ongoing arguments is often to start having more of them, rather than less. By agreeing regular 'ventilation sessions', either daily, twice-weekly, weekly or whatever suits the couple, conflict can begin to be contained. The principle is that up to an hour is set aside and the time is split between the couple. One partner may use their time to express their thoughts and feelings in any non-abusive way they choose. The other partner listens attentively but does not respond. When it is their turn they may respond as they wish or share other thoughts and feelings that are around. At the end of the allotted time the couple agree to go their separate ways for a while to cool off. Over time the ventilation sessions usually become shorter and less frequent as more and more is aired.

Another benefit of these sessions is that it allows other times of conversation to be protected and hence there can be at least some semblance of normality.

Another way to minimise conflict is to become more attuned to when emotions are beginning to run high. Couples can discuss the signs that each may display when tensions begin to arise – for example, physical signs such as clenched teeth or stomping feet, verbal clues such as sarcasm or silence or relational changes such as irritability or withholding affection. Many people instinctively want to withdraw when they notice these signs in a partner, but taking proactive action not only demonstrates empathy and care, it can also prevent the situation from escalating. My advice to couples is not to ignore their partner's tension signs but to verbally acknowledge them and ask if they would like to arrange a time to talk. If a partner says they're ok or they're not ready to talk then this needs to be respected, but at least awareness and care has been demonstrated.

Ultimately, both couples and therapists need to remember that it takes two people to improve communication and two people to have a row. If a conversation is becoming destructive, then I would always suggest that couples take a rain check. It may be frustrating at the time, but in the interests of each of their emotional safety, this is often the wisest choice.

12   Satisfying sexuality

Being in recovery means giving up addiction, not giving up sex. Sex is great. It's fun, exciting, exhilarating, relaxing, romantic, intimate, erotic and esteem building. What's more, research suggests that it's good for our emotional and physical health as well as for our relationships (Whipple, 2003). Unfortunately, this is not true of *all* sex, as those who've suffered from sex addiction and previous chapters of this book testify. But 'good' sex brings with it many benefits and like healthy relationships that we looked at in the previous chapter, a satisfying sex life is one of the most powerful relapse prevention strategies available.

When we talk about 'good' sex or 'satisfying sexuality', we are not assuming this will be within a heterosexual monogamous relationship. People with sex addiction come from every orientation and some choose open non-monogamous sexual relationships, while others are single, or find themselves single. Whatever the relationship status, it's essential that the right to sexual expression is not ignored or minimised. Unlike any other addiction, the goal is not abstinence but healthy integration of satisfying sexuality. This means all expressions of sexuality should be considered including the choice of celibacy, casual sexual relationships, partnered sex, fetishes and masturbation. Each potential avenue needs to be explored in light of the impact it may have on the addiction, and whether the behaviour will perpetuate the cycle or help to break it.

In this chapter we will look at how satisfying sexuality can be achieved, whether someone is single or in a monogamous or open non-monogamous relationship. We will also explore how celibacy can be a positive sexual choice. You won't find any prescription for how to achieve satisfying sexuality as it differs for every individual and every relationship, and it is something that constantly evolves. But there is general information to guide your thinking and further reading suggestions are available in the resources section at the end of this book.

Defining 'satisfying' sexuality

Sexuality is the global term we use to describe our gender, our thoughts and our feelings about sex, be they positive or negative, our sexual orientation and desires, our sexual behaviours, including the choice of celibacy, and our sexual potential for reproduction and pleasure. We are all sexual in the same way as we are all emotional and we are all intellectual. Our emotional and intellectual capacity and expression may vary, but it nonetheless exists.

Being sexual is part of the nature of being human and like emotion and thought it is morally neutral. This is an important fact to acknowledge as it helps to break through shame, especially for those who experience fetishes or paraphilias. The state of 'being' is autonomous and affects no one. It is only when we are 'doing' that we begin to impact others. On the whole we don't make moral judgements about how others think and feel. Indeed, unless they choose to express it, we are unaware that there is anything to judge. It is only when emotion, thoughts and/or sexuality are expressed to the detriment of others that we should even consider making a judgement. Like emotion and intellect, our sexuality is one of the strategies we can call on for survival or we can use it for our individual pleasure or to communicate and build relationships with others. And in the same way as our emotions and thinking are not fully within our conscious control, neither is our sexuality. We are responsible for how we express and manage our sexuality, but we may not always be able to control how we experience it.

Learning to be comfortable with our sexuality is a crucial element of good mental and emotional health. Being comfortable does not necessarily mean we can express our sexuality anyway our genitals desire, but means that we're able to acknowledge and respect our sexual feelings and choose to express them in ways that fit with our values and our chosen lifestyle.

So what is satisfying sexuality? In a nutshell it is any kind of sexual expression that is fulfilling emotionally, physically, psychologically and spiritually. I include 'spiritually' because for many people sex has a spiritual component. Whether that's linked to a faith, or a way of articulating the profound feelings of intimacy and wellbeing that sex can evoke. Sexual addiction can rob a person of seeing sex as a fulfilling part of their life, but when it's such an integral part of being human, re-discovering this experience is a fundamental component of long-term recovery.

Setting sexual boundaries

The circle exercise described in Chapter 7 (see Figure 7.2) is a useful tool for setting sexual boundaries; in addition it's important to ensure that the activities listed in the OK circle are non-triggering and can be described as 'satisfying'.

Satisfying sexual behaviours are:

- in line with personal values
- respectful of self and others
- pleasurable
- mutually fulfilling (when partnered)
- not shameful
- confidence and esteem building.

As highlighted in Chapter 7, it's a good idea to go through the final boundary list with someone who can challenge the behaviours that are in the OK circle. It can be far too easy to allow cognitive distortions and optimism to creep in along with behaviours that are not tenable. It may be that some behaviours also need to be contextualised to ensure clarity. For example, if someone who is single has put 'intercourse with my partner' in their OK circle, it will be important to clarify how a 'partner' will be defined. Similarly, if someone has put 'mild BDSM' as OK, the word 'mild' will need to be made clear. The more detail there is, the easier it will be to stick to. Many people also find it helpful to allocate timescales or markers based on length of time in recovery. Such as deciding that masturbation is ok, but not until six months of full sobriety has been achieved. Or sexy underwear and role play is ok in a couple relationship, but not until there has been a minimum of four months absence of fantasy. Every boundary list will be personal to the individual, and will of course need to take into consideration the needs of partners. The boundary list can then be seen not just as a tool for maintaining sobriety but also a template for satisfying sexuality.

Sex when you are single

Struggling with sex addiction when you're single can present particular challenges when it comes to developing satisfying sexuality. Unlike the partnered addict who may just be stopping extra-relational sex, most single addicts will have to completely give up the sexual lifestyle they've previously experienced. For most, a period of celibacy and abstinence from masturbation can be useful to allow old neural pathways to begin to die; however, if masturbation was never compulsive or a contributory factor, this may not be required. For those whose masturbatory habits need to change, a period of 90 days is the standard recommendation (Laaser, 2002), but this needs to be considered on an individual basis.

Like someone who's in a relationship, it's essential to define 'satisfying' sexuality and to ensure that desired behaviours are in line with personal values. Since sexual activity is almost inevitably going to be limited, if not absent for a while, alternative ways of achieving physical satisfaction should be explored. For some that might include taking up a new physical activity such as sport or exercise, or a body-awareness practice such as yoga or Qiqong. For those who have given up masturbation, a new mindfulness or sensate focused approach, that precludes fantasy, needs to be established before restarting to ensure the cycle is not re-triggered. Any psychosexual therapist should be well equipped to offer a masturbatory programme to suit individual needs.

Understandably, many single addicts are keen to find a new relationship, but dating can offer additional dilemmas to someone who is in early recovery. If casual sexual encounters have been part of the acting out behaviour, then it's essential that a new sexual relationship is not entered into until there is absolute confidence that the relationship has some kind of future. This may be difficult for a prospective partner to understand who has no awareness of sexual addiction. Similarly, there may be some behaviours within a new relationship that could be triggering and hence need to be avoided, such as watching pornography together or dressing up or perhaps particular fetishes or sexual practices. This may be difficult to do without being open about the problem with a new partner. In my experience, most people with an addiction would prefer their new partner to know of their history. Not only does this allow a truer experience of intimacy but it also opens the door for additional support and encouragement. However, timing is important and unfortunately it must be accepted that there is a risk that some prospective partners will choose to walk away.

Monogamous couple sex

For addicts who are continuing in a monogamous couple relationship, their list of OK behaviours needs to be explored in consultation with their partner. If there are activities missing that a partner would enjoy it will be necessary to explain that this could be triggering for the addict and hence needs to be avoided – at least in early recovery.

The discovery of sexual addiction can provide an opportunity for couples to fully explore their sexual relationship and consider how they would like it to improve and grow. It can also be helpful to discuss what role sex has played in the couple relationship in the past and how they want it to feature in the future, remembering that sex changes over the course of a relationship and as we age. And that sex will inevitably mean different things at different times. Couples who have previously had an open or non-monogamous relationship who are committing to monogamy for the first time will also need to consider the implications and challenges of doing this and how they will be faced.

Many couples find it helpful to consider each of the following aspects of their sexual relationship as listed below, and talk about what each means to them and in which areas they each would like improvement.

* Affection and intimacy
* Sensuality
* Romance
* Playfulness
* Eroticism
* Adventure
* Initiation
* Stimulation
* Talking about sex.

The timing of these conversations needs to be considered sensitively as some couples are not ready to think about their sexual relationship for quite some time after disclosure, whereas others see it as a priority. Working through this highly sensitive area is often best done with a psychosexual therapist who can address the physical, emotional and relational aspects of sexuality.

Open non-monogamy

Some people with sex addiction are in open non-monogamous relationships. For those unfamiliar with the term, it is a general label that covers any kind of relationship where partners who are committed to each other have agreed that complete sexual fidelity is not part of their contract. Some will have made this agreement when they first met while others may have changed from a monogamous to a non-monogamous agreement. The terminology seems to differ depending on the context but broadly speaking there are three types of non-monogamy. Polyamory covers any kind of relationship where multiple partners have a romantic involvement as well as sex with each other. Typically, this will be a group of two or three people, sometimes of differing sexual orientations, who commit to each other and agree boundaries for their relationship. An open relationship is one where each individual may have sex or date other people and swinging refers to couples who agree they will have sex with others, but usually only when they are together.

Open non-monogamy only works where there are clear boundaries that have been agreed between all involved. Most commonly this will be agreements around the amount of non-sexual involvement allowed and the types of sexual behaviours. For example, some swingers agree that they will be sexual with other people but preserve intercourse for their own relationship. When those boundaries are broken then there is a breach of trust and all the accompanying difficulties that happen in any other intimate relationship. When one partner within a non-monogamous relationship discloses sex addiction, the boundaries need to be redrawn by both. It is likely that the addicted partner will need to put firm restrictions on their own behaviour because they have broken the agreed boundaries. This will have an impact on everyone else within the relationship and hence agreeing new terms of engagement will be a larger task than for those in monogamous relationships. Often a primary partner's reaction is to see the addiction as proof that non-monogamy does not work for them and they may want to switch to monogamy. When this happens, both must seriously consider if this is viable for them as individuals and explore what will be lost, as well as what will be gained, if they become monogamous. For couples who have been openly non-monogamous for a long time, especially those on the gay or kink scene, the switch to monogamy may also have significant social implications.

Celibacy

Most people will not see celibacy as a sexual choice, but for many people recovering from addiction, especially those who are single, celibacy is an option to be seriously considered – at least for a while. Celibacy is a personal commitment to avoid any sexual relationship and traditionally would previously have been a life-time vow linked to a religious faith. Nowadays, many people choose celibacy, or abstinence, as an alternative to casual sex or non-relational sex, and put fulfilment of their sexual desires on hold until they're in a committed relationship.

It would be nice to say that the key advantage of celibacy is that it is unambiguous, and while it is with regard to no partner sex, masturbation is a contested issue. Some believe that celibacy should not include any kind of self stimulation whereas others believe that releasing the occasional urge is ok. Ultimately each person must decide for themselves. The key to celibacy is that sex is taken out of the frame. If there is occasional masturbation, it is about scratching a biological itch to eliminate the urge rather than wanting sex per se, so that celibacy can be enjoyed again. The advantage of celibacy for someone recovering from sex addiction is that it allows time and energy to be fully focused on other areas of life. Having made the decision that sex is not on the agenda, there is space to grow and develop in other areas. Most find the discomfort of sexual desire gradually declines and relationships, new and old, take on a different quality when there are no sexual connotations. Like monogamy, and non-monogamy, celibacy has its challenges, but for some it's the simplest option.

Overcoming sexual challenges

Most people in recovery will face sexual challenges. For some this will be an immediate and on going problem, especially in early recovery, while for others it may be something that occurs just occasionally. The challenges listed below are often difficult to discuss and manage in a couple situation without creating potential alarm and anxiety for partners, and hence it's usually better for these to be dealt with individually. If issues are particularly entrenched or persistent referral to a psychosexual therapist would be advised.

Dealing with fantasies

Whether you call it fantasies or memories, the problem is the same, as visual images of what's been seen or experienced during acting out can become imprinted on the brain. These images can then arrive uninvited into sexual activity, whether that's with a partner or alone, and blocking these images out takes time and perseverance. The most successful technique is to develop a habit of mindfulness during sex. This means staying fully present in the room with all the senses. Focusing on sight, smell, hearing, taste and especially physical sensation. This can be harder to achieve during masturbation when there is less sensory input and for this reason many addicts who are in a relationship choose not to masturbate. For those who are single, it's often best to set a period of abstinence during early recovery and only introduce masturbation when mindfulness skills have been developed and visual images can be controlled.

Fetishes and paraphilias

There is an ever growing list of fetishes and paraphilias and most people will have played with at least some of them during their sexual history. The term 'fetish' is used to describe an attraction to an object, body part or situation that's not normally considered sexual and is one of the paraphilias. Most fetishes do not cause any emotional or psychological difficulty and indeed, many are now commonplace in society as we can see from high street stores such as Ann Summers. On the other hand, paraphilia is a medical term that is used for anything non-normative that creates sexual arousal and also causes psychological distress. This means that something that is a fetish to one person, such as bondage or pain exchange sex, may be a paraphilia to someone else. The current list of example paraphilias includes voyeurism, exhibitionism, sado-masochism, transvestism, fetishism and paedophilia and hence a paraphilia may, or may not be, legal. It's important to be aware that this list has changed over the years as sexual diversity has become more widely accepted, with homosexuality being top of the list until relatively recently.

It is not understood how and why some people have fetishes and paraphilias and some do not. As previously explored, our sexuality is highly complex and is influenced by many factors including hormones, childhood experiences, individual personality and relational and social contexts. There is some evidence that childhood trauma can result in development of a fetish or paraphilia but there are also many people with different sexual preferences with no history of abuse of any kind. Unfortunately, there are many who prefer to pathologise or ridicule people with different sexual tastes, rather than accept that human sexuality is still beyond our comprehension.

Some people with sex addiction also experience a paraphilia and are very distressed by their sexual attraction. When this is the case, work can be done with a therapist to reduce dependency on the distressing stimulant and develop a 'satisfying' sexuality. Others may not experience any distress about their attraction and be happy to incorporate it into their recovered sexual lifestyle. On some occasions it is the partner who experiences the distress. During disclosure it may be revealed that the person with the addiction has a fetish attraction that they have privately and secretly engaged in outside of the relationship. Some partners may be able to accept a difference in taste but not want to participate, while others may be comfortable incorporating it into the relationship. If a behaviour can not be tolerated by a partner, for whatever reason, this should be respected and supported while considering what impact this may have on the viability of the relationship's future.

It is often a challenging task to decide if a non normative sexual behaviour is significant to the addiction or not. Many people feel shame about their 'unusual' attractions, but that may be the result of societal, cultural and relational stigma rather than because the behaviour is compulsive. Therapy is often required to help to decide where the behaviour belongs in the three circle boundary exercise and as always, ultimately the individual must decide if they want the behaviour to be part of their sexual repertoire as they move forward in their recovery.

Diverting sexual frustration

Although sexual addiction is primarily used as a way of anaesthetising against negative emotions there's no denying the fact that for many it also provides sexual release. In the early stages of recovery some addicts experience a reduction in their sex drive, in part due to feelings of sexual shame and also due to the stress of recovery – but many others struggle with unmet sexual needs. In order to manage the cravings for sexual satiation it first needs to be established that the need is truly sexual, rather than emotional. As discussed previously, when sexual release has been a bi-product of negative emotions it becomes a conditional response and hence difficult feelings trigger arousal. Therefore, when arousal is felt the first question needs to be whether or not there is another unmet need that is being stimulated. For example, if strong feelings of arousal happen after a stressful day at work, could the deeper need be for expressing frustration or having a friend to share the burden with. If sexual frustration is a significant issue then physical diversion such as exercise is generally considered the most effective solution, but if feelings do not begin to subside within a few weeks, then this is best worked through during therapy where incidents can be explored in depth and practical strategies can be tailored to the individual.

Resolving sexual dysfunctions

Clinical experience continues to assert that excessive use of pornography can result in erectile dysfunction and/or delayed ejaculation. A fact that is also supported by countless personal stories on the excellent yourbrainonporn. com website. This is because the regular use of highly stimulating material can raise the orgasmic threshold. A period of abstinence may be all that's required to resolve the problem, but it does take time. Additional help can be provided by a psychosexual therapist, who can provide sensate-focused masturbatory or couple programmes.

Another common problem is low sexual desire. Some people with an addiction may have split off their sexuality to such an extent that couple sex was almost non-existent. Others feel so much shame about their behaviours that they can't bear to be intimate with a loved one. Some develop what's known as the Madonna/whore syndrome where women are split into either good girls who don't or bad girls that do. When this thinking is ingrained it can be difficult to feel desire for a partner who is seen as too special for sex while arousal is still present for others. This is another situation that is often best worked through as a couple within psychosexual therapy.

13 Developing a healthy lifestyle

Back in Chapter 6 we explored the importance of committing to a personal value system that gives meaning and purpose to life and developing a vision of the future that incorporates those values. Any addiction can quickly become part of someone's lifestyle and some struggle to imagine a life without it. For long-term recovery to be successful, that lifestyle has to change.

We have talked at length throughout this book about the harmful consequences of sex addiction, but it must also be recognised that there are a lot of gains too – however fleeting they may be. As well as being a powerful tool to relax and soothe both body and brain, sex is also exhilarating and empowering. Addiction is also a place where many people experience what's known as 'flow'. Flow is used to describe the state of mind when we're totally absorbed by an activity that we're good at, also known as being 'in the zone', or 'in the groove'. Most people with an addiction are very good at what they do. They become experts at finding and collecting pornography or making show reels, or they become experts at researching sex workers or picking up sex partners. Quite aside from sexual satiation, there's often a real satisfaction and sense of being alive that's found when lost in the addiction. Long-term recovery means finding alternative ways to experience these positive emotions. In reality, many things are poor substitutes and it's important to accept this fact. There may be little that can replace the intense high of sexual arousal, but when the bigger picture of life is taken into account, and additional pleasures are added, the gains definitely outweigh the losses. We have also considered at length how addiction is used to anaesthetise against negative emotions and cope with the stresses and strains of life. Unfortunately, there are no known ways of completely avoiding life's challenges, but a healthy lifestyle can minimise their impact.

In this chapter we will explore what a healthy lifestyle looks like, from an emotional, physical, spiritual and relational perspective. We will also look at how to maintain a balanced life through increased personal awareness, emotional intelligence and assertiveness.

Being physically healthy

'Healthy body, healthy mind' is a well-known cliché that we increasingly accept as truth. When our body is strong we're more resilient to physical and emotional stress. We're more able to fight off viruses and infections, and we have more willpower to fight off triggers and temptations. Physical and mental agility allows us to remain vigilant to threat of every kind and, when recovering from addiction, that's vital.

Some people with sex addiction are already incredibly fit and active. Maintaining optimum physical health may have been part of the addiction and used for attracting partners. It's important that this is not lost during recovery, but that the motivation is changed to keeping healthy for one's own personal satisfaction, rather than purely for sexual gain. Those whose sex addiction has not been partner-based may have neglected their health for many years. Indeed, some who have been caught up in deprivation addictions, such as those that include shaming and painful encounters or binge pornography, may have deliberately ignored their physical health. And some will use physical negligence as a way of punishing themselves during the regret phase of the cycle.

Our physical health can be optimised by paying attention to the following three areas.

- Sleep – It's well known that sleep is essential for our physical health and wellbeing, and it's recommended that adults get 8 hours sleep per night. Many people with sex addiction will have lost their natural sleep routine, as the early hours are often a popular time for porn. Developing a good sleeping habit will not only aid physical health but also provide the means for enough energy to pursue more productive pleasures.
- Exercise – When we exercise we automatically trigger our natural feel-good chemicals. Whether that's running, going to the gym, playing competitive sports or something more peaceful like Pilates or tai chi. Exercise can help relieve stress and reduce depression, both of which are common factors in addiction and it can be a great way of filling time that had previously been taken up with acting out.
- Diet – In addition to maintaining a healthy diet of sufficient calorific intake and an appropriate balance of proteins, complex carbohydrates and fresh fruit and vegetables, supplements are also thought to aid recovery. As yet there is no clinical evidence to support the claims,

but some believe that the addition of appropriate amino acids that serve as the building blocks for serotonin, dopamine and GABA can help in relapse prevention. Supplements may help restore deficiencies in these neurotransmitters and hence spur cravings and assist in finding alternative natural 'highs'. The main recommendations are L-Tyrophan, L-Tryptophan and L-Glutamine. If you would like further advice or information I would recommend seeing a reputable dietician.

Establishing a balanced life

The great writer and social activist Thomas Merton said: 'Happiness is not a matter of intensity, but of balance and order and rhythm and harmony.' Most people with sex addiction have relied on intensity to provide a sense of happiness, and in recovery the challenge is to find happiness within a balanced life. When our lives are in balance it is easier to maintain an emotional equilibrium. That's not to say there won't be times of extreme pleasure and extreme pain, but when a life is balanced we're better able to manage, or avoid, polarities of emotion. A balanced life is also a life that is rich with variety and focuses on the needs of every aspect of being human.

There are a number of different opinions on what constitutes a balanced life, but most agree it's a combination of work, rest and play – sometimes alone, sometimes with others. In my experience, a balanced life includes eight elements – relationship, friendship, family, fun, relaxation, work, personal growth and social contribution. The importance of each of these areas will vary from individual to individual and change over the course of life. To maintain balance, we must be ready to adapt when circumstances dictate, but no element should be entirely absent. We will now explore what each of these areas of life means in more depth.

1   Relationship – This refers to a primary couple relationship. As we saw in Chapter 11, a happy and fulfilling couple relationship can be an invaluable source of comfort and motivation in recovery. And indeed, a stable couple relationship is an important part of many people's lives. It is a well-known fact that many otherwise happy relationships fail due to lack of attention and effort, and therefore it's important to work at our couple relationships. There are of course many people who are single and some who choose to remain so, either temporarily or long term. In this case the relationship area of life would best describe the most significant friendship. The person who you feel closest to and has most influence in your life.

2 Friends – A friend in need is a friend indeed, or so the saying goes, and recovery is a time when friends can play an especially important role. Many people with an attachment-induced addiction would say they've never really had any close friends and all tend to find that their compulsive behaviours has meant that they've kept people at arms length. The shame of sex addiction often leaves people unable to fully relax in others' company and inevitably this can affect the bond of friendship. Friendships fulfil many different functions, which is fortunate since no single relationship could ever fulfil all our needs. Reflecting on existing friendships within the context of the categories below can be a useful way of exploring desired change.

- *Best friends* – someone, or if you're lucky, a few people who you can be totally honest with, without risk of judgement. Someone who you can trust who will always have your best interests at heart.
- *Functional friends* – these friends tend to play a particular role in your life. You like each other and help each other out but neither of you would describe yourselves as particularly close. You may share a common interest such as a sport or hobby, or being parents or living on the same street. These are recreational relationships which may develop into a deeper friendship, or may continue happily as they are for many, many years.
- *Casual acquaintances* – these are people you work with and friends of friends who may drift in and out of your life and you probably don't know very well. You may suspect that you would become good friends if the circumstances were right. But perhaps because of time or geographic distance or office politics, they remain a warm smile and a handshake away.

Whatever the type of friend, having someone who can lend a listening ear or a helping hand, or someone who can share a laugh or encouragement is an invaluable asset in recovery. Building and re-building friendships often takes little more than time and effort, and once the acting out behaviour has stopped, there will be much more of both to go around. Hence creating a varied and satisfying friendship base can become a goal.

3 Family – Nowadays, families come in many different shapes and sizes. Parents, step-parents, grandparents, step-grandparents, siblings, half-siblings, step-siblings, aunts, uncles, cousins, nieces, nephews and a whole load of other second or in-law relations. There might also be other family friends who play, or have played, a significant role in family life and of course, children of whatever age. A crisis such as recovering from an addiction will bring some family members closer, and make others pull away.

Family relationships vary considerably between different cultures and each of us has a different expectation of how a family 'should' operate. The discovery, or disclosure, of addiction may highlight problems that have been around for many years, or may reveal a depth of understanding and support that had hitherto gone unnoticed or been taken for granted. Either way, family in whatever way you define it, or experience it, is an inevitable part of life that can be maximised for optimum reward.

4   Fun and recreation – When sex, or any other compulsive substance or activity, has been a part of someone's lifestyle for a long time, other pastimes often lose their appeal or disappear all together. Play is part of being human. From birth to old age, the desire to have fun, to laugh and be creative, is universal. In terms of transactional analysis, this area of life emanates from the free child. The shame of addiction often robs people of their ability to get in touch with their inner free child and innocent fun may be a dim and distant memory. Getting back in touch with this part of ourselves and giving it a place to express itself in our lifestyle is a key component of becoming whole and healthy again.

In order to reintroduce fun, some people find it helpful to think back to activities that used to be enjoyed before the addiction took grip. Or to remember the things that you were always going to do 'one day'. This is where group work can often be beneficial as others share the things they enjoy and members can encourage each other to have fun again. Many recreational activities also have a social component which can support the growth in friendship and some will also have a competitive and/or physical element which can provide a helpful release for adrenalin and testosterone. There are an endless list of things that might be classed as fun and recreational, but broadly speaking they will be pursuits that include some element of physical or mental energy, such as sport or physical exercise, a creative hobby, travelling or visiting places, further education, competitive games, DIY, gardening, laughing with friends, cooking, wine making, bee keeping, playing an instrument, singing and so on and so on.

5   Rest and relaxation – Many activities that might be classed fun and recreational are not necessarily relaxing. While it's important to have activities that stimulate us, it's also important to have periods of time that are devoted to slowing down. Busyness seems to be a curse of 21st-century living and many people feel guilty if they're not doing something perceived as productive with their time. But relaxing is productive, because it allows us to recharge our batteries and gives space for inspiration to be born. For those who used their addiction to anaesthetise against stress and anxiety, learning new ways to relax is

especially important. Like fun and recreation, some people find it easier to relax in the company of other people and others prefer to be alone. Either is fine as long as both the body and mind are able to be relaxed. For some, relaxation has a spiritual quality and is best enjoyed in religious practices or in communion with nature. Other typical activities might include reading, listening to music, gentle exercise, meditation, watching TV or film, playing chess, enjoying scenery and so on.

6 Work – Another area of our lives that can give satisfaction is work, and for some, work is the place where creativity and 'flow' can also be found. That could be voluntary work, paid employment, part time or full time. Whatever form work takes, it is a place where you have the potential to feel good about what you give and produce, and what you receive in terms of financial and/or emotional reward. Unfortunately work can also be a significant trigger for some people with addiction, either due to the opportunity it provides to act out, or because of the negative emotions it creates. When work is a problem area, ideally energy should be focused on improving the current situation or changing career, but if that's not possible expanding in other areas of life can make an unsatisfactory job more tolerable.

7 Personal growth – Where work is not a source of pleasure, it is especially important to take time to focus on personal growth. It is the nature of being human that we enjoy learning. We like to expand our knowledge and our skill set. To feel a sense of achievement that comes from personal endeavour. And since this is an area of life that is not dependent on other people, it provides an opportunity to be completely focused on personal needs and desires. Some will be fortunate enough to gain personal growth from their employment, but since most jobs require working on behalf of the team or the company, an additional element of self-focused growth can be beneficial. Personal growth means different things to different people. It may be learning a new skill such as a language or playing an instrument, or a new craft such as painting or carpentry. Or it might mean emotional growth through therapy, or reading or mindfulness exercises and meditation; alternatively it could be spiritual growth through prayer or other religious practices. It doesn't matter what it is as long as there is a sense of self-improvement and progress.

8 Contribution – Contribution is perhaps the opposite of personal growth. It refers to the part of life where we give to others or give back to society. It is the place where we can develop our empathy and enjoy the rewards of altruism. When we give to others, it also allows us to step outside of ourselves and see the world from another perspective. Depending on the activity it can also provide a positive

sense of agency and influence. Making a contribution may mean getting more involved in a political party, either as a supporter or a candidate. Or maybe a social issue such as poverty, housing, immigration, children and young people's welfare, physical or mental health, the elderly, education or public services. Or perhaps helping a charity that specialises in environmental projects, working in the third world, fighting for human rights or animal welfare. Many recovering addicts, especially those in 12-step communities, make a commitment to give back in some way to support fellow addiction sufferers.

These eight areas of life are not in order of importance and it may be that one area, such as relationship or employment, is at times completely missing. If that is the case then other areas can be focused on to ensure that life is still experienced as fulfilling. In fact, it is often when one of these key areas is taken away, as so often happens as a result of sex addiction, that the importance of the other areas of life becomes apparent. Unfortunately, it is not always possible to have a balanced life, but we can endeavour to do so.

In Figure 13.1 you'll see an illustration of a life wheel. This is a concept widely used in life coaching as a tool to discover which areas of life may need more attention. The principle is that by looking at the wheel and marking your degree of satisfaction between 1 and 10 on each axis (with 1 is at the centre and 10 on the outside), you can see how balanced your life is and therefore how smoothly the wheel of life will turn. And the more high marks you're able to score yourself, the richer your life will be and the more overall satisfaction you're likely to gain from it.

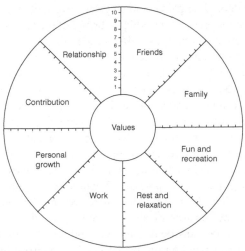

Figure 13.1 Life wheel

Completing the life wheel can provide valuable information about the areas of life where change is both desired and required. As you can see from Figure 13.1, all of these eight areas of life should come from a central point of your value system. As we explored in Chapter 7, our personal value system should underpin everything we do, including our priorities and the decisions we make, and when we live in line with our values, our lives will have meaning and purpose.

Developing a balanced life that is rich in each of the eight areas is just part of the work of developing a healthy lifestyle. The other key component is keeping it that way. At times our lives gets out of kilter and while we may know that our life wheel is not rolling as smoothly as it should, often we leave it too late before making amends. An excellent tool that Patrick Carnes incorporates as part of his Recovery Start Kit is what he calls the Personal Craziness Index (Carnes 2005). He describes how there are times in our lives when we feel 'in the zone'. Our wheel is turning smoothly and all seems right with the world. But unless we are vigilant and continue to take care of ourselves, disorder can creep in and destructive patterns of self-soothing can return. Below is an adapted UK version that can serve as a valuable life assessment tool to help us notice when life is getting out of balance and we need to refocus and get back 'in the zone'. I would recommend that this exercise is done on a monthly basis in the early stages of recovery and perhaps 6-monthly thereafter. But, as you will see, this is a tool that can be a valuable resource for everyone – not just those in recovery.

Box 13.1 Life balance inventory

Read through the examples below, then list the things that happen to you when your life is getting out of balance and you need to get yourself back on track again.

- Physical health – How do you know when you're not looking after yourself physically? For example, do you smoke, drink too much alcohol or coffee, have trouble sleeping, suffer with headaches or stomach complaints, forget to cut your toe nails or skip shaving?
- Relationship – What signs do you see when your relationship is not getting the attention it needs? For example do you feel more distant from your partner or find yourself becoming more needy or jealous. Or perhaps you argue more easily over little things or you find yourself being less tolerant than usual? What impact does being out of balance have on your sexual relationship?

continued...

Box 13.1 continued

- Friends – When life is out of balance, what impact does it have on your friendships? For example, do you spend less time with them? Are there some friends that you particularly miss or activities you miss out on? Do you find yourself less able to fit in when you do meet up with people or losing confidence in social situations? Do you find yourself becoming more dependent on social stimulation from other sources such as a partner, family or even the TV?
- Family – What are the signs that you're not spending enough time with members of your family, whether that's children, parents or siblings? Do you find yourself being nagged to spend more time with them or do you notice that you feel guilty when you're spending time on other things because you should be with them. Do your children behave differently when they have less of your attention?
- Fun and recreation – How do you know when you're not getting your needs for fun and recreation met? For example, do you feel bored and boring, behave restlessly such as pacing around or flicking between TV channels bored and restless? Do you get irritable and enviable of others who seem to be doing more? Or feel lethargic or apathetic?
- Rest and relaxation – What are the signs that you might be burning the candle at both ends too often and need to get more quiet time? For example, do you find yourself getting irritable and crotchety, feeling anxious for no particular reason, feeling frustrated when others want your time or withdrawing into silence? Or do you find you are fidgety and can't sit still?
- Work – What are the signs that you're struggling at work? For example, do you start working crazily long hours, not returning phone calls, getting disorganised, start being late or find it difficult to concentrate and focus on individual tasks. With more time at work and less at home, maybe you notice differences in your home environment such as no food in the fridge, or washing left undone and bills left unopened.
- Personal growth – When you're not making time to focus on your personal development do you find yourself feeling less satisfied in other areas of life such as work and with your partner? Do you have a sense of feeling unfulfilled or unstimulated? Do you let spiritual practices slip such as prayer or meditation?
- Contribution – When you're not finding time to give back or connect to the wider world, what do you notice? Does life begin to get out of perspective, or do you find yourself grumbling about trivia, losing the ability to be grateful for what you have, struggling with compassion fatigue? Do you feel less tolerant of others and out of touch with the world outside of your own?

Increasing emotional intelligence

The term 'emotional intelligence' has been buzzing around and growing in popularity since the early 1980s and the majority of people now accept the importance of the concept. Emotional intelligence is essential for navigating relationships and developing the lifestyle that we desire. There are dozens of different definitions of EI but they all basically boil down to this: 'Emotional Intelligence is the ability to identify, understand, manage and take appropriate action on the emotions of self and others.' It's easy to see that someone with good emotional intelligence will be in a stronger position to determine their own destiny, communicate with others and avoid coercion. And if, or perhaps when, hardship strikes they'll also be equipped to healthily manage and express their feelings and gain the support of others. EI is a skill that some seem to be born with whereas others have to learn and develop it.

The first requirement of emotional intelligence is to learn to identify our emotional needs. In the world of emotional intelligence this is known as emotional literacy and it's a notion that has been embraced by workers with young people where it's been proven that learning a language of emotion helps young people's mental stability. When a teenager is taught the language to recognise and express their rage they're less inclined to hit out physically. And when they can differentiate between their feelings of fear, sadness and frustration they can consider their options and make a decision about the best course of action to take.

Once we have identified and named our emotional needs, including any underlying primary needs, we can begin to understand them. Once we know *how* we feel we can ask *why* we feel. In the realms of emotional intelligence this is where someone, having recognised their feelings of anger or sadness or fear, might ask themselves what has caused that emotion. What is going on in their inner and outer world that has evoked this emotional state?

How we manage our emotional feelings is essential, not only for our own sense of self-worth, autonomy and personal satisfaction, but also for our relationships and our society. When emotions are out of control it affects those around us. It's obvious to see how uncontrolled anger can have a negative effect and to a certain extent, sadness and pessimism. But it's also true of positive feeling states such as happiness. Being around someone who is overflowing with happiness may inspire you to be happy, or it may make you feel more miserable by comparison or even irritated. That's not to say that managing our emotion will mean that we keep it hidden but we should be aware of its impact and therefore ensure that its communication is within our control.

As explored in previous chapters, all addictions are a method of emotional regulation. They either create a positive emotion or eliminate a negative one. Increasing emotional intelligence can help people recovering from addiction to become better at identifying, understanding, managing and expressing their emotions. All of us have some emotions that are harder to manage than others and these will probably be the very ones that someone with an addiction will be left struggling with once the anaesthetic has been removed. The exercise in Box 13.2 can be a helpful way of identifying what those emotions are, along with any others that may require work. The exercise also identifies the areas where emotions are harder to manage. For example, someone may find it easy to identify and manage feelings of frustration with a partner but may ignore them in the workplace, or fears may be openly acknowledged with friends but hidden with parents. By identifying not only the emotion, but also the environment within which the problem lies, underlying causes or dynamics can also be explored.

Developing assertiveness

One of the casualties of shame is loss of assertiveness. As sex addiction slowly erodes self-esteem, many sufferers lose their capacity to stand up for themselves and say how they feel and what they need. Many feel they have lost the right to assert themselves and drift into passivity and inertia. A few swing the other way towards aggression. A common defence mechanism against shame is grandiosity and self-entitlement and this means that some people in recovery becoming overly demanding and aggressive. It's important to recognise that being assertive is not about putting your needs ahead of someone else's, but putting them on an equal level. It is about respecting self and others.

Developing assertiveness is essential for maintaining a balanced and fulfilling life. When we're assertive we're able to express our opinions and feelings, say 'No' without feeling guilty and prioritise our time to fit with our values and needs. Without assertiveness we're likely to say 'Yes' to things that we don't want to do and put up with situations that are unfair. The result is a life that is governed by others needs and desires, rather than our own. Lack of assertiveness also damages intimacy in relationships as real needs and feelings are suppressed and partners, friends and family may never get to know the real person. For someone recovering from addiction it is particularly important to learn assertiveness so that needs and emotions that were previously soothed with the addiction are managed healthily.

The first task in developing assertiveness is to identify the times and places where being assertive is a problem. If the emotional intelligence inventory has been completed this will highlight where emotions are difficult to express and where assertiveness might be a useful tool to help the process. Once identified, the thoughts and cognitive distortions that block assertiveness can then be explored. For example, someone might recognise that they don't ever say no to friends because they fear they won't be liked. Or they don't ask their partner for more time alone because they fear it would hurt their feelings or turn into an argument. These thoughts can then be tested for their validity and either reframed or taken into account.

The next step is to consider what an assertive approach to these situations would be. Most often this includes a combination of appropriate body language, communicating thoughts and feelings in an open and calm way and being consistent and persistent if necessary. There are many books written on assertiveness as well as a wide range of online tools. Ultimately developing assertiveness takes practice but once the rewards of a more fulfilling life are experienced, there is plenty of incentive to do so.

Box 13.2 Emotional intelligence inventory

Consider the emotions listed in Table 13.1 overleaf in the vertical column, and place a tick in the appropriate column to indicate in which areas of your life you experience each particular emotion. Once you have completed this, go back and circle the ticks that are helping you in your life – bearing in mind that a negative feeling may also be useful sometimes. For example, when you feel bored or apathetic with a partner it might motivate you to do something new together. Or feeling frustrated at work might encourage you to learn a new skill or take on more responsibility. If you notice that there is an emotion that you have not ticked at all, that might indicate a feeling that is being denied. Similarly, if you have ticked very few emotions in one column, this might indicate that you find it particularly difficult to show emotion in this environment. The results of this inventory can then be shared with a therapist or with a trusted friend to consider how you might increase your emotional intelligence in these areas.

Table 13.1 Emotional intelligence inventory

Feeling	When alone	With my partner	With family	With friends	At work	Needs Attention
Hurt						
Betrayed						
Let down						
Embarrassed						
Ashamed						
Worthless						
Stupid						
Guilty						
Lonely						
Alone						
Isolated						
Unwanted						
Alienated						
Redundant						
Misunderstood						
Unheard						
Rejected						
Self-conscious						
Angry						
Frustrated						
Irritated						
Enraged						
Annoyed						
Volatile						
Violent						
Manipulated						
Controlled						
Empty						
Numb						
Cold						
Useless						
Invisible						
Apathetic						
Bored						
Sad						
Depressed						
Used						
Distressed						
Disorientated						
Weary						
Insecure						
Hopeless						

Feeling	When alone	With my partner	With family	With friends	At work	Needs Attention
Fear						
Scared						
Confused						
Worried						
Nervous						
Suspicious						
Defensive						
Jealous						
Powerless						
Trapped						
Overwhelmed						
Love						
Tender						
Passionate						
Supportive						
Supported						
Loved						
Loving						
Valued						
Respected						
Wanted						
Affectionate						
Caring						
Generous						
Grateful						
Happy						
Satisfied						
Content						
Proud						
Secure						
Relaxed						
Confident						
Wanted						
Needed						
In control						
Hopeful						
Free						
Excited						
Total number of circled ticks						
Total left uncircled						
Needs Attention						

14 Recognising and overcoming blocks to recovery

Unfortunately, addiction is not an easy problem to overcome and most people can expect to experience a few slip-ups on the road to recovery. As long as these slip-ups, or even the occasional relapse, are accompanied by greater self-awareness, improved relapse-prevention techniques and renewed commitment to recovery, they can reluctantly be accepted as par for the course. However, continuing relapses or any escalation in behaviour may be the result of an underlying block that has not yet been recognised.

One of the most common blocks is an unresolved psychological issue, as explored in Chapter 9. Until the deeper causes of sex addiction are dealt with, an anaesthetic will still be sought. If someone has a complex trauma and attachment-induced addiction, then it may take years of therapy to resolve the underlying problem. Although a cognitive understanding of the problem may have been reached, this knowledge takes time to filter into emotions and behaviour. And unfortunately the nature of the cycle of addiction is that each relapse may reinforce negative emotions and hence create more triggers. This means that relapse prevention strategies will need to be constantly revised throughout the therapeutic process.

Another common block is lack of motivation or commitment to change. One researcher discovered that 70 per cent of his sample who had sought help for sex addiction were ambivalent about change (Reid, 2007). Back in Chapter 2 we looked at the importance of assessing motivation and the therapeutic strategies that work best at each stage. If someone is still in the contemplation stage of change, or has slipped back to this stage, then the focus of work needs to be appropriately adjusted. However, even the most committed person may find that their motivation waivers if they've continued to experience relapse. One of the slogans of the 12-step movement is 'progress not perfection' – absorbing the truth of this statement can help someone to get back on the wagon again.

In this final chapter we explore some of the most common blocks to recovery and how they can be overcome. Some are psychological, some relational and some physical. They are challenges that many people in recovery face, so even if you're not experiencing a block at this present moment, reading this chapter now would be a good idea to ensure you know what to watch out for.

Denial

There are many different forms of denial and each can wreck recovery. Some are obvious and easy to confront, though not necessarily easy to change, and others are more subtle. Broadly speaking you can break denial down into two statements: 'It's not that bad'; and 'The pain ain't worth the gain'. The first statement includes a longer list of emotions and cognitions that either deny the consequences of the addiction all together, or deny the impact of the consequences, whereas the second statement accepts the consequences but either does not acknowledge the benefits of recovery or denies their ability to change.

'It's not that bad'

On the whole, us humans are a pretty resilient species but unfortunately that can go against us when it comes to beating addiction. Most of us have at least some success at leaving painful memories in the past and a healthy optimism allows us to forge ahead with life without constantly worrying about what's round the corner. In some respects, people with a healthy resilience to life, who also struggle with addiction, can be the hardest to treat. It may be that a crisis of some sort is what initiated seeking help but when life is back on track, the pain may be forgotten and the initial incentive to change lost. And stressing about the 'what if's' may not be in that person's nature.

Another common accompaniment to this kind of denial is the cognitive distortion of minimisation. Acting out behaviours may have been reduced so they are also 'not that bad' and hence risk may be seen to be minimised as well. Some people with this denial are within the honeymoon period of recovery and having survived what they thought might be the end of their life as they knew it, feel temporarily safe. In short, they 'got away with it' and may feel that as long as they're careful, they can continue to 'get away with it'. Ultimately, it is, of course, the individual's prerogative to decide if they recover completely from their addiction or just cut down. But before making that decision, it's important to have all the facts and to have considered every possible outcome. To do this, both the actual and the potential consequences of continuing the addictive behaviour need to be considered.

Box 14.1 is an exercise that provides an opportunity to list the worst consequences of past acting out behaviour and to remember the feelings associated with the event then, and also now.

There is something incredibly powerful about seeing the worst pain of the past all written down together in black and white along with its emotional impact. What most people find as they consider how they feel now when they reflect is that much of the pain is the same. A few express relief that the secrecy is over and the truth has been revealed, but the pain often does not diminish. In some senses, completing this exercise is a bit like returning to the scene of the crime or going back to the wreckage of the car. You may have survived, but the devastation is no less real. When completing this exercise with someone who has either a trauma or attachment-induced addiction, be prepared for the return of powerful negative emotions. Feelings of anxiety and/or attachment pain may resurface and will need to be soothed in a healthy way to avoid slipping back into denial.

Box 14.1 Rock bottoms

Take a sheet of paper and write down four or five of the rock bottom times that have been caused by your sexual addiction. They may be rock bottom because of an actual physical consequence such as losing your job or going into debt, or because of the pain caused to a loved one, or of course both. Or it might be a rock bottom moment that was purely emotional – such as the terror you felt when you nearly got caught or the acute sense of shame you felt around a particular event, such as missing a special occasion because of your addiction or having to pretend to be someone you're not. In your mind's eye, go back to each of those times and write down every precise detail of what happened. As well as writing the facts, also write down exactly how you felt while it was happening and how you felt over the subsequent hours and days. When you have completed this, spend some time reading back over the rock bottom events you've listed and write down how you feel now as you bring them back into your conscious memory. Once you've done that, take another sheet of paper and write down how each of those events could have been worse. How much worse might you have felt if x, y or z had happened? If it's not possible for those events to have been any worse, ask yourself how many times you are willing to put yourself through those emotions? And how many times you're willing to put loved ones through those emotions?

Once the past consequences have been assessed, the potential cost of continuing to act out needs to be explored. Back in Chapter 1 we talked about the importance of recognising not just actual consequences but also potential ones. Just because someone has not yet been killed roller skating in the fast lane of the motorway does not mean it's a safe sport and while a very small minority of people have been killed in air crashes, knowing the probability allows us to continue to take a calculated risk each time we fly. The following exercise can be useful to provide the information required to ensure the risks of continuing to act out are fully calculated.

Box 14.2 Harmful consequences

On a scale of 1 to 10, where 1 is no risk at all and 10 is inevitable, complete these tables.

What is the risk of the following happening if you are *not* found out	1	2	3	4	5	6	7	8	9	10
Hurting people you love										
Not developing a relationship										
Spending less time with people you love such as a partner, family and friends										
Spending less time on health and fitness, hobbies and personal growth										
Wasting money										
Compromising your work or career										
Catching an STI										
Developing a sexual dysfunction										
Damaging your self esteem										

What is the risk of the following happening if you *are* found out	1	2	3	4	5	6	7	8	9	10
Hurting people you love										
Losing your partner										
Having less contact with your children										
Having less contact with other family members										
Losing friends										
Losing your home										
Losing your job										
Reducing your disposable income										
Damaging your self esteem										
Wanting to end your life										

Completing these exercises can serve as a harsh reality check, especially if they're completed with a trusted friend, therapist or 12-step sponsor who can challenge any minimisations or other cognitive distortions. Although there may be a sense of 'getting away with it now', is that really true? Is there really no cost or is it being denied? And what would the cost be of getting caught? Is it worth the risk? If the answer is yes, then the second denial statement should also be explored.

'The pain ain't worth the gain'

If the consequences, actual and potential, have been accurately calculated, then either now is not the right time for giving up the addiction because there is insufficient motivation, or recovery does not seem worth it. It's important to acknowledge that part of recovery includes loss and it is often this loss that feels 'not worth it'. That may be loss of sexual excitement, loss of freedom, loss of power or loss of self-identity. These feelings of loss need to be taken seriously, empathised with and mourned – and where possible, rebuilt or replaced. This can be particularly difficult when the benefits of recovery are a lifestyle that has never been experienced, not even as part of a double life.

Geoff's story

Geoff had always been a successful ladies' man. He had been a very attractive boy who grew into a very good-looking man and he had never been short of female attention. He loved women and he loved sex – and he had enjoyed plenty of both. He recognised he was addicted in his early 30s as his increasing efforts to commit to a steady relationship failed. Geoff had a few attachment issues as the result of seeing his parents' marriage fail, but primarily his addiction was opportunity-induced. He had the looks, the charm, the money and a job that gave him ample access to what he called 'an endless flow of willing pussy'. A year into recovery, Geoff had 'cut back' considerably, but he was still acting out. As much as he longed for a committed relationship and children, he couldn't imagine only ever sleeping with one woman. He also worried that without the drive to conquer and the thrill of the chase, he would become boring. He wondered if he was just one of those people who were born to be a Lothario and perhaps he should focus his therapy on mourning the fact that he might never have a 'normal' life.

When giving up the addiction doesn't seem worth it, denial is accompanied by ambivalence. The Matrix question can be a useful way of exploring this and providing a direction for future work. Those of you who have seen the film *The Matrix* will remember that the hero, Neo, was offered a choice. The blue pill would allow him to remain unchanged and stay in blissful ignorance, whereas the red pill, which represented painful reality, would eventually lead to true freedom. Someone struggling to decide if recovery is worth it can choose the blue pill, which would take them back to their pre-recovery days where much of their acting out happened without the conscious awareness of addiction. Or they could choose the red pill, which guarantees eventual freedom but comes with further work and the loss of some of what had been held dear. Those who choose the blue pill can be further helped to consider what they'll lose if they go back to their old life through the previous exercises and those who choose the red can focus on building benefits and self-belief. Geoff was very sure he wanted the red pill and hence we were able to focus on overcoming his self-doubt and building an image of the future he most deeply desired.

The life wheel as described in the previous chapter can be a good way of exploring the benefits of overcoming addiction as can the exercises on values and life vision in Chapter 7. But unless someone believes they have the capacity to achieve the life vision or chosen lifestyle, it may feel like an empty dream rather than an achievable reality. General work on increasing self-esteem can be beneficial as will neuro-cognitive restructuring as discussed in Chapter 10. If ongoing feelings of low self-esteem and worthlessness are not able to be resolved, then the problem may be undiagnosed depression. There's more on concurrent mental health problems later in this chapter.

Unforgiveness

Throughout this book I have talked about how shame is one of the biggest problems people with sex addiction have to face and overcome. When shame has not been overcome, unforgiveness will inevitably take hold and can rob a person of any sense of deserving to recover. Unforgiveness may be of the self or it may be a partner who refuses to forgive. When this happens it is impossible to escape the regret phase of the cycle. And even though acting out may have stopped a long time ago, and triggers may be healthily managed, someone who remains unforgiven, remains trapped in the cycle of addiction.

Framing forgiveness as an essential part of recovery can, in itself, give permission for forgiveness to happen, but many feel that to forgive themselves, or forgive a partner, would be synonymous with saying what happened didn't matter. Forgiveness is often wrongly perceived as being 'let off the hook' and some feel that being constantly reminded of the pain that's been caused is a price they must pay. Withholding forgiveness is often used as a punishment and in these situations it is often referred to as accusatory suffering. The person with the addiction remains accused of their crime and must continue to suffer lest they reoffend. In reality, the opposite is more probable, as suffering is much more likely to trigger addiction than forgiveness. Forgiveness does not mean that the crime will be forgotten or that work on rebuilding relationships and self-esteem has been concluded. On the contrary, it makes space and frees energy for that work to begin.

Forgiveness is easy to talk about but much, much harder to do. The first step is to understand and recognise the benefits of forgiveness and then decide if you want to forgive. When it is a partner who cannot forgive, they can be helped to recognise that the key benefit of forgiving will be for themselves. To 'let themselves off the hook' of anger and bitterness. There will still be ongoing work to manage fears and anxieties, but having forgiven, the focus can be on the future rather than on the past. For the person with the addiction, the benefits are more obvious, but some will feel they must continue to blame themselves in order to demonstrate remorse and responsibility. Where this is the case then a reality check may be required with those who they feel responsible to. Do they really want their loved one to live in guilt and shame? If so, to what end? It's also helpful to ask if someone could forgive if it had happened to someone else? The answer is nearly always 'Yes' and so the logic of why someone else who had done exactly the same things is worthy of forgiveness can be explored.

As well as exploring the pros and cons of forgiveness it can be helpful to look at what precisely it is that can be forgiven and to understand that forgiveness is not a one-off event, but an ongoing process. Hence a choice may be made to forgive some things, but not others – or to forgive some things now, and some things later. If you're trying to ask yourself 'Can I forgive myself or my partner for their sex addiction?' – this is just too big a question. However, you may be able to ask one of the following.

Can I forgive myself – or my partner – for …

- having an addiction?
- not knowing they had an addiction?
- having a sex addiction?
- not recognising their problem sooner?
- not getting help sooner?
- not admitting to the problem sooner?
- some of the acting out behaviours (for example, perhaps viewing pornography may be easier to forgive than seeing a sex worker)?

- being deceitful?
- some of the lies (these could be broken down further to individual events)?

Many of these questions need to be put within the context of the relationship. There may have been times within the relationship that were especially difficult or when confessing the addiction may have been even more destructive. And in terms of the societal context, at the time of writing, there are many people with sex addiction who had no idea the problem existed and hence did not take their problem seriously. Similarly, for many there was no professional help to be sought, while others did seek help only to be misunderstood and/or turned away. As said previously, sex addiction is not widely recognised and pornography comes with no health warnings. While it might be reasonable to say to a drug user or an alcoholic 'You should have known better', often this is not the case for people struggling with sex addiction.

Forgiveness takes time and unfortunately it can be withdrawn as well as given. By breaking down the task of forgiveness into more manageable chunks, the gradual process can begin and self-esteem and trust can be given emotional room to grow.

Cross-addictions

There is growing evidence that cross addiction is widespread within sex addiction sufferers (Carnes et al., 2005), with a significant number of people either concurrently, or previously, struggling with drug dependency, alcoholism, gambling, eating disorders or another compulsive behaviour. My survey of the UK indicated that 36.3 per cent of people with sex addiction had experience of another addiction or compulsive behaviour which is broken down as indicated in Table 14.1.

When another addiction or compulsion is present it's important that there is understanding of how the addictions may interact with each other and that they are worked through simultaneously. Failure to do this will either result in continual relapse or in other addictions being escalated. Relapse prevention strategies need to be focused not just on stopping sexual behaviours, but other addictive processes or substances as well. Even if extensive work has already been done on stopping the sexual addiction if it is part of a package of addictions, then these also need addressing.

In the seminal paper 'Bargains with Chaos' (2005), Patrick Carnes and fellow clinicians Robert Murray and Louis Charpentier talk about 11 different ways that addictions can interact with each other. These are as follows.

Table 14.1 Cross addictions

	Currently experience	Previously experienced
Drug addiction	8.3%	58.3%
Alcohol problems	21.5%	31.0%
Nicotine	42.9%	33.3%
Gambling	16.7%	29.2%
Compulsive exercise	25.0%	57.1%
Compulsive working	45.1%	45.1%
Compulsive gaming	16.7%	37.5%
Compulsive spending	41.5%	48.8%
Compulsive hand washing/cleaning	21.4%	32.1%
Eating disorder	32.5%	47.5%

- Cross-tolerance – when one addiction increases the ability to engage in another. For example, the more you drink the easier it is to chat women up online, and the more you chat online the more you're likely to drink.
- Withdrawal mediation – when one addiction is used to help stop another, such as engaging in compulsive working to stop visiting sex workers.
- Replacement – when one addiction replaces the other such as internet gaming instead of internet pornography.
- Alternating cycles – when addictions interchange with each other, for example when someone alternates months or even years of binge eating with multiple affairs, and then swaps back again.
- Masking – using an addiction to hide another one such as blaming the stress of over-working for pornography use and never addressing the work compulsion.
- Rituals – often this is when a chemical addiction is used as part of the ritual of acting out, such as taking cocaine before seeing a sex worker and smoking a cigarette afterwards.
- Fusing – when one addiction amplifies the impact of another such as using MDMA/ecstasy or cocaine to heighten orgasm during sexual acting out.
- Numbing – needing to use another drug or behaviour to numb out the effect of another, such as drowning out the shame of sexual acting out with alcohol or using hours of pornography to come down from using amphetamines.
- Disinhibiting – using an addiction to gain confidence to engage in another, such as getting drunk before having sex with a stranger or viewing pornography to feel more confident in bed with a partner.

- Combining – where a number of addictions are combined to give the perfect 'high' cocktail, such as an evening of alcohol, nicotine, pornography, social media and then cybersex.
- Inhibiting – when one addiction is seen as 'the lesser of two evils', such as drinking more or taking up smoking again when stopping sex addiction.

Once other compulsive behaviours and substances have been named and their interaction identified, relapse prevention strategies can be developed that can work across each addiction. Or if necessary, additional help can be sought through pharmacological interventions to help overcome chemical dependency.

Co-morbidity

'Co-morbidity' is the term that describes when one or two other disorders, or diseases, are present at the same time as the primary disease or disorder. Sex addiction is sometimes a symptom of another mental health problem, or is triggered by it. Unless this other problem is identified and treated, the addiction will probably continue.

There have been a couple of studies that have explored the prevalence of other mental health problems with sex addiction (Black et al., 1997; Raymond et al., 2003). Both studies were relatively small but each showed a significant level of co-morbidity with other mental health disorders. These disorders were most commonly either another addiction, as discussed previously, or an Axis I anxiety or mood disorder. Some also showed symptoms of an Axis II personality disorder.

The most common concurrent mental health problems are depression, generalised anxiety and anxiety caused by specific phobias. Addiction may be an effective tool for soothing the symptoms of these problems and consequently it will be hard to stay stopped until these underlying problems are resolved. The addiction may also cause them as the resulting shame can fuel both depression and anxiety. If there are any concerns that depression or anxiety are a problem then a GP needs to be consulted for appropriate treatment. The following list of symptoms may offer a helpful guideline.

Common symptoms of depression

The symptoms of depression can be complex and vary widely from person to person, but generally if you're depressed, you feel sad, hopeless and have no interest in the things you used to enjoy. Of course everyone can *feel* depressed at times, but if you're *suffering* from depression you're likely to have noticed feeling some of the following symptoms for more than a month.

Emotional symptoms

- Sadness
- Hopelessness
- Low self-esteem
- Feeling tearful
- Guilt
- Irritability
- Anxiety
- No motivation
- Difficulty making decisions
- Having suicidal thoughts or thoughts of harming yourself

Physical symptoms

- Being slow and sluggish
- Speaking slowly
- General lethargy
- Loss or increase in appetite
- Changes in sleep patterns
- Unexplained aches and pains
- Lack of energy or lack of interest in sex
- Changes to your menstrual cycle

Social symptoms

- Losing interest in friends and family
- Struggling at work
- Missing social activities
- Neglecting hobbies and interests
- Ignoring household chores
- Struggling with couple relationships

Common symptoms of anxiety

The symptoms of General Anxiety Disorder (GAD) often develop slowly and like depression, vary from person to person. The severity of symptoms also varies and some will experience far more of the psychological while others experience more physical ones. If you're suffering from a phobic anxiety then the symptoms will be similar but noticeably triggered by particular environments such as confined or open spaces or social events.

Emotional symptoms

- Restlessness
- Being hypervigilent
- Feeling 'on edge'
- A sense of doom
- Worrying
- Constant brain busyness
- Difficulty concentrating
- Irritability
- Impatience

Physical symptoms

- Nausea
- Stomach ache
- Diarrhoea
- Tiredness
- Pins and needles
- Palpitations
- Dry mouth
- Muscle aches and tensions
- Breathlessness
- Sweating
- Going and/or cold
- Headaches
- Painful or missed periods
- Changes in eating patters
- Difficulty sleeping

Social symptoms

- Feeling nervous or anxious with friends
- Avoiding going to busy places and/or being alone
- Struggling to concentrate on conversations

If you think another mental health problem may be complicating recovery then it's essential to arrange an appointment with a GP who can make the necessary referral for professional diagnosis and treatment.

Opportunity

The last, but by no means the least, block to recovery is the ultimate enemy, opportunity. Many people with sex addiction talk about going weeks or even months without a craving or perhaps without even thinking about their addiction, until opportunity came and knocked at their door. The house is empty and someone has left their unprotected laptop sitting on the side. Or a meeting is cancelled and you're alone in a town where you know a sex worker is just a phone call or text away. Or a beautiful stranger approaches you and it's obvious that no-strings-attached sex is on the agenda. When opportunity strikes, resolve can disappear out of the window and endless cognitive distortions can flood the mind along with euphoric recall of how fantastic acting out used to feel. If opportunities come one at a time, hopefully they can be managed with relapse prevention strategies, but if life is one big opportunity, such as for those in certain professions or within certain social groups, the challenge is much, much tougher. For these people the only route to full recovery may be a complete change of lifestyle that eliminates, or at least significantly limits, opportunity.

And so it seems we have come full circle from the start of this book. We undoubtedly live in a world where there is more sexual freedom and opportunity than at any other time on earth. The internet provides us with endless variety and unlimited access to sexual exploration. Progressive social standards accept a range of sexual lifestyles, some of which are profoundly challenging to those who struggle with sex addiction. Ultimately recovering from sex addiction is a choice. A daily choice, to overcome childhood difficulties, triggers, urges and blocks and develop healthy relationships, satisfying sexuality and a fulfilling lifestyle.

Conclusion

Sex addiction is a devastating condition that affects many millions of innocent people. Not just those who personally struggle with it, but also those who love them. Relationships and families can be torn apart, jobs lost, health and personal values compromised and self-esteem left in tatters. It is my belief that sex addiction can be overcome completely, but for some, recovery is a life long process of beating triggers, maintaining integrity and claiming life.

My hope is that this book will have gone some way to increasing understanding of sex addiction and thereby raising compassion and generating hope, and that the exercises provided within these pages will help to provide both a compass and a map to full recovery.

The serenity prayer, first composed by theologian Reinhold Niebuhr and adopted by the 12-step community, sums up both the struggle and the solution for all in addiction recovery. And indeed, for all who strive to manage the complexities of life. We must all learn to accept that there are things in life that we will never be able to change, and find the courage to change the things that are our responsibility.

> God, grant me the Serenity to
> Accept the things I cannot change,
> the Courage to change the things I can,
> and the Wisdom to know the difference.
> Amen.

Further reading and resources

Books

About sex addiction

Clinical Management of Sex Addiction, edited by Patrick Carnes and Kenneth Adams (New York: Brunner Routledge)

Cruise Control – Understanding Sex Addiction in Gay Men, Robert Weiss (New York: Alyson Publications Inc.)

Don't Call it Love – Recovery from Sexual Addiction, Patrick Carnes (New York: Bantam)

Erotic Intelligence – Igniting Hot, Healthy Sex While in Recovery from Sex Addiction, Alexandra Katehakis (Deerfield Beach, FL: Health Communications Inc.)

In the Shadows of the Net – Breaking Free from Compulsive Online Sexual Behaviour, Patrick Carnes, David Delmonico and Elizabeth Griffin (Center City, MN: Hazelden)

Mending a Shattered Heart – A Guide for Partners of Sex Addicts, edited by Stefanie Carnes (Carefree, AZ: Gentle Path Press)

Out of the Shadows – Understanding Sex Addiction, Patrick Carnes (Center City, MN: Hazelden)

Sexual Addiction – An Integrated Approach, Aviel Goodman (Madison, CT: International Universities Press)

The Porn Trap – The Essential Guide to Overcoming Problems Caused by Pornography, Wendy Maltz and Larry Maltz (New York: Harper)

Untangling the Web – Sex, Porn and Fantasy Obsession in the Internet Age, Robert Weiss, Jenifer Schneider (New York: Alyson Books)

Your Sexually Addicted Spouse, Barbara Steffens and Martha Means (Far Hills, NJ: New Horizon Press)

About addiction

Addiction as an Attachment Disorder, Philip J. Flores (Lanham, MD: Aronson)

Learning the Language of Addiction Counseling, Geri Miller (London: Wiley)

Psychological Trauma and Addiction Treatment, edited by Bruce Carruth (New York: Routledge)

The Fix – How Addiction is Invading our Lives and Taking over Your World, Damien Thompson (London: Harper Collins)

Theory of Addiction, Robert West (Oxford: Wiley-Blackwell)

About general psychology and self-help

A Toolkit of Motivational Skills, Catherine Fuller and Phil Taylor (Oxford: Wiley-Blackwell)

Beyond Empathy – A Therapy of Contact-in-Relationship, Richard Erskine (New York: Routledge)

Boosting Self-esteem for Dummies, Rhena Branch and Rob Willson (London: Wiley)

Emotional Intelligence – Why it Can Matter More than IQ, Daniel Goleman (London: Bloomsbury)

Flow: The Psychology of Optimal Experience, Mihaly Csikszentmihalyi (London: Harper Collins)

Infant Losses, Adult Searches – A Neural and Developmental Perspective on Psychpathology and Sexual Offending, Glyn Hudson Allez (London: Karnac)

Managing Anger – Simple Steps for Dealing with Frustration and Threat, Gael Lindenfield (London: Thorsons)

People Skills – How to Assert Yourself, Listen to Others and Resolve Conflicts, Robert Bolton (New York: Touchstone)

Super Normal Stimuli – How Primal Urges Overran Their Evolutionary Purpose, Deirdre Barrett (Norton USA)

The Body Remembers – The Psychophysiology of Trauma and Trauma Treatment, Babette Rothschild (New York: W.W. Norton)

The Mindful Brain, Daniel Siegel (New York: W.W. Norton)

The Neuroscience of Psychotherapy: Building and Rebuilding the Human Brain, Louis Cozolino (New York: W.W. Norton)

Wherever You Go, There You Are, Jon Kabat-Zinn (New York: Hyperion)

About relationships and sexuality

Attached – The New Science of Adult Attachment and How it Can Help You Find and Keep Love, Amir Levine and Rachel Heller (New York: Tarcher)

Better than Ever – Love and Sex at Midlife, Bernie Zilbergeld (Bancyfelin: Crown House Publishing)

Couples and Sex – An Introduction to Relationship Dynamics and Psychosexual Concepts, Carol Martin-Sperry (London: Routledge)

Games People Play, Eric Berne (London: Penguin)

Improving Your Relationship for Dummies, Paula Hall (London: Wiley Press)

I'm OK, You're OK, Thomas Harris (London: Arrow)

Help Your Children Cope with Your Divorce, Paula Hall (London: Vermillion)

How to Have a Healthy Divorce, Paula Hall (London: Vermillion)

Loving Yourself, Loving Another – The Importance of Self-esteem for Successful Relationships, Julia Cole (London: Vermillion)

Recovering Intimacy in Love Relationships – A Clinician's Guide, Jon Carlson and Len Sperry (London: Routledge)

Rekindling Desire, A Step-by-Step Program to Help Low Sex and No-Sex Marriages, Barry and Emly McCarthy (New York: Brunner-Routledge)

Rewriting the Rules – A New Guide to Love, Sex and Relationships, Meg Barker (London: Routledge)

Stop Arguing. Start Talking – The 10 Point Plan for Couples in Conflict, Susan Quilliam (London: Vermillion)

The Guide to Getting it On, Paul Joannides (Waldport, OR: Goofy Foot Press)

Treating Infidelity – Therapeutic Dilemmas and Effective Strategies, Gerald R. Weeks, Nancy Gambescia and Robert Jenkins (London: Norton)

Psychotherapy, counselling and treatment services

For sex addiction

ATSAC (Association for the Treatment of Sexual Addiction and Compulsivity) – www.ATSAC.co.uk
The UK's professional association for sex addiction professionals provides a register of therapists specialising in sex addiction treatment and training for professionals.

IITAP (International Institute for Trauma and Addiction Professionals) – www. IITAP.com
An American-based organisation founded by Dr Patrick Carnes that provides a register of therapists specialising in sex addiction treatment and training for professionals.

SAA (Sex Addicts Anonymous) – www.saa-recovery.org.uk
Peer support groups for sex addicts following the 12 step principles. Meetings around the UK.

SLAA (Sex and Love Addicts Anonymous) – www.slaauk.org
Peer support groups for sex addicts following the 12 step principles. Meetings around the UK.

The Hall Recovery Course – www.thehallrecoverycourse.co.uk
A recovery course for sex addiction developed by Paula Hall in the UK, both weekly and intensives. Available at a growing number of locations around the UK.

The Priory Group – www.priorygroup.com
A group of multi-disciplinary treatment centres around the UK that provide residential and outpatient treatment for sex addiction.

Recovery Nation – www.recoverynation.com
A recovery website that provides online recovery tools for sex addicts, partners and couples along with expert coaching and community support.

The Kick Start Recovery Programme – www.sexaddictionhelp.co.uk
A free online self-help resource to help overcome sex addiction, based on the BERSC Model and exercises from The Hall Recovery Course.

www.yourbrainonporn.com
A science-based website that provides information about the impact of pornography and recovery advice for those whose porn use is a problem.

For individual and relationship issues

College of Sexual and Relationship Therapy – www.cosrt.org.uk
Provides information on sexual problems and a register of private therapists who specialise in relationship and sexual problems.

Pink Therapy – www.pinktherapy.com
The UK's largest independent therapy organisation working with gender and sexual minority clients.

Relate – www.relate.org.uk
The UK's largest counselling service for couples and individuals with sexual or relationship difficulties. Also provides services for young people and families.

Relationships Scotland – www.relationships-scotland.org.uk
Provide counselling for relationship and sexual problems to individuals and couples throughout Scotland.

The British Association of Counselling and Psychotherapy – www.bacp.co.uk
Provides a register of private counsellors and psychotherapists who can work with a wide range of problems.

References

Addiction Today, December 2011, Article – The Latest Definition of Addiction from ASAM (American Association of Addiction Medicine).

Bartholomew, Kim and Horowitz, Leonard M. (1991) Attachment Styles Among Young Adults: A Test of a Four-category Model. *Journal of Personality and Social Psychology*, Vol. 61(2), August 1991, 226–244.

Berke, J. D. and Hyman, S. E. (2000) Addiction, Dopamine, and the Review Molecular Mechanisms of Memory. *Neuron,* 25, 515–532.

Birchard, T. (2011) Sexual Addiction and the Paraphilias. *Sexual Addiction & Compulsivity,* 18, 3, 157–187.

Black, D. W., Kehrberg, L. L. D., Flumerfelt, D. L. and Schlosser, S. S. (1997) Characteristics of 36 Subjects Reporting Compulsive Sexual Behaviour. *American Journal of Psychiatry*, 154(2), 243–249.

Blanchard, G. (1990) Differential Diagnosis of Sexual Offenders: Distinguising Characteristics of the Sex Addict. *American Journal of preventative Psychiatry & Neurology,* 2, 45–47.

Bechara, A. and Damasio, H. (2002) Decision-making and Addiction (part 1): Impaired Motivation of Somatic States in Substance Dependent Individuals When Pondering Decisions with Negative Future Consequences. *Neuropsychologia,* 40, 1675–1689.

Blankenship, R. and Lasser, M. (2004) Sexual Addiction and ADHD: Is There a Connection? *Sexual Addiction & Compusivity*, 11, 7–20.

Blum, K. Braverman, E. R., Holder, J. M., Lubar, J., Monastra, V. J., Miller, D., Lubar, J., Chen, T., Comings, D. E. (2000) Reward Deficiency Syndrome: A Biogenetic Model for the Diagnosis and Treatment of Impulsive, Addictive, and Compulsive Behaviors. *Journal of Psychoactive Drugs*, 32 (Suppl.), 1–112.

Carnes, P (1991) *Don't Call it Love: Recovery from Sexual Addiction*, New York: Bantam.

Carnes, P. (2001) *Out of the Shadows*, Center City, MN: Hazelden.

Carnes, P. (2005) *Facing the Shadow* 2nd edition, Carefree, AZ: Gentle Path Press.

Carnes, P. and Adams, K. (2002) *Clinical Management of Sex Addiction*, New York: Routledge.

Carnes, P., Murray, R. and Charpentier, L. (2005) Bargains with Chaos: Sex Addicts and Addiction Interaction Disorder. *Sexual Addiction & Compulsivity*, 12, 79–120.

Carruth, B. (2011) *Psychological Trauma and Addiction Treatment*, New York: Routledge.

Courtwright, D. (1982) *Dark Paradise: Opiate Addiction in America before 1940*, Cambridge, UK: Cambridge University Press.

Cozolino, L. (2002) *The Neuroscience of Psychotherapy: Building and Rebuilding the Human Brain*, New York: Norton.

Crenshaw, T. L. (1996) *The Alchemy of Love and Lust*, New York: Pocket Books.

Dickson, L., Derevensky, J. amd Gupta, R. (2002) The Prevention of Gambling Problems in Youth: A Conceptual Framework. *Journal of Gambling Studies*, 18, 97–159.

Dodes, l. (2002) *The Heart of Addiction A New Approach to Understanding and Managing Alcoholism and Other Addictive Behaviours*, New York: HarperCollins.

Duvauchelle, C., Ikegami, L., Edward, A. C. (2000) Conditioned Increases in Behavioural Activity and Accumbens Dopamine Levels Produced by Intravenous Cocaine. *Behavioural Neuroscience*, 114(6), 1156–1166.

Ershe, K. et al. (2012) Abnormal Brain Structure Implicated in Stimulant Drug Addiction. *Journal of Science*, 335(6068), 601–604.

Erskine, R. (1999) *Beyond Empathy – A Therapy of Contact-in-Relationship*, Philadelphia, PA: Brunner-Mazel.

Ferree, M. C. (2002) Females – The Forgotten Sex Addicts, published in *Clinical Management of Sex Addiction*, New York: Routledge.

Fisher, J. (2007) *Addictions and Trauma Recovery*, New York: Basic Books.

Flores, P. J. (2004) *Addiction as an Attachment Disorder*, Lanham, MD: Aronson.

Fossum, Merle A., Mason, Marilyn J. (1986) *Facing Shame: Families in Recovery*, New York: W.W. Norton.

Fowler, J. (2006) Psychoneurobiology of Co-occurring Trauma and Addictions. *Journal of Chemical Dependency Treatment*, 8(2), 129–152.

Franklin, T. R., Acton, P. D., Maldjian J. A., Gray, J. D., Croft, J. R., Dackis, C. A., O'Brien, C. P. and Childress, A. R. (2002) Deceased Gray Matter Concentration in Insular, Orbitofrontal, Cingulate, and Temporal Cortices of Cocaine Patients. *Biological Psychiatry*, 51, 134–143.

Gilliland, R. D., South, M., Carpenter, B. and Hardy, S. (2011) The Roles of Shame and Guilt in Hypersexual Behaviour. *Sexual Addiction & Compulsivity*, 18,12–29.

Goldstein, R. Z., Volkow, N. D., Wang, G-J., Fowler, J. S. and Rajaram, S. (2001) Addiction Changes in Orbitofrontal Gyrus Function: Involvement in Response Inhibition. *Neuroreport*, 8;12(11): 2595–2599.

Goodman, A. (1993) Diagnosis and Treatment of Sexual Addiction. *Journal of Sex 6 Marital Therapy*, 19, 225–251.

Griffin-Shelley, E. (2002) Adolescent Sex and Love Addicts, published in *Clinical Management of Sex Addiction*, New York: Routledge.

Grov, C., Parsons, J.T., Bimbi, D. S. (2010) Sexual Compulsivity and Sexual Risk in Gay and Bisexual Men. *Archive of Sexual Behaviour*, 39(4), 940–949.

Hall, P., (2011) A Bio Psychosocial View of Sex Addiction, *Sexual & Relationship Therapy*, 26(3), 217–228

Hall, P. (2012) Survey of 350 UK People Who Identify as Suffering with Sex Addiction, conducted via Survey Monkey.

Hudson Allez, G. (2009) *Infant Searches, Adult Losses*, London: Karnac.

Krentzman, A. R., 2007. The Evidence Base for the Effectiveness of Alcoholics Anonymous: Implications for Social Work Practice. *Journal of Social Work Practice in the Addictions*, 7(4), 27–48.

Laaser, M. R. (2002) Recovery for Couples, published in *Clinical Management of Sex Addiction*, New York: Routledge.

Manning, V., Best, D., Rawaf, S., Rowley, J., Floyd, K. and Strang, J. (2001) Drug Use in Adolescence: The Relationship Between Opportunity, Initial Use and Continuation of Use of Four Illicit Drugs in a Cohort of 14–16-yr-olds in South London. *Drugs: Education, Prevention & Policy*, Vol. 8(4), 397–405.

Miller, G. (2005) *Learning the Language of Addiction Counselling*, London: John Wiley and Sons.

Money, J. (1989) *Vandalised Love Maps*, Buffalo NY: Prometheus Books.

Nerenberg, A. (2002) The Value of Group Psychotherapy for Sexual Addicts, published in *Clinical Management of Sex Addiction*, New York: Routledge.

Ogden, P., Minton, K. and Pain, C. (2006) *Trauma and the Body: A Sensorimotor Approach to Psychotherapy*, New York: W.W. Norton.

Potter-Efron, R. (2006) Attachment, Trauma and Addiction, published in *Psychological Trauma and Addiction Treatment*, New York: Routledge.

Prochaska, J. and Di Clemente, C. C. (1982) Trans-theoretical Therapy; Towards a More Integrative Model of Change. *Psychotherapy; Theory, Research and Practice*, 19, 276–299.

Raymond, N. C., Coleman, E, and Miner M. H. (2003) Psychiatric Comorbidity and Compulsive/Impulsive Traits in Compulsive Sexual Behaviours. *Comprehensive Psychiatry*, 44(5).

Reid, R. C. (2007) Assessing Readiness to Change among Clients Seeking Help for hypersexual behaviour. *Sexual Addiction & Compulsivity*, 14:167–186.

Robbins, T. and Everitt, B. (eds) (2010) *The Neurobiology of Addiction*, Oxford: Oxford University Press.

Rosenthal, R. (1992) Pathological Gambling. *Psychiatric Annals, 22*, 72–78.

Schneider, J. P., Corley, D. and Irons, R. (1998) Surviving Disclosure of Infidelity: Results of an International Survey of 164 Recovery Sex Addicts and Partners. *Sexual Addiction & Compulsivity*, 5: 189–217.

Schore, A. N. (2003) *Affect Regulation and Disorders of the Self*, New York: Norton.

Seigel, D.J. (2007) *The Mindful Brain*, New York, W.W. Norton.

Sex Addicts Anonymous, *The Bubble, An Analogy about Sex Addiction*, Houston, TX: SAA Publications.

Soloman, R. (1980) The Opponent Process Theory of Acquired Motivation. The Costs of Pleasure and the Benefits of Pain, *American Psychologist, 35*(8), 691–712.

Steffens, B. and Means, M. (2009) *Your Sexually Addicted Spouse*, Far Hills, NJ: New Horizon Press

Sussman, S. (2007) Sex Addiction Among Teens: A Review. *Sexual Addiction & Compulsivity*, 14(4), 257–278.

Sussman, S. (2010) Love Addiction: Definition, Etiology, Treatment. *Sexual Addiction & Compulsivity*, 17(1), 31–45.

Taber, J., McCormick, R., Russo, A., Adkins, B. and Ramirez, L. (1987) Follow-up of Pathological Gamblers After Treatment. *American Journal of Psychiatry*, 144, 757–761.

Van der Kolk, Bessel. (1996) *Traumatic Stress*. New York: The Guilford Press.

Weiss, R. (2002) Treatment Concerns for Gay Male Sex Addicts, published in *Clinical Management of Sex Addiction*, New York: Routledge.

Whipple, B. (2003) White Paper – The Health Benefits of Sexual Expression, published by *Planned Parenthood Federation of America in Cooperation with the Society for the Scientific Study of Sexuality*.

Ybarra, M.L. and Mitchell, K.J. (2005) Exposure to Internet Pornography among Children and Adolescents: A National Survey. *Cyber Psychology & Behaviour*, 8(5), 473–486.

Zapf, J. L., Greiner, J., Carroll, J., (2008). Attachment Styles and Male Sex Addiction. *Sexual Addiction & Compulsivity*, 15, 158–175.

Index

Page references in *italics* indicate figures, tables and boxes

12-step and other self-support groups 88
30-task model 86

abstinence 97
abuse 43–4
abusive relationships 21
accountability contract *148*
acting out 9, 12; attachment-induced addiction 57–8; case examples *114*; cycles of addiction 111, *112*; and emotions *113*; risks *181*; six-phase cycle 53, *57*, 58; trauma-induced addiction 57
action stage: stages of change model 20–1
addiction: and adolescence 13; books on 192–3; defining *see* defining sex addiction; and emotional pain 57
addictive cycles: case examples 59–60
addictive personality 37–8
adolescence: and addiction 13; loneliness 40–1; masturbation 40; porn use 24; sex addiction 23–4; survey results 24, 41
adrenalin 12
Ali: childhood issues 119–20, 121, 122, 124
ambivalent attacher 48, 58
amygdala and trauma 45
anxiety 14, 38, 188–9
anxious/pre-occupied attacher 48, 57

arousal threshold 14
assault 44
assertiveness, developing 174–5
assessment and diagnosis 18–32; assessment process 28–9, *30*; classifications 24, *25*, 26–8; defining the type 30–2; measuring severity 29, *30*; motivation for change 19–21; questionnaires 28–9, *30*; special populations 22–4; variations of addiction 21–2
attachment-induced addiction 26–7, 125–8; acting out 57–8; adult attachment styles 48–9; the brain 47; case studies 48, 128; core beliefs 92; cyber chat 59–60; dormant phase 54; how it starts 46–9; parenting 30, 47–8; partner's perspective 71, 72; questionnaires 30–1; separation 30; sexual desire 55; triggers 54–5, *108*
attachment issues: relational needs 127; unresolved issues and unmet needs 125–8
attachment styles, adult 48–9
avoidant attacher 48, 57–8

balanced lifestyle 166–9, *170*, *171–2*; contribution 169–70; couple relationship 166; family 168; friends 167; fun and recreation 168; life balance inventory *171–2*; life wheel *170*, *171*; personal growth 169; rest and relaxation 168–9; work 169

behaviour chain 111, *112*
behavioural addiction 7–8
behaviours: reconstitution phase *116*
Berne, E. *150*
BERSC model 34, *35*
Bill: attachment-induced addiction 48
Birchard, T. 86–7
blame *110*
blocks to recovery 178–90; case
    examples 182, 183; co-morbidity
    187–9; cross-addictions 185, *186*,
    187; denial 179–83; opportunity
    190; rock bottoms *180*;
    unforgiveness 183–5
books (resources) 192–4
boundaries, childhood 121–2
boundaries, sexual 97, *98*
the brain: attachment-induced addiction
    47; chemistry and the internet 13;
    development of 36; how triggers
    affect 131–2
The Bubble 12

Carnes, P. 86, 91, *141–2*, *171*, 185
case studies: addictive cycles 59–60;
    attachment-induced addiction 48;
    blocks to recovery 182; cycle of
    addiction 59–60, 104, *106*, *109*,
    112, *114*, *115*, *116*, 117; denial 182,
    183; maintenance and reinforcement
    59–60; partner's perspective 63–4,
    65, 69, 72, 75; sex drive 9, 10;
    trauma-induced addiction 46
causes 33–49; attachment-induced
    addiction 46–9; BERSC model 34,
    35; opportunity-induced addiction
    35–42;trauma-induced addiction
    42–6
celibacy 160
Charpentier, L. 185
chemical addiction 12
child protection 22
childhood issues 118–22; attachment
    26–7; cases studies 119–20, 121,
    122; lifelines 119, *120*; managing
    negative emotions 121
circle exercise *98*, 156–7
classifications of sex addiction 24–8;
    attachment-induced addiction 26–7,
    30–1; OAT classification model
    25; opportunity-induced addiction

25, 27–8, 31–2; trauma-induced
    addiction 26, 31
co-addiction and co-dependency 70–3
co-morbidity 187–9
cognitive distortions 55, *56*, *109–11*
cognitive-neural restructuring 132–6
*Cognitive Neural Restructuring
    Therapy for the Treatment of
    Sexually Compulsive Disorders*
    (Hedelius and Freestone) 136
comments, personal: reclaiming
    personal values 94–5; treatment
    89–90
commitment to recovery 91–102;
    creating a vision for life *99–102*;
    identifying core beliefs 91–2, *93*,
    94; reclaiming personal values
    94–5, *96*; setting sexual boundaries
    97, *98*; treatment 82, 91–102
communication: couple relationships
    151–2, *153*
compulsive sexual behaviour *51*
conflict, relationship 152–4
consequences of addiction 14, *15*,
    16–17
contemplative stage 20
contribution: balanced lifestyle
    169–70, *172*
control/release cycle 51, *52*
core beliefs, identifying 91–2, *93*, 94
couple relationships: balanced lifestyle
    166; books on 193–4; building
    better 148–54; communication
    151–2, *153*; conflict 152–4;
    healthy 148–54; disclosure 145–6;
    evaluating quality *105*; healthy
    144–54; intimacy 151; life balance
    inventory *171*; problems *15*;
    services for 195; trust 146–7,
    148; unconscious couple collusions
    149–51
couple therapy 85
Craig: cycle of addiction 104, *106*,
    109, 112, *114*, *115*, *116*, 117
creating a vision for life *99–102*
cross-addictions 185, *186*, 187
cyber chat addiction: Tim 59–60
cycles of addiction 51–9, 103–17;
    acting out 111, *112*, *113*; behaviour
    chain 111, *112*; case examples
    59–60, 104, *106*, *109*, 112, *114*,

115, *116*, 117; cognitive distortions
109–11; dormant phase *105–6*;
emotional regulation *105*; four-
step cycle *51–2*; identifying
regrets *115*; life balance *106*;
maintenance and reinforcement
51–9; oscillating release/control
cycle 51, *52*; preparation phase
109–12; reconstitution phase
115–17; regret phase 114, *115*;
relationships *105*; six-phase cycle
52, *53*, 54–5, *56–7*, 58–9, *104*;
SUDs 111, *112*; treatment 103–17;
triggers *107–8*

D day (disclosure day) 145
debt *15*
decision making, boundaries and self-
control 121–2
defining sex addiction 3–17;
addiction: terminology 7–9; case
examples 9, 10; consequences of
14, *15*, 16–17; function of addiction
11–12; neurochemistry 12–14;
sexual behaviours 6–7; what it is
6–7; what it is not *9–10*, 11
denial 18–19, *111*; blocks to recovery
179–83; case examples 182, 183;
minimisation 179
depression 14, 187–8
despair *51*
Diagnostic and Statistic Manual of the
American Psychiatric Association
(DSM) 8–9
DiClemente, C. C. *19*
diet 165–6
disclosure, managing 145–6
discovery, impact of 51–65
dismissing/avoidant attacher 48
domestic violence 31
Don't Call it Love (Carnes) 43
dopamine 12, 13, 36–7
dormant phase 52, 53–4, *105–6*;
attachment-induced addiction 54;
opportunity-induced sex addiction
54; trauma-induced addiction 54
drama triangle *149*
drug addiction 7
DSM (Diagnostic and Statistic Manual
of the American Psychiatric
Association) 7–9

eating disorders, comparisons with
10–11, 13
emergency stops: managing triggers
141–2
emotional abuse 31, 43
emotional intelligence, increasing
173–4, *175*, *176–7*
emotional intelligence inventory *175*,
176–7
emotional issues, unresolved 118–28;
attachment 125–8; childhood
118–22; sexual messages 122–4;
trauma 124–5
emotional pain 57
emotional regulation, evaluating *105*
emotional triggers, avoiding 136–9;
emergency stops *141–2*; emotions
138–9; letter to self *141–2*; physical
urges 139; RUN 140–1
emotions: avoiding triggers 138–9;
managing negative 121;
opportunity-induced addiction 39;
survey results 39; when acting out
113
employment *15*
endorphins 12
entitlement (cognitive distortion) *110*
environmental triggers, avoiding: people
and places 136–7; porn protection
137–8; time and money 137
erectile problems 14, 163
Erskine, R. 127
Eryk: attachment-induced addiction
128
escalation 14, 22
evaluation: unmet needs *105–6*
exercise 165
externalisation 140

Facing the Shadow (Carnes) *141–2*
family: balanced lifestyle 168, *172*
fantasies 161
fearful/avoidant attacher 48
feelings, managing difficult 39
female sex addiction 22–3
fetishes and paraphilias 161–2
financial difficulties 14
food: comparison with sex 13
forgiveness 183–5
Fossum, M. A. 51, *52*
four-step cycle of addiction *50*

Frank: sex drive 9
Freestone, A, T. 136
friends: balanced lifestyle 167, *172*
fun and recreation: balanced lifestyle
   168, *172*
function of addiction 11–12

Generalised Anxiety Disorder (GAD)
   38, 188–9
Geoff: blocks to recovery 182, 183
group therapy 85
guilt 80–1

Hall Recovery Course 87, *99–102*, 194
health concerns 14
health problems *15*
healthy lifestyle, developing a 84,
   164–77; assertiveness 174–5;
   balance 166–9, *170*, *171–2*;
   emotional intelligence 173–4, *175*,
   176–7; physical health 165–6
Hedelius, M. 136
helplessness *111*
high sex drive 9
hyperarousal *57*
Hypersexual Disorder 9
hypersexuality 9
hypoarousal *57*

illness and disability 44
individual therapy 84–5
integrative cognitive behavioural
   therapy 86
internet: brain chemistry 13;
   opportunity-induced sex addiction
   27–8; sex addiction and 13; sex
   offending 22
internet pornography 31
intimacy, strengthening 151

job loss 44
Joe: trauma-induced addiction 126
Julian: low sex drive 10
justification *110*

Karpman, S. 149
Kick Start Recovery 88

legal actions *15*
lesbian, gay, bisexual, transgender and
   queer people (LGBTQ) 24

letter to self *141–2*
life balance, evaluating *106*
life balance inventory *171–2*
life wheel *170*, *171*
lifelines: childhood issues 119, *120*
Lorna: partner's perspective 63, 65,
   69, 72, 75
love addiction 9, 21
'love map' 14
low sex drive 9–10
low sexual desire 163

magnifying *110*
maintenance and reinforcement 50–60;
   case examples 59 60; cycles of
   addiction 51–9
Mason, M. J. 51, *52*
masturbation 31, 40, 156–7
Matrix question 183
mental filter *110–11*
mental health problems *15*, 186
Mike: pornography addiction 41–2
mindfulness 140
minimisation *110*, 179
Minton, K. *57*
misdiagnosis 18
money *15*
monogamous couple sex 158–9
Motivational Interviewing 93–4
Murray, R. 185

Nadine: partner's perspective 63–4, 65,
   69, 72, 75
neural pathways 131–2
neurochemistry: sex addiction 12–14
neurogenesis 132
Niebuhr, R. 191
normalisation *111*

OAT classification model *25*
Ogden, P. *57*
online recovery programmes 87–8
open non-monogamy 159–60
open relationship 159
'The Opponent Process Theory of
   Acquired Motivation' (Solomon)
   45
opportunity and recovery 190
opportunity-induced sex addiction *25*,
   27–8, 31; adolescent loneliness
   40–1; brain development 36; case

204   *Index*

examples 41–2; core beliefs 92;
developing self-control 38–9;
dopamine dysregulation 36–7;
dormant phase 54; emotions 39;
how it starts 35–42; internet 27–8,
31; masturbation 31; partner's
perspective 70–1; personality 37–
8; pornography 31; questionnaires
31; secrets and shame 39–40; sex
education 40; sexual desire 55;
triggers 54
opportunity-related triggers *107*
oscillating release/control cycle 51, *52*

the PAC model *150*
Pain, C. *57*
paraphilias 161–2
parent/child relationship *150*
parental control software 137
parenting: attachment-induced
addiction 30; impaired *15*; styles
of 47–8; survey results 38–9
parking illegally example *56*
partner therapy 88–9
partner's perspective 61–75; addiction
recovery 74–5; attachment-induced
addiction 71, 72; case studies 63–
4, 65, 69, 72, 75; co-addiction and
co-dependency 70–3; continuing
the relationship 67; coping with the
fallout 66–9; emotional reactions
61; impact of discovery 51–65;
opportunity-induced addiction
70–1; patterns of disclosure 64–5;
professional support 68–9; recovery
for partners 73–4; sex life 67–8;
telling others 66–7; trauma-induced
addiction 71–3; trust 68
in-patient programmes and treatment
centres 87
patterns of disclosure 64–5
personal growth: balanced lifestyle
169, *172*
personal relationship problems 14
personal values 93–4
personality and sex addiction 37–8
Peter: trauma-induced addiction 46
physical abuse 31, 43
physical health: health lifestyle
165–6; life balance inventory *171*;
problems *15*

physical urges, triggers 139
pillars (cognitive-neural restructuring)
133–6
polyamory 159
pornography: addiction 41–2;
adolescent use of 24; early
exposure to 37; internet 31;
opportunity-induced addiction 31;
survey results 40; technological
protection 137–8
pre-contemplative stage *19*, 20
premature deaths, effects of 44
preoccupation step *51*
preparation phase 53, 55, *56*, *109–12*
preparation stage 20
press exposure *15*
Prochaska, J. *19*
professional support: for partner's 68–9
profile of sex addicts 28
psycho-educational treatment groups
86–7
psychological purpose of addiction
11–12
psychology: books 192–3
psychotherapy, counselling and
treatment services 194–5

questionnaires: assessment and
diagnosis 28–9, *30*; attachment-
induced addiction 30–1;
opportunity-induced sex addiction
31; trauma-induced addiction 31

rationalisation *109*
re-wiring the brain 132–6
reclaiming personal values 94–5, *96*
reconstitution phase 53, 115–17;
identifying behaviours *116*; self-
esteem 59
recovery: blocks to *see* blocks to
recovery; effect partners have 74–5;
for partners 73–4
Recovery Nation 88, *99–102*, 194
Recovery Start Kit (Carnes) *171*
regret phase 53, 58, 114, *115*
reinforcement *see* maintenance and
reinforcement
relapse 21, 143
relapse prevention strategies 83–4,
129–90; blocks to recovery 178–90;
healthy couple relationships

144–54; healthy lifestyle 164–77; satisfying sexuality 155–63; triggers 131–43
relational needs, identifying 127
release/control cycle 51, *52*
resources 192–5
rest and relaxation 168–9, *172*
risks (acting out) *181*
ritualisation step *51*
rock bottoms *180*
RUN 140–1

secrets and shame 39–40
Seemingly Unimportant Decisions (S.U.D.s) 55, 111, *112*
self-control: childhood issues 121–2; developing 38–9
self-esteem 14, *15*, 59
self help: books about 192–3
separation (attachment-induced addiction) 30
serenity prayer 191
severity, measuring 29, *30*
sex addiction: assessment and diagnosis 18–32; books on 192; classifications of 30–2; definition 3–17; how it starts 33–49; how its maintained and reinforced 50–60; internet and 13; lesbian, gay, bisexual, transgender and queer people (LGBTQ) 24; partner's perspective 50–60; psychotherapy, counselling and treatment services 194–5; terminology 8–9; types of 30–2; variation of 21–2
Sex Addiction Screening Test (Carne) 20
Sex Addicts Anonymous 12
sex addicts, profile of 28
sex drive 9–10
sex education 40
sex life: partner's perspective 67–8
Sex Offences Act 22
sex offending 22
sexual abuse 31, 43
sexual behaviours 6–7, 45
sexual belief systems 122–4
sexual boundaries, setting 97, *98*, 156–7
sexual challenges, overcoming 161–3; fantasies 161; fetishes and paraphilias 161–2; sexual

dysfunctions 163; sexual frustrations 162–3
sexual desire 12, 13, 55
sexual dysfunctions *15*, 163
sexual frustrations, diverting 162–3
sexual messages 122–4
sexual offending behaviour 14
sexuality: books on 193–4
sexuality, satisfying 155–63; celibacy 160; defining 156–7; monogamous couples 158–9; open non-monogamy 159–60; overcoming challenges 161–3; setting boundaries 156–7; single people 157–8
sexually transmitted infections (STIs) 14
shame 14, *15*; core beliefs 92–3; reducing 80; regret phase 58; survey results 39–40; treatment objectives 80–2
sharing (disclosure) 146
single people: masturbation 156–7; satisfying sexuality 157–8
six-phase cycle *104*; acting out 53, *57*, 58; dormant phase 52, 53–4; preparation phase 53, 55, *56*; reconstitution 53, 59; regret phase 53, 58; triggers 52, 54–5
sleep 165
slip ups and relapse 143
Solomon, R. 45
stages of change model *19*, 20–1
Stephens, E. 86
STIs *15*
S.U.D.s (Seemingly Unimportant Decisions) 55, 111, *112*
sugar example 27–8
suicide *15*
Supernormal Stimuli 27
supplements 165–6
survey results: abuse 43–4; adolescent loneliness 41; adolescent sex addiction 24; consequences of sex addiction 16–17; cross-addictions 185, *186*; emotions 39; female sex addiction 23; parenting 38–9; pornography 40; secrets and shame 39–40; sex education 40; sex offending 22; shame 39–40; terms 9, 21; treatment 89–90

swinging 159

technology: porn protection 137–8
telling others: partner's perspective
    66–7
terminology 8–9, 21
'therapeutic disclosure' 145
Tim: cyber chat addiction 59–60
time and money, triggers 137
time wasting *15*
'tolerance and escalation' 12–13
trauma 124–5; effect on the brain
    45; impact of 44; and sexual
    behaviours 45; triggers *108*;
    working with 124–5
trauma-induced addiction 124–5;
    abuse 43–4; acting out 57;
    assault 44; case examples 46,
    126; classifications of sex
    addiction 26; core beliefs 92;
    domestic violence 31; dormant
    phase 54; emotional abuse 31,
    43; how it starts 42–6; illness
    and disability 44; impact of
    trauma 44; job loss 44; partner's
    perspective 71–3; physical abuse
    31, 43; premature deaths 44;
    questionnaires 31; sexual abuse
    31, 43; sexual desire 55; triggers
    54, *108*
trauma-related triggers *108*
treatment 77–128; commitment
    to recovery 91–102; cycles of
    addiction 103–17; objectives
    and options 79–90; personal
    comments 89–90; survey results
    89–90; unresolved issues and
    unmet needs 118–28
treatment approaches 11, 37, 43,
    85–9; 12-step 88; 30-task model
    86; four-step cycle 51; integrative
    cognitive behavioural therapy
    86; online programmes 87–8;
    partner therapy 88–9; in-patient
    87; psycho-educational treatment

groups 86–7; self-support groups
    88
treatment objectives: commit to
    recovery 82; develop a healthy life
    84; establish relapse prevention
    strategies 83–4; reduce shame
    80; resolve underlying issues 83;
    shame 80–2; understand and
    personalise the cycle of addiction
    83; understand sex addiction 80
treatment options: couple therapy
    85; group therapy 85; individual
    therapy 84–5; specialist
    approaches 85–9
trigger phase *107–8*
triggers: attachment-induced addiction
    54–5; avoiding and managing
    131–43; avoiding environmental
    and emotional 136–9; effect on the
    brain 131–2; identifying *107–8*;
    managing unavoidable 139–42;
    opportunity-induced addiction 54;
    re-wiring the brain 132–6; sexual
    desire 55; six-phase cycle 52,
    54–5; trauma-induced addiction 54
trust 68, 146–7, *148*
types of sex addiction 30–2

unconscious couple collusions
    149–51
underlying issues, resolving 83
unforgiveness 183–5
uniqueness (cognitive distortion) *110*
unresolved issues and unmet needs
    118–28
'UR-CURED' 80

values list 96
victim stance *111*

window of tolerance 57
work: balanced lifestyle 169, *172*
workplace difficulties 14

Zapf, J. L. 48